George Warrington Steevens

Naval Policy with Some Account of the Warships of the Principal

Powers

George Warrington Steevens

Naval Policy with Some Account of the Warships of the Principal Powers

ISBN/EAN: 9783337032555

Printed in Europe, USA, Canada, Australia, Japan

Cover: Foto ©Suzi / pixelio.de

More available books at **www.hansebooks.com**

NAVAL POLICY

WITH SOME ACCOUNT OF

THE WARSHIPS OF THE PRINCIPAL POWERS

BY

G. W. STEEVENS

FELLOW OF PEMBROKE COLLEGE, OXFORD

METHUEN & CO.
36, ESSEX STREET, W.C.
LONDON
1896

PREFACE

THE unkindest fate that this book or its author could encounter, is that the one should be accounted an attempt at original theory and research, or the other dubbed a naval expert. I am not an expert, and the following pages are not written for experts. They are merely an endeavour to interpret in some measure such sources of information upon naval matters as are open to the general public. But even these, unfortunately, make up a good body of print; and most men and women have neither the time nor the inclination to study and collate them. I have endeavoured to present their essence here in such a way that those who disagree with my opinions may be able to form conclusions of their own.

A book of this kind must needs scamp a full recognition of its borrowings; it is wholly made up of borrowings. Many of these have been set down in their proper place. But there are others too great and too perpetually recurrent to be dealt with thus, unless the whole book were to be made up of footnotes and cross-references. For statistical matter I have pillaged without scruple the successive volumes of *Brassey's Naval Annual*, and Mr. Laird Clowes's *Naval Pocket Book*, as well as the principal newspapers.

PREFACE

In points of policy and strategical theory I am equally indebted to the great works of Admiral P. H. Colomb, the various strategical essays of Mr. J. R. Thursfield, and the writings of Mr. W. H. Wilson. Above all, it is impossible to give any detailed acknowledgment of my debts to Mr. Spenser Wilkinson and Sir Charles Dilke. Supposing this book were to prove an introduction to the works here named, it will have more than succeeded, and ought to prove of some small but real service to the political direction of this country.

G. W. STEEVENS.

CONTENTS

I. THE PROBLEM.

A Parliamentary Paper examined—The Debate on the 1896 Estimates—Speeches by Mr. Goschen, Sir Charles Dilke, Mr. Balfour, and others—The necessity for an analysis of official figures . *Page* 1

II. THE ELEMENTS OF FORCE IN WARSHIPS.

Mechanical invention the controlling influence in the history of war—Requisites of a fighting ship—Rifled guns, armour, steam—Continuity of progress—Introduction of rifled cannon—Of slow-burning powder and breech-loaders—Wire guns—The secondary armament—Introduction of quick-firers: their power, their construction—The dynamite gun—The torpedo: its position in war still undefined—Introduction of compound plating—Harveyed steel: its power of resistance—Steam power: progress of engines—Forced draught and its dangers—Water-tube boilers 13

III. THE BRITISH NAVY.

The fighting force—Theory of offence and defence: the command of the sea—The *Majestic* class described—The group system—Unarmoured ends of British battleships—The *Royal Sovereign*, *Centurion*, *Renown*, *Canopus* class, *Nile*, *Sanspareil*—Size of heavy guns—The "Admiral" class—Second-class and third-class battleships—Coast-defence ships—The functions of cruisers—The *Armstrong* type—The *Terrible*: compared with foreign types—First-class cruisers described—Second-class cruisers: their inferiority in gun-power to French types—Third-class cruisers—Torpedo-gunboats—Torpedo-boat destroyers: their fragility, their functions—Torpedo-boats 51

IV. FOREIGN NAVIES.

FRANCE—Character of the French Navy—Description of *Charlemagne*, *Masséna*, *Carnot*, *Brennus*, *Marceau*, etc.—The French battle fleet compared with the British—Armoured cruisers—Can they replace the battleship?—Other cruisers—Torpedo craft. RUSSIA—The Russian Navy exists for aggression—Russian battleships described—Cruisers and torpedo craft. GERMANY—The best kept Navy in Europe—German battleships, cruisers and torpedo boats.

CONTENTS

ITALY—Decline of Italian naval power—Deficiency of armour—Description of battleships, cruisers, torpedo-craft. UNITED STATES—Aggressive naval policy—Description of battleships and cruisers
Page 107

V. RELATIVE STRENGTH.

The element of uncertainty—Tabular comparisons of the vessels of the principal Powers 158

VI. SHIPBUILDING POLICY.

Mr. Goschen's intentions—Policy and estimates—Our possible enemies—Necessity for increase of armament—Necessity for meeting coast-defence ships with British battleships—Defence of our commerce—The theory and practice of blockade—We want five battleships to an enemy's three—Deficiencies of our existing battle-fleet—Deficiencies in our force of cruisers: of torpedo craft—The German menace—Necessity for continuous progress . . . 179

VII. OFFICERS AND MEN.

The personal equation—Necessity of training—Numbers kept at sea by the principal Powers—Impossibility of manning our existing fleet—The Royal Naval Reserve—Foreign reserves—Schemes for making up our deficiencies: additions to permanent force, short service, reform of present reserve, increase of marines, volunteers—Mr. Goschen's intentions 212

VIII. COLONIES AND COALING STATIONS.

The command of the sea the best Colonial defence—Our distant squadrons—Obsolete ships on foreign stations—Local defence: Australia, New Zealand, The Far East, India, South Africa, Canada, The West Indies—Importance of coaling stations—Weakness of present garrisons—Sierra Leone an example—Malta and Gibraltar 237

IX. ARE WE READY FOR WAR?

The Mediterranean Squadron—Strategical advantage of France—Should we abandon the Mediterranean?—Defective arrangements for mobilization—Divided command of our naval ports—Divided responsibility for the Navy generally—Necessity for a General Staff with a responsible Chief—The function of public opinion in Naval Policy—War must be left to experts . . . 267

APPENDIX . . 291

INDEX . 321

NAVAL POLICY

I.

THE PROBLEM.

TOWARDS the end of January, 1896, there was issued —a year late—a Parliamentary Return of the naval strength of Great Britain and the other principal maritime Powers. Compiled, as we must presume, from the most authoritative sources by the most competent experts, it was intended for the information of the men who have to vote our money for the one effective arm of defence we possess against foreign aggression. It is natural, and surely most essential to our health as a nation, that both Members of Parliament and their constituents should wish to be accurately and clearly informed upon the exact strength of our Navy, and its relation to the strength of others. The Return in question was presumably issued to satisfy this most commendable curiosity. It is not necessary to reproduce it here, for one very good reason: that it can convey no information to anybody.

It could mean almost anything, according to the taste and fancy of the interpreter; which means that it means nothing. For example: that large body of public opinion which regards a ship as a ship, and

NAVAL POLICY

one ship as good as another, could extract from the Return very great consolation. It appears therein that Great Britain owns 384 ships above the size of a torpedo-boat; while France (160), Russia (90), and Germany (81), have between them only 331. On this calculation, we thus possess a comfortable superiority over the three next naval Powers put together: a very comfortable reflexion for the taxpayer to sleep on. Other critics, more discriminating, would consider the classification under which these numbers were submitted to Parliament. There were four heads: battleships, coast-defence ships, cruisers, and other ships. To the believer in battleships it was doubtless interesting to learn that Great Britain, with 46 of these craft completed and 10 building, holds at present a clear lead of the next two Powers — France, with 25, and 9 building; and Germany, with 20, and 3 — but will have lost it by the time the ships building are ready to go to sea. On the other hand, if you count coast-defence ships in the fleet available for battle, we are at present 9 ships behind, and will shortly be 11. It would also be instructive to notice that Germany is at present appreciably more powerful than Russia, both in battleships alone and in battleships and coast defenders together; and also in cruisers. But in cruisers the figures of the Return—and, of course, the Return affords no criterion but figures—give Her Majesty's Navy 126 ships, against 131 of the five other European Great Powers together. In "other ships" our position is not quite so satisfactory, the figures standing at 131 to 167, both Russia and Italy being relatively strong in "other ships." All these conclusions might be drawn by the first two rules of simple

THE PROBLEM

arithmetic from the Parliamentary Return under consideration. No doubt they are all interesting; but, unfortunately, they are all demonstrably misleading. And, indeed, it requires no very great acumen to discern that one battleship may differ from another in capacity for battle, one cruiser from another in fitness for cruising; while even one "other ship" may be other than another. It is so obvious, that it may seem rather poor spirit to make such cheap and obvious mockery of the Return. Yet a Parliamentary Paper purports to be a thing of some weight and dignity. Why, then, on the most important question with which Parliament has to deal is information conveyed to it in a form so manifestly open to ridicule?

For about six weeks Honourable Members had the opportunity of digesting the intelligence thus conveyed to them, and then came on the Navy Estimates. It is not necessary to recapitulate the peculiar circumstances of the international situation at the beginning of March, 1896. The country was beset by a crowd of difficulties with Foreign Powers to which living memory can hardly find a parallel later than the Napoleonic War. In addition to France and Russia, who hold an honorary position as our probable assailants, we were involved in acute differences with Germany and with the United States. On the face of things it was not wholly inconceivable that we might have to make head at sea against a combination of these four Powers. In this crisis, if ever, it was plainly necessary that those who provide our means of defence should be quite clearly aware of our own naval strength, and of its relation to that of our possible enemies. The provision of our means of defence depends, first, on the naval advisers of the First Lord of the Admiralty; second, on the First Lord; third, on the Cabinet; fourth, on the House; lastly, on the country as a whole. In theory the technical knowledge of the five factors may be considered to go, roughly, in a descending scale. The Sea Lords may be presumed to know what the Navy should be better than the First Lord; he, better than the Cabinet Minister; he, better than the plain M.P.; and he, better than the plain constituent. But in practice all knowledge ought to be common to all. Certainly all are equally interested in the adequacy of the Navy. And it is surely not too much to ask that even the meanest voter, though he must needs take much on trust, should have some sort of idea what are the functions our fleet is meant to discharge, and what is its capacity for discharging them. There ought to be an accepted standard of necessary strength, if such can be arrived at. There should be in any case a common understanding as to our actual strength at sea relatively to the navies against which we might possibly have to defend ourselves.

A brief retrospect of the discursive debate on the Naval Estimates of 1896 shows only too well that this common understanding is completely absent. How completely, a few extracts will prove. Mr. Goschen began by frankly declining to flatter our intelligence by entering into any details at all.

"I am not going," he said, "to place before the House comparative lists of the navies of foreign countries and of our own. It is, no doubt, a matter which has to be done, and we at the Admiralty have given days and weeks and months to the consideration of the relative strength of the

THE PROBLEM

different navies. I propose, not to place before the House the processes or figures by which we have arrived at our results; I propose only to give those results, with some indication of the system which we have followed. We have proceeded by analyzing, as regards battleships, all such forces as ought to be taken into consideration. We have been aware of this fact: that there are first-class battleships belonging to ourselves which are at present not much more efficient than some second-class battleships; and, on the other hand, that there are some second-class battleships which may be ranked, in certain circumstances, as equal to first-class battleships. We look at the matter as a whole. We take a second-class battleship which is capable, as regards armament, armour, and speed, of competing with the first-class battleship. You must send the first-class battleship against it. Nevertheless, that second-class ship is unequal to the first class, because it has not got the coal-carrying capacity; and, therefore, it is only under certain given circumstances that the second-class ship is equal to the first class. In the construction of battleships there are four *desiderata*—speed, armament, defensive armour, and coal-carrying capacity. To secure these objects—if you want to secure them all in their fullest efficiency—you require vessels of a certain size; and when you want to decrease the size of that vessel you must make up your minds which of those four *desiderata* you are prepared to sacrifice, and that sacrifice you will choose according to the special circumstances of the nation. Those who are prepared with defensive naval strategy may leave out coal-carrying capacity; those who believe that theirs must be an offensive policy must on no account surrender coal-carrying capacity; and so it happens, when you compare one of our ships, having large coal-carrying capacity, and also considerable capacity for carrying ammunition, with a foreign ship, you may find that the foreign ship has thicker armour; but what is her coal-carrying capacity? You must make a sacrifice on one side or the other; and it is only when you bear in mind these first principles, you will do justice to your own ships, or be able to form a proper opinion."

NAVAL POLICY

At a later point in his speech he added: "A broad view has been taken of the Navy, and we believe that now"—that is to say, in 1899, by which time the 1896 programme is to be carried into effect—"we have arrived at some point on which we may stand."

The considerations enounced by the First Lord are very lucid and very true. But unluckily we find Sir Charles Dilke, upon the continuation of the debate, declaring with equal lucidity and truth that we are very far indeed from any point on which we may stand.

"A very large proportion of our fleet," he pointed out, "now extending to a half of the lowest class but one and the whole of the lowest class is entirely armed with the old guns; and yet they are counted in all comparisons between the force of this country and Foreign Powers as battleships capable of taking their place in the line. The two main points in all Naval Estimates must be battleships and guns. No other test will stand the investigation of sound sense. I cannot see in this programme of the Government as regards battleships in 1899 that any standard of comparison has been taken by the Admiralty as between ourselves and Foreign Powers which could be accepted by those who hold views similar to my own as a sufficient standard for defence. The programme this year seems to me to be a hand-to-mouth programme, a mere continuation programme, a France and Russia programme."

Mr. Balfour, in answer, was even more explicit as to the absolute adequacy, so far as the present position goes, of Mr. Goschen's estimates.

"I think, therefore, that we must content ourselves with the general standard which has been quite sufficient in the past, and, without taking a vast, though not absolutely impossible, combination against us, simply contemplate bringing up our fleet to a strength which would enable us to contend on satis-

THE PROBLEM

factory terms with the two largest fleets that could be brought against us. I believe that that standard has been attained, and will be attained, by the efforts of the late Government, and by our efforts during the three coming years. The facts are extremely simple. You may take as first-class battleships, ships which, from their armament, speed, and defensive armour, are capable of fighting in the first line against any other ships of a similar class, irrespective of coal supply, of height of free-board, or other conditions which make a ship valuable for distant service or service in a rough sea and on the ocean; or you may proceed on a different principle, and you may say that no ship can be described as a first-class battleship which is not capable of fighting anywhere in the first line of battle, that has not a very large coal supply, as well as powerful armament, and that is not therefore capable of joining in a combination of fleets very far distant from its base of operations. According as you take one or other of these principles of calculation no doubt you will get different results in making comparisons with foreign navies. But let it be observed that there is so far this justification for the narrow definition advanced by the late Chancellor of the Exchequer. You are dealing by hypothesis with a single nation—with Great Britain—fighting a combination of Powers, choose what Powers you like. Those two Powers, if you mean to include the second-class battleships—second-class in point of size—with very heavy armament among their first-class ships, undoubtedly cannot bring together in combination a fleet equal to your own. Those ships are only first-class ships in their own waters, and not first-class ships far from their base, and therefore do not form part of a fleet which can work with another nation very far from the base of operations. Therefore it is manifest that, though it would be rash for this House to say that, because some of these smaller and powerfully-armoured ships cannot act far from their own port, they ought under no circumstances to be regarded as first-class battleships, for all purposes they are not first-class battleships, and some of these purposes are the very purposes that become important when you are considering the combined action of two foreign fleets. If you take a rigid definition of a first-class battleship, requiring not merely powerful armament, but powerful armour, speed, and coal endurance, we shall have, as I make out, in 1898-99 a very considerable superiority over the two largest fleets that may be brought against us."

Sir William Harcourt followed on the same side.

"The First Lord of the Treasury has said truly that it depends upon how you compare your ships. We see a small ship of, say, 10,000 tons compared with a ship of 14,000 tons, and we are told that the foreign ship is equal to the English ship of 14,000 tons; it is said the only difference is in the coal-carrying capacity of the vessel. The fact is the small ship has got thicker armour and heavier guns, and therefore it is of as much use in its own waters, as the First Lord has said, as is the larger ship. I daresay that is quite true; but are you going to have no ships of your own in your own waters? If not, why are you not? Are you not going to have in your own waters constantly vessels which you will not send to a great distance? In my belief, the nation will always demand that you shall have a number, and a considerable number, of vessels in the Channel, which are not to go to the other end of the world in case of war. I do not believe that the nation ever will again run the risk which was nearly fatal to it just before the battle of Trafalgar when the Channel was left without a protective fleet, the great ships having gone to a distance. If so, there is an easy method of obtaining a larger number of ships which, for defensive purposes, may be made as powerful as, or more powerful than, much larger ships of other nations. There is a policy by which you can get a far larger number of ships in your own Channel, and that is a policy which is well deserving of consideration."

And then he apologized to the House "for having gone so far with the details of the matter"—a very significant hint as to the spirit in which it was

THE PROBLEM

considered decent that the House should treat such affairs.

All this sounds very confident and very comforting. But next follow Sir John Colomb, and later Mr. Arnold Forster, both able and assiduous students of naval affairs. On their showing the matter does not seem quite so simple as Mr. Balfour would make out, and they appear to differ from Sir William Harcourt in holding the view that it is possible that the British Navy might find it advisable to act in force in other seas than its "own Channel." Sir John Colomb

"Regretted to hear the First Lord of the Treasury hark back to the fallacious idea that if our fleet was equal to the two fleets of the greatest Foreign Powers, therefore this country was safe. The strategical equality of ships was a question quite separate from individual fighting power, and he submitted that if ten battleships were in a port they could not be kept in by ten other battleships. In some ports he could name it would take twenty and even thirty to give any guarantee of producing that moral effect which would keep the ten ships in. If that was so, he maintained it was false to base our naval policy on the abstract comparison of battleships."

And Mr. Arnold Forster followed (a day or two afterwards) with a tribute to Sir Charles Dilke's speech.

"It struck every one who heard it as a lucid, well-conceived statement of a case which might be strong or weak, according as the facts stood. Until the facts were overthrown it was a strong case, and one to which a little more consideration ought to be devoted. The leader of the Opposition said that we were to accept the proposals of the Government, because they were proposed by a responsible Government with their knowledge of the necessities of the case. Was it not an elementary fact that during the last ten years everything that had been conceded had been forced by agitation from the responsible Government, and had been something they did not intend to give? The increase of the Navy Estimates had proved that the Estimates made by former responsible Governments did not cover the necessities of the case. To tell them that they must accept these Estimates, because they were proposed by a responsible Government, was to fly in the face of all experience."

Now what is the plain Englishman—to whom, after all, the naval power of England is a matter of vital concern—to make of all this? What can he make of it? Simply that the First Lord of the Admiralty and the First Lord of the Treasury think that the Navy Estimates of 1896 put the country in a satisfactory state of defence; from which it should follow that there will be next to no Navy Estimates in 1897. The leader of the Opposition seems to tend towards the same view; while Sir Charles Dilke, Sir John Colomb, and Mr. Arnold Forster hold a diametrically opposite opinion. He will see that the men in high authority say one thing, and the men who have made a study of the subject say the other. But, beyond this, the four days of debate tell him absolutely nothing. The men who represent him and govern him are at loggerheads, and of the opinions of the Sea Lords of the Admiralty— the men of practical experience and knowledge—there is no sign. The Parliamentary Returns fog him with figures which carry no meaning with them; the Parliamentary speeches exhibit nothing but a conflict of the opinions on which it is his custom to rely. We must attempt to get beyond these levelling figures which make one ship as good as another, and these speeches which cannot determine what is a first-class battleship and what is not. "It depends what you count," said Sir

THE PROBLEM

Charles Dilke, and the phrase was the keynote of the whole debate. It seems worth while to ask what there is to count, and what reason there is why you should count it.

In other words, we ought to go behind arbitrary classifications, and inquire what are the elements of naval force which the classifications represent. We must analyze. It may be granted at once that the analysis can never be quite certain or quite final. There has not been sufficient experience of naval war to determine the relative value of one factor and another with strict exactness. Still less can we put down on paper such indeterminate equations as the value—the skill and coolness—of one fighting man in reference to another. War, like sport, must always have this element of human uncertainty, which is the cause of the charm of both. But without presuming to absolute mathematical certainty, we can, and should, get some way further towards it. We can ask what it is that makes one fighting-ship superior to another; why one ship is superior for one particular purpose to another; how our own country stands in reference to these qualifications. There is a reason for everything, if we can only ferret it out; and there must be a reason why one ship, or one fleet, should conquer another. Also there is a purpose for everything, and everything is what it is in order that it may fulfil a certain purpose. If we can find out what reasons there are why one ship or fleet can be made superior to another, and in what particular ways British ships and fleets ought to be superior to any other ships and fleets that may be pitted against them, then we shall have advanced some way to the solution of the most important problem that confronts us as a nation. We want to find out as well as we can, first, what our Navy can do relatively to other navies, and, second, what it ought to be able to do. And having found this out as well as we can, at all costs, if we are to remain the greatest nation of the world, we must fit the Navy to do its work. We exist as a great nation by reason of our colonies, our trade, and our daily bread, and, once we lose the sea, we lose all three of them.

II.

THE ELEMENTS OF FORCE IN WARSHIPS.

THE history of warfare is the history of a struggle for existence among weapons. If the world has chosen to fix its attention upon those who have used weapons in battle, those who devised them have been the real makers of military history. The fighting man has been as resolute and cunning in one age as in another; the manner of his fighting, and, within limits, the chances of his success, have been governed by the inventor. The battle of Crecy, to use a commonplace of the school books, was less a victory of Englishmen over Frenchmen than a victory of the light archer over the armoured horseman. The battle of Falkirk before it, where the English bowmen broke up the square of Scottish spearmen, was a victory of organized long-range weapons over an organization of weapons useful only at close quarters. Bannockburn, where the English bowmen were broken by cavalry, was a set-back in the true line of progress, due, probably, rather to bad generalship than to the defects of the bow as a weapon; the bow, at any rate, reaped a rich revenge at Halidon Hill. The invention of gunpowder still further increased the disadvantage of the close fighting weapons, until, for highly-organized warfare, the bayonet is like to become as obsolete as the battle-axe. This and similar gigantic changes in the conditions of war are the work of the inventor, and of the inventor alone. The rulers of battle have been the inventors of steel-forging, of body-armour, of gunpowder, and the like; the great tacticians have been merely those captains who had the insight and the coolness to turn the inventor's ingenuity to best account in the field. It would be futile to deny that courage or skill, or even numbers, have often given the victory to the less perfectly equipped force. But on the whole, and in the long run, the military nations of the world seem so nearly equal in bravery and generalship, that the possessors of the best machines are certain to win in the long run. Valour marches in the iron grip of science, and must either obey or perish.

It is only in our own age, with its astonishing harvest of inventions in every field, that physical science has thus clearly disengaged itself as the tyrant of war. In earlier days progress in the instruments of war was so slow that a nation could easily be a century or two out of date in its equipment without the certainty of defeat. To-day progress is so bewilderingly rapid that the failure to keep up with the scientific developments of a single year might very conceivably ruin a great empire. If this is true of war by land, it is a thousand-fold truer of war by sea, and that for a very obvious reason. It results from a fundamental law of hydrostatics, that you cannot put more weight into a ship than the weight of the water it displaces. In a ship of any given size the amount of destructive and protective power that can be put on board is necessarily and immutably limited by this law. Moreover, the size

ELEMENTS OF FORCE IN WARSHIPS

of a ship itself, theoretically unlimited, is limited in practice by such considerations as handiness in turning, draught of water, capability of approaching land, facility of docking, and the like. In the ship of war, therefore, we find the very paradise of the inventor. It is the essence of mechanical invention to concentrate the greatest possible energy into the least possible weight and space: an engine of fifty horse-power is preferable to fifty horses, not because it is more powerful—for by hypothesis it is not—but because it is more compact and manageable. The ship of war cries out for such compacted power, and the inventor has most abundantly responded to the appeal. The modern warship is such a maze of complicated machines, that the ordinary Briton, who is not engineer, chemist, mathematician, and electrician all in one, may well give up the attempt to unravel the appalling tangle. Yet it is his business to know, at least, the most important factors in the efficiency of Her Majesty's ships of war, which are also his own. On their efficiency depends his daily bread, to say nothing of his national self-esteem and honour. And this efficiency depends, nowadays, on a never-ceasing development of new forces of attack and defence, in which the smallest pause may at any moment mean defeat and ruin.

The primary requisites for a fighting-ship are obviously two—the ability to get to the point where she is to fight, and the ability to fight when she gets there. The first function is the subject-matter of strategy, the second of tactics. Neither can be preferred before the other, since no quality can be more than indispensable. But it is obvious that, in any ship, they can be combined in various degrees, and attained by various means. The ability to get to the point of action depends on sea-worthiness, speed, and staying-power; ability to defeat the enemy, mainly on power to destroy his ships, protection for the ship's self, and speed to enable it to bring its offensive qualities into play to the best advantage, and to assist its means of defence. In three words, offensive, defensive, and locomotive power, are the principal necessities of a warship; and the best ship is that which affords the most advantageous combination of the three.

It so happens that a point, which may be roughly placed about forty years ago, marked a great step forward in each of these respects. This was the almost simultaneous introduction of steam propulsion, armoured ships and rifled guns, and the epoch may be taken as the birth of the modern warship.* These three elements combine into the battleship; that is, the ship capable, by reason of her offensive and defensive power, to sustain the stress of a fleet action. With a different distribution of the armour from that first adopted — by the horizontal protection offered by a steel deck, instead of vertical plating on the side—the three elements are as indispensable to the modern cruiser. The terrible example which the *Merrimac*, possessed of armour, steam, and rifled guns, made of

---

* In strict accuracy the first steam vessel in the British Navy was the *Comet*, in 1821, and the first screw steamer, the *Rattler* 1841. The first armoured ships were five floating batteries built by France in 1854, and their first appearance in action was at the capture of Kinburn, in the Crimea, the following year. Rifled small arms were issued to British troops in 1851, but Lord Armstrong did not complete the first rifled cannon till 1856. It is acutely observed by Mr. H. W. Wilson (*Ironclads in Action*, ii. 210) that the steam-engine, making exact perfection of work possible, and enabling large masses of metal to be treated, is really responsible both for armour-plates and rifled guns.

the *Cumberland* and *Congress*, which lacked them, settled the question of this indispensability once and for all. Without them, in short, no ship of any size could possibly take the sea, in war-time, without the certainty of destruction.

But since the well-marked epoch which saw this great revolution in the construction of warships, progress has not been stayed. It is easy to fix this point as the birth of the modern fighting-ship, but since then its growth, if less readily marked down at any particular period, has been continuous. During the last forty years, indeed, the transformation has been as complete, if more gradual, than was effected by the three great inventions which rendered the old man-of-war obsolete in every respect, almost at a blow. The *Warrior*, of 1859, which (after the substitution of rifles for smooth-bores) embodied all the progress of her day, would be almost as helpless against the *Majestic* as the *Victory* would be against the *Warrior*. The *Achilles* (1869), which is the oldest armoured ship supposed to be fit for service, carries armour whose resisting power is less than one-third of that of our newest, the *Majestic;* her heaviest guns have less than one-tenth of the power of the *Majestic's*, while her speed is to that of the *Majestic*, roughly, as five to seven, and to that of our fastest vessels, as five to twelve. Obviously the *Achilles* is hopelessly obsolete as compared with the *Majestic*. Moreover the thirty years between the two gave birth to a long series of vessels, which mark the line of evolution from the one to the other. Each of these vessels is obsolete, in a greater or less degree, as compared with the type that succeeded her. As compared with the very latest type, they are all, in a sense, obsolete; and it must ever be remembered that to engage in naval war with an obsolete fleet is to invite disaster. It will be replied, and with perfect truth, that the absence of the one or two latest modifications does not necessarily incapacitate a ship for war. That being admitted, the method by which we can arrive, as nearly as possible, at the actual fighting value of a fleet is very plain. We must analyze the various steps in naval progress marked by each type, with a view to determining the value of each. We must then examine the existing fleet, and discuss to what extent it is equipped with each progressive element of efficiency.

To take first attacking power. The superiority of rifled small-arms was demonstrated in the Crimea; the superiority of rifled cannon as decisively in the American Civil War. The smooth-bore gun had two immense disadvantages—inaccuracy of aim, and shortness of range. For facility of loading, a certain amount of what is known to artillerists as windage was necessary; that is to say, there was necessarily a space between the projectile and the bore of the gun. When the gun was fired the projectile bounded from side to side of the barrel, and was naturally deflected to one side or another, according to the spot where it last struck before leaving the gun. Thus, if it struck at the right, close to the muzzle, it bounded away to the left. With such a machine precision in shooting was obviously impossible. Furthermore, no projectile could be used with the smooth-bore but a spherical one. This had two disadvantages, as compared with the long projectiles now in use. If its diameter was the same, its weight was less; if its weight was to be the same, its diameter had to be greater. Now the resistance of the air varies directly with the square of the diameter of a body, and inversely with its weight. Consequently the larger and lighter spherical shot was sooner stopped by the air, which means that its range was less. If the long projectile had been used in a smooth-bore, it would have spun over and over on leaving the gun; whereas the rifled barrel spun it about its axis in the gun, so that it preserved the original direction in its flight. The first rifled cannon, built by Lord Armstrong, was breech-loading, and made of steel. But both these improvements, which have since become essentials of efficient ordnance, were somewhat in advance of their time. Steel could not yet be cast with sufficient perfection, and though the difficulties and accidents that resulted from the breech-loading method could have been overcome, guns were then so short that it made little difference whether they were loaded from one end or the other. Hence the British Admiralty's preference for muzzle-loaders, which to begin with was not unreasonable. What was unreasonable, and might easily have been fatal, was the belated stubbornness with which the muzzle-loader was clung to after the last shred of justification for it disappeared.

This last shred went in 1878—again, so far as concerned this country, through the agency of Lord Armstrong. In that year experiments were conducted with slow-burning powder and long guns. The advantage of this invention—which had been first proposed in America, and first used in Russia—was great and obvious. A small-grained quick-burning powder ignited instantaneously, exerting a prodigious pressure on the gun in the immediate vicinity of the explosion, but a comparatively small and momentary impulse on the projectile in its journey down the barrel. The large-grained powder took longer to ignite; the gas was given off gradually, and thus drove the projectile down the gun with steadily increasing force. In a short gun slow-burning powder was useless; the projectile was gone while the powder was still igniting, so that much energy was lost. In a long gun this powder got more work on the projectile, with a vast resultant gain in energy. For example, the long gun, even of twenty years ago, drove the shot from the muzzle at the rate of 2000 feet a second, whereas none of the short muzzle-loaders had ever attained 1600; to-day France has guns eighty times the length of their calibre, which give a muzzle-velocity of over 3200 feet a second. This enormous gain could not be sacrificed; consequently long guns became a necessity. As a further consequence, these guns had to be breech-loaders, for on board ship there was no room to run in the long guns until the muzzle was in a possible position for loading. As the breech-loader had not to be run right in, there was also a gain in quickness of loading. A third advantage lay in the protection given to the gun's crews, since the loading could be done behind a better protection of armour. With these three advantages—superior velocity, giving increased range and power of penetration, quickness of loading, and protection for the crews, the breech-loader was plainly certain to drive its competitor off the sea. To-day the muzzle-loader is only less antiquated than the smooth-bore. How heavily the British Admiralty has handicapped the Navy by its long-continued refusal to recognize this fact we shall see later.

ELEMENTS OF FORCE IN WARSHIPS

As soon as steel became sufficiently well known to be worked with precision and confidence, iron was abandoned in the manufacture of heavy guns. The superior strength of steel enabled it to resist a more violent explosion, and thus the steel gun could fire a higher charge. A further advance in this direction was the introduction of wire guns. Until recently, guns were made by shrinking hoops on to the barrel. The barrel was first built of steel; then a steel cylinder was taken, whose inner diameter, when it was cool, was less than the outer diameter of the barrel. This cylinder, or hoop, or jacket, was then heated until it expanded sufficiently to be placed round the barrel. Then, as it cooled, it shrank on to the barrel, which was compressed, while the hoop was expanded. This gave enormous strength to both. In wire construction, on the other hand, the steel is applied in the form of a continuous wire, instead of hoops, and is wound round the barrel at a very high tension. This method has the disadvantage of being slow, since the gun must all be made in one piece, so to speak; whereas previously the barrel and half-a-dozen hoops could all be prepared simultaneously. On the other hand, the wire gun is immensely stronger, and the introduction of new smokeless powders, of great explosive force, has made strength a matter of prime importance. The 12-inch wire gun of the British Navy, for example, as compared with the older hoop-shrunk weapon of the same calibre, will stand, without damage, an explosion powerful enough to give a muzzle-velocity of 2400 ft.-secs. to 1914, and a muzzle-energy of 33,940 ft.-tons to 18,130. With this enormous gain in power, wire guns will, doubtless, in time replace all others; they are already being built of various calibres for the British Navy. As yet, however, comparatively few are mounted aboard ship. Moreover, although the wire gun is vastly more powerful than the older guns of the same calibre, there are many guns mounted in all the principal navies equal, or superior, in power to the heaviest wire guns afloat. Thus the energy with which the projectile leaves the muzzle of our own $13\frac{1}{2}$-inch 67-ton guns, as carried by the *Royal Sovereign* and her sister ships, is slightly greater than that attained by the 12-inch 46-ton wire guns of the *Majestic* and similar ships. On these grounds it would not be proper to consider an armament of hoop-shrunk guns as necessarily inferior to one of wire guns in the same way as an armament of muzzle-loaders is necessarily inferior to one of breech-loaders. The muzzle-loader is outclassed for purposes of modern war, and any ship that carries it is unfit for the battle of to-day or to-morrow; whereas this is far from being the case with the guns of the *Royal Sovereign*.

The next important development in gun-power, after the introduction of breech-loaders, was not, properly speaking, an improvement in artillery, though it led indirectly, and in combination with other causes, to a step forward in gunnery so great as to amount almost to a revolution. This development, which at first appeared only to concern the naval architect, was the introduction of the secondary armament in battleships. To explain the meaning of this, it is necessary to hark back a little. The earliest ironclads resembled the old three-deckers in carrying almost all their guns on the broadside. But the ironclads of this type were very large, and especially very long, otherwise they would not have had broadside enough to carry a battery of any power. As a consequence they were clumsy at turning, and generally unhandy; also they could neither direct any fire to speak of ahead or astern, nor were they protected from raking fire. To remedy these defects Sir Edward Reed designed a series of central-battery ships. In these the guns were concentrated amidships, protected by armoured bulkheads from fire ahead or astern, and capable of firing several heavy guns in the same direction. With the same idea of securing all-round protection and all-round fire, a series of turret-ships was built concurrently with the central-battery type. These carried four heavy guns, mounted close together amidships, in revolving turrets adapted to give them the widest possible arc of fire. It was on these four heavy guns—the primary armament—that the earlier turret-ships wholly depended for their offensive power. But in the later vessels of this class the secondary armament began to be introduced—that is to say, a number of guns not powerful enough to pierce thick armour, and yet more powerful than was necessary to repel torpedo-boats. These guns, which would evidently be very effective in attacking the unarmoured parts of large ships, first appeared in the *Inflexible*, which was completed in 1880. The turret-ship, however, with all her offensive and defensive power crowded up into a comparatively small space amidships, was ill-adapted for the development of the secondary armament. At the worst, it masked the fire of the heavy guns, and, at the best, it was not shielded by armour, so that the secondary guns could easily be put out of action in a few minutes. But in 1880 a vessel of a very different type was laid down—the

Collingwood — designed by Mr. (now Sir William) White. She carried her four heavy guns, not in turrets, but in barbettes, which are armoured turrets without any top to them :* the breech of the gun is lowered to the loading position, which is under cover, and the gun is then raised above the barbette to fire. Instead of being set close together amidships, like the earlier turrets, the *Collingwood's* two barbettes are at the forward and after end respectively of a long armoured citadel, and the secondary armament of six 6-inch guns is mounted between them. All British battleships since laid down have followed the main lines of the *Collingwood* in respect of the disposition of the armament, and the type is now being largely copied abroad. Meanwhile, the number of secondary pieces has been increased from six in the *Collingwood* to twelve in the *Majestic;* they are now mounted so as to secure a better all-round fire, and in all the latest vessels behind armour.

At first the function of the secondary battery was not altogether plain. No doubt it could plug a certain number of leisurely shells into the unarmoured parts of an antagonist. But the ships of 1880 were built with a view to let the whole of their unarmoured parts be shattered, and yet to remain afloat and able to fight their heavy guns as serenely as ever. In a few years, however, came an invention that revolutionized, and is still revolutionizing, the whole art of naval architecture and the whole science of naval tactics. This was the quick-firing gun; and it need hardly be said that it owed its birth to the insatiable genius of Lord

---

* In some later ships there is a heavy steel shield over the top of the barbette.

ELEMENTS OF FORCE IN WARSHIPS

Armstrong. The quick-firing cannon may be called the child of the machine-gun, of which the first to see active service was the mitrailleuse in the Franco-German war. But perhaps it may, with even greater point, be called the child of the torpedo-boat. Everywhere it is the demand that begets the supply, the attack that suggests the defence; and we have already seen that this is nowhere more true than in naval war.

As soon as the torpedo-boat appeared on the scene as a recognized factor in fighting by sea, it was plainly necessary that the larger ship should be supplied with a weapon to beat off the assailant. The earliest exploits of torpedo-boats were in the Russo-Turkish war of 1877; the heavy guns of the Turks were too slow and clumsy to hit the Russian boats, and rifle fire was too light to stop them. Plainly some intermediate weapon was wanted. Accordingly in 1877 Mr. Nordenfeldt invented a machine gun, with four barrels, one inch in calibre: this fired in a minute 216 shots quite large enough to sink any torpedo-boat of the day. When the torpedo-boat became faster, and protected her vitals with coal, the Hotchkiss three- and six-pounder cannon were invented. These guns can fire thirty and twenty-five rounds a minute respectively, and are adapted to the use of shell, which would be more effective against a torpedo-boat than shot. As it is reckoned that an attacking torpedo-boat would only be under fire of these guns for about a minute, this rate of fire, wonderful and even appalling as it is, is plainly none too high. Yet when the Hotchkiss six-pounder is compared with older slow-firing guns, it will be seen at once how tremendous was the revolution it

NAVAL POLICY

implied. Six of these tiny machines, whose calibre is two inches and a-quarter, can fire in a minute exactly the same weight of metal as the $16\frac{1}{4}$-in. 110-ton gun, which is the most powerful in the world. Of course, one round from this monster will penetrate a thickness of material which the six-pounder might bombard resultlessly for ever; on the other hand, the Hotchkisses can perform many services of which the big gun is incapable. The fact remains that these six guns, weighing between them—and remember the vital importance of economy of weight aboard ship—a little over two tons, can spit out metal upon the enemy at exactly the same rate as the gun which weighs over 110 tons.

To get this amount of power at this economy of weight and money was evidently enough for a torpedo-boat. Even if only a couple of six-pounders bear on an attacking torpedo-boat, they can fire fifty shots at her during the minute she is under fire. But there are torpedo craft in existence which the Hotchkiss gun is not sufficient to stop. These are the craft called indifferently torpedo-catchers and torpedo-gunboats—very fast vessels of anything from 400 to 1200 tons. They were originally designed to destroy torpedo-boats with the light quick-fire guns which they carry; but they are also fitted with torpedo gear for the attack of larger vessels. Now the Hotchkiss is useless to stop a vessel of this kind, as was very clearly demonstrated in 1891, when the Balmacedist gunboats, *Almirante Lynch* and *Almirante Condell*, torpedoed and sank the *Blanco Encalada* in Caldera Bay. The ironclad carried three six-pounders, and hit her assailants more than once, but without doing them any damage. Three years later the *Aquidaban* was similarly sunk by the torpedo-gunboat *Sémpaio* off Desterro, in Brazil; the *Sempaio* was hit thirty times by machine guns, but suffered no disabling hurt of any kind. Here, then, was a new demand for a larger quick-firing gun, and the demand was duly supplied by Lord Armstrong. It was supplied, indeed, before the practical demonstration of its necessity afforded in Caldera Bay—almost as soon as the new form of torpedo craft was designed. The new weapon was the 4·7-in. quick-firer, an enormous advance on anything that had been seen before. In a competitive trial, at Portsmouth, between one of the new guns and the 5-in. service breech-loader, the quick-fire piece fired ten rounds at sea in 47 secs., while the slow-firer took 5 mins. 7 secs. for the same task. That is to say, that a battleship, with the new gun, could plant twelve shots into an approaching torpedo-catcher, where the old gun could only discharge two. The advantage is not represented by these figures alone: there is also the serious addition to it, that whereas the aim need only be altered slightly between each of the quick-firer's shots, the attacking boat will have advanced so far between the rounds of the slow-firer that a considerable adjustment will be needed, and the charge may far more easily be wasted. Twelve shots a minute, again, seeing that these shots weighed 45 lbs. apiece, with shell corresponding, was plainly good enough for these torpedo-gunboats with anything like shooting. If this was so with the 4·7-in. gun, how much more so with the 6-in., introduced immediately after, which throws shot of 100 lbs. as against 45, and exerts an energy of 3356 ft.-tons as against 995? Indeed, it may be said that the invention of the quick-fire gun—and that more especially since the advent of smokeless powder—has robbed the torpedo of half its terrors. It is still the same tremendous and irresistible force when it can get home. But it has lost the attribute of silent mysterious power which it won in the days of its earliest successes; there now exists a weapon which can face it, given vigilance and skill, with something more than an even chance of victory. It is now no longer necessary to grope after such helpless, clumsy devices as torpedo netting. The quick-fire gun has, assuredly, not killed the torpedo. But it has brought it down to the level of other weapons whose possibilities can be estimated, and which can be resisted, and even conquered, by recognized and definite means.

By the time the quick-firer had advanced to such relatively high calibres as 4·7 and 6 inches, new possibilities and new functions began to open out before it. If it was good enough to destroy the steel-built unarmoured torpedo-catcher, it was also good enough to destroy the unarmoured portions of steel-built battleships. Before the introduction of the larger quick-firers, the armour of battleships was concentrated on certain definite positions. Over the whole water-line in most foreign warships, over the side and the transverse bulkheads of the central citadel in English vessels, and over the heavy gun positions in all, was piled armour so thick as to defeat, so far as possible, the attack of the heaviest guns afloat. The rest of the ship was left unarmoured. Considerations of weight forbade that anything but the vitals should be efficiently protected against the great guns, and if it could not be armoured against these, it was as well left unarmoured altogether.

ELEMENTS OF FORCE IN WARSHIPS

The large quick-firer changed these conditions completely. The 6-inch Armstrong quick-firer can penetrate 15 inches of wrought iron at the muzzle, and 9 inches at 2000 yards; this means $7\frac{1}{2}$ inches at the muzzle, and about $4\frac{1}{2}$ at 2000 yards, of the hardest and most impenetrable steel armour at present known. Obviously a gun of this power, firing six rounds a minute, can do enormous damage to the finest battleship ever launched. It can riddle the unarmoured ends of British battleships, thereby decreasing their speed, and with it their tactical value, even if it does not disable them altogether. It can destroy ammunition hoists and hydraulic mountings, thereby as good as destroying the guns. It can burst under barbettes or turrets, which it could not attack directly, and possibly disable half, or even in some cases all, the great guns of a ship at a single blow. The naked or lightly-protected secondary armament it can put out of action infallibly. It must in any case deal awful destruction to life, and sow wild confusion and disorganization in any ship against which it is directed in any strength. And if this is so with gunpowder, it would be tenfold more so with the high explosives now tentatively adopted by the leading naval powers. These compounds have a detonating energy vastly greater than that of gunpowder: wherever they penetrate they will tear a huge rent in a ship's side, the concussion will be awful, smashing everything within reach, and any man who is so unhappy as to escape instant death will indubitably be suffocated by their poisonous fumes. An engine which can deal six such blows in a minute could not but revolutionize naval warfare. It did not want the recent lesson of the China-Japan war to demonstrate its power, but that demonstration was complete and final. The quick-fire guns of the Japanese riddled the Chinese vessels and tore them open, mowing down every man before them. Many were set afire, and two were actually sunk by Japanese shell. It is true that these were unarmoured cruisers, but what the cruiser suffered here the unarmoured parts of the battleships may look to suffer elsewhere.

It may be said here that the quick-firing gun is not differentiated from the ordinary slow-firer by any one clearly-defined principle, as is the breech-loader from the muzzle-loader. The superior rapidity of fire is obtained by the combination of several expedients affecting most of the component parts of a big gun. The breech-piece is so arranged that it can be opened more readily, in one motion instead of two; a cartridge case is used, which disposes of the necessity of sponging out the gun after each round; the recoil takes place directly in the line of fire; springs are used to return the gun at once from the recoil to the firing position, and the sights are placed on the carriage instead of on the body of the gun, thus enabling the gunner to take his aim while the piece is being loaded. All these inventions unite to make up the quick-firer. In principle, therefore, there is no limit to the size of this kind of ordnance, and the French Navy now claims to possess quick-fire guns of 9·4 inches calibre, while Lord Armstrong's firm goes no further than 8 inches, and the British Navy only to 6. But in practice a limit is fixed by the weight of the projectile. For a genuine quick-firer this must be of a weight to be handled by one man with the rapidity which the performances of these guns exact. The British 6-in. gun is served by five

ELEMENTS OF FORCE IN WARSHIPS

men, one of whom gives all his energies to handling the 100 lb. shot; and to do this six times a minute is probably as much as any man could comfortably stand for many minutes together. The Armstrong 8-in. gun has a projectile of over 200 lbs., and the Canet 9·4-in. one of 330, which is too heavy for rapid handling. Nevertheless, one pattern of the Elswick 8-in. gun fires 250 lb. four times a minute, while the 9·2-in. British service gun fires 380 lbs. five times in six minutes. The energies of the discharges are 10,226 and 10,910 foot-tons respectively, so that in six minutes the destruction done by the smaller quick-firer is to that of the larger slow-firer as 245,424 to 54,550. With this enormous balance to play with, the quick-fire gun can easily afford to lose a little of its nominal rapidity through the unhandy weight of the shot, and still maintain a vast superiority in offensive power. From all this it is quite plain that, bearing in mind the original question as to the relative efficiency secured by modern improvements, the ship that lacks heavy quick-fire pieces must be considered obsolete relatively to the ship that possesses them.

With regard to offensive power, so far as it resides in guns, there is no need to pursue the analysis further. There is, indeed, a weapon which, in the near future, may conceivably create the completest transformation that war has yet seen—the pneumatic dynamite gun, invented by Lieutenant Zalinski, of the U.S. Navy. This weapon discharges huge flying torpedoes, as they may most appropriately be called, by means of compressed air. The gun is fifty feet long, of 15 inches calibre; the full charge is 500 lbs. of dynamite. With this charge fair practice can be made at about a mile and a-half, while by using an 8-inch projectile, with 100 lbs. of dynamite, the range can be increased to two miles. It is claimed that the dynamite shell does not need actually to strike a ship, but that if it struck the water and exploded, no vessel could live within thirty yards of it. But even so it has as yet been found difficult to make accurate practice with this gun, and the flight of the projectile is so slow that this difficulty, in aiming at a body in motion, is much enhanced. For this reason, as well as the very treacherous character of dynamite, most nations are at present rather shy of the pneumatic gun. It is mounted as a shore defence in various harbours of the United States, which Government also, with commendable enterprise, fitted out the *Vesuvius* with the Zalinski guns, and sent her to sea to destroy derelicts. The *Nictheroy* was also armed with one of these weapons in the recent Brazilian Civil War. But the experience of the *Vesuvius* was not conclusive, and the *Nictheroy* never fired her gun in action. At present, therefore, this weapon need not be taken into account as a factor in naval strength.

The locomotive torpedo—which is in its essence a submarine gun—is still, although it has had many more years of development, in something the same dubious position as the Zalinski tube. That it can wreck the stoutest ship, if it explodes against the bottom, is obvious. But despite the fact that recent naval war has given us more experience of torpedo actions than of any others, the potentialities and limits of this weapon remain largely obscure. That torpedo-boats can destroy ships lying at anchor, keeping only a slack watch, or unprovided with suitable quick-fire guns, was proved by the fate of the Turkish *Seifé* in the Danube nearly twenty years ago, and by the cases of the *Blanco Encalada*, the *Aquidaban*, and the Chinese vessels in Wei-hai-Wei harbour since; but the truth is so obvious that it hardly needed demonstration. Mr. H. W. Wilson has compiled an interesting tabular statement* of the result of the twenty-seven actions in which the torpedo has been used, from which it appears that out of twenty-one ships attacked when at anchor, twelve were sunk. Assailant boats were lost only in six instances, of which three were in the American Civil War, before the torpedo-boat had as yet developed itself into a highly specialized craft. On the other hand, there is no extant case in which a ship in motion has ever sustained the slightest damage from a torpedo. The first time such an attempt was made was by the British *Shah* against the *Huascar*, while later, at the Yalu, more than one of the Chinese vessels fired nearly every torpedo (probably for fear they might be exploded by the enemy's shell) without the slightest result. The deeds of the Chinese boats were equally futile, though had they been handled by skilful and resolute men, the dense smoke of the battle would probably have given them admirable openings. As it was, the sole result of the torpedo in the only fleet action fought since its birth is the unconfirmed conjecture that a Chinese cruiser may have been sunk by a stray floating Whitehead, or else by one of her own torpedoes exploded in its tube. What results could be attained by torpedo craft accompanying a fleet to sea, or by the torpedo equipment of larger ships in action, we have at present no data to determine. Six torpedo-boats safely crossed the Atlantic in 1894 to the seat of hostilities in Brazil; but the numerous break-

* *Ironclads in Action*, vol. ii, table xxv.

NAVAL POLICY

downs of such craft in any sea raise the doubt whether this performance, though most creditable in any case, was not also somewhat lucky. Our own torpedo-boat-destroyers could doubtless in some cases accompany a squadron to sea, and act as enlarged torpedo-boats; but even the destroyers, as will be shewn in the next chapter, have still to make their reputation for soundness of machinery. Nor is there any experience to go on as to the part 'these vessels would play in action between squadrons of battleships. They would doubtless be used for this purpose in the event of war, and should at least neutralize any sea-going torpedo-boats that might be with the enemy; to say more than this is to prophesy without knowing. As for larger ships, it can be said confidently that any torpedo above the water would be a good deal more dangerous to its possessor than to the enemy. Apart from this, the principal point to notice is that as the torpedo has been partly neutralized by the quick-fire, so it has itself almost wholly superseded the ram. If a ship is immobile enough and near enough to the enemy to be rammed, she is still more certainly immobile enough and near enough to be torpedoed; moreover, she should be able herself to torpedo the enemy before the moment of collision. This fact does not, perhaps, amount to very much, for the ram is hardly a more trustworthy weapon than the torpedo.* Whatever, in fact, may be the ultimate fate of the torpedo, it is too deadly a weapon to ignore in any fleet. And for one boon we may all be grateful to it. The torpedo-boat swooping through a hail of shot and shell upon its huge prey, has restored all, and more than all, the romance that went out of naval war with

* See Mr. Laird Clowes (*Journal of the United Service Institution*, 1894).

the cutting-out expeditions and boarding fights of the old days.* What is almost as important is that, in the day of great ships, torpedoes have restored to the junior officer that opportunity of developing responsibility and resource that comes of an independent command.

It is hardly necessary to insist further on the intimate way in which progress in one department of naval efficiency is associated with progress in another. As soon as one weapon attains a commanding position, there rises another to counteract it. Similar to this struggle is the long duel between offence and defence, between armour and the gun. The contest has had various phases. At one moment armour has defied penetration by the most powerful gun in existence; at another it has seemed on the brink of as complete an obsolescence as has overtaken body-armour by land; at the present moment attack and defence are more or less in equilibrium. Armour, in the first instance, followed naturally upon the invention of shell. But, although shrapnel came into use in 1808, it was only at Sinope, in 1853, that its awful effects were clearly demonstrated, and only in 1854 that mechanical progress enabled the long-existing idea of defence to be put into execution. The earliest armour, though not exceeding four or five inches of iron plating, proved a world-awakening success. The ships that bore it were nothing less than impregnable. At Kinburn the French floating batteries bombarded and silenced strong forts at half-a-mile range—a feat impossible either before or since—with a loss of only two men killed and twenty-five wounded—almost all hit by

* See Mr. F. T. Jane's *Blake of the Rattlesnake*, for a fine, lurid, blood-and-dynamite romance on these lines.

projectiles entering the port-holes. The *Merrimac* and *Monitor* hammered each other steadily for three hours, with no worse result than stunning one or two men; the only blood shed in the engagement was from the nose, through concussion. But the general introduction of rifled ordnance, along with its increasing weight and power, soon changed the relation between gun and armour. The corslet of iron grew heavier and heavier, to resist the increasing violence of the attack: the limit was reached about 1880 with the enormous thickness of 24 inches in the *Inflexible*, and $21\frac{1}{2}$ in the French *Formidable* and Italian *Duilio*. Meanwhile the gun was still increasing its power, and, unless the ship was to be all armour, the laying on of ton after ton of iron could clearly not go on for ever. A substance was required which should possess equal or greater resistance, with less weight and thickness—an economy of weight, in fact, for such is the essence of all progress in naval architecture. The requirement was fulfilled by the introduction of compound armour-plates of soft iron faced with hard steel. This was manufactured either by running steel, at a great heat, over a wrought-iron plate, or by placing a thin steel plate at a distance from the iron foundation, and filling up the interval with molten steel, which bound the two plates together. In both processes the iron was about twice the thickness of the steel, and the compound plate was compressed to about half its original thickness, so as to give it toughness. The effect of the hard steel face was that the plate could not be penetrated by shot; it had to be cracked and broken up before the area behind it could be efficiently attacked. With this great advantage to its account, compound armour became the standard protection for British ships for about ten years. There was, however, always a doubt as to the relative merits of compound plates and solid steel, and several competitive trials were carried out all over Europe in the early Eighties, with a view to the decision of this question. As all the armour engaged is now more or less obsolete, it is not necessary to enter into the details of these competitions. Roughly, the conclusion was that compound plates were the best up to 12 inches thickness. Beyond this, solid steel showed a considerable superiority. The whole problem was simple enough to state, but difficult to solve. Projectiles were becoming harder and harder every year; chilled iron gave place to cast-steel, and cast-steel, in turn, to the forged steel Holtzer shot. In the meantime, as artillery increased in power, the force with which shot could be propelled advanced, step for step, with the improvement of the shot itself. The problem for the armourer was to make a plate hard enough in the face to break up steel shot, but, at the same time, tough enough in the back to hold together, if the shot got through. Compound plates were not hard enough at the surface; solid steel was too brittle at the back.

The problem was solved by the Harvey process, which gives to a single steel plate a very hard face, with a soft and tenacious back. This process consists in planing one surface of steel plates, and sandwiching between two of them a layer of animal charcoal equal to their own thickness. They are then covered over with sand, and heated for a fortnight at a temperature of 1800 degrees. During this process the charcoal is transferred to the surface of the steel plates, and gives them great hardness. After cooling for a week, they are re-heated, and chilled with water. The surface thus obtained is so hard that it is difficult to drill holes in it; these have, therefore, to be made in the plate before the Harvey treatment. Experience with this armour has given results which may fairly be called extraordinary. One of the plates for the American battleship *Massachusetts*, 17 inches thick, was attacked by two 12-in. 880 lb. forged steel shot, with striking velocities of 1410 and 1853 ft.-secs., and energies of 11,715 and 20,240 ft.-tons respectively. The first round was calculated to pierce about 20 inches of iron, and 14·4 of steel; the second to pierce 24·2 inches of iron, and 19·4 of steel. Both projectiles broke up against the hard face: the first penetrated 8, and the second 11 inches, slightly cracking the plate. Better still was the success of a 14-in. double-forged Harvey plate last year. Projectiles reckoned to pierce 20·4 inches of iron, or 16·3 of steel, were defeated by it, without even a crack; and even an 830 lb. shot, with 1800 ft.-secs. velocity—all but the standard test in the United States for 17-in. armour—failed to get through it. This 14-in. plate thus virtually passed the trial for 17 inches; and its resistance to penetration was, roughly, two-fifths as much again as that of untreated steel. The most astonishing result of all was obtained by a Carnegie plate, which, last year, resisted a projectile which would have passed through two and a-half times its own thickness of iron. It should be said that all these plates were reinforced either by the use of nickel, or by being reforged after the carburizing process, or by both. Without this it has been found that the Harvey treatment, while hardening the face, tends to soften the back of armour considerably. Nickel enables the carburization to penetrate deeper into the plate, and also toughens the whole mass: reforging has the same effect on the body of the steel. The net result of the Harvey process is, as was said above, that armour has regained its equality with the gun: although projectiles like the Carpenter and Wheeler-Sterling American shot grow more and more formidable, attack and defence are roughly in equilibrium. This does not mean to-day, of course, that there are not guns and shot which, on the proving-ground, can break up any plate on earth; but in action many blows would be oblique, and it is not likely that many fair hits would be concentrated upon a single plate. And even if Harveyed steel armour were quite incapable of keeping out steel shot, it would still be indispensable against the shells of quick-firing guns—by far the deadliest agency of modern battle.

The elements of force hitherto considered, armament and armour, are purely tactical; their function consists in enabling a ship to fight. Steam power has a double value. It both brings a ship into touch with the enemy, and fits her to fight to the best advantage when she gets there. In respect of steam power the advance of the last forty years has been as striking as in offensive force; so that the steamers of the Crimean War would be as obsolete by the side of the vessels of to-day as were the old sailing ships beside them. The first great development in steam propulsion was the substitution of the screw for the paddle. This point was very practically settled by making fast the screw steamer *Rattler* by her stern to the stern of a paddle steamer of equal horse power, and sending both ahead at full steam; the *Rattler* won this tug-of-war at the rate of 2·8 knots an hour. This point settled, there followed great improvements in engines. The old engines were of the simple or common kind; that is to say, that steam of a comparatively low pressure was passed from the boilers direct into each cylinder. In 1886 appeared the ironclad *Pallas*, which was fitted with compound engines. Her engines had two cylinders, one of them four times the size of the other; steam passed at high pressure into the smaller, and thence to the larger, which it filled by its expansion. The pressure was lower here, but it acted upon four times the area of cylinder; so that if the pressure in the larger cylinder of the *Pallas* were one-fourth that of the smaller, the power developed in the two would be exactly equal. In the same ship were introduced surface condensers, by which the steam that had done its work was condensed and passed back to the boiler. This expedient did away with the necessity for the old method of condensing steam by mixing it with sea-water, and the consequent waste of energy involved in pumping out part of this brackish water after it had been heated, lest the salt incrustation should spoil the boilers. This double advance secured a vast economy in coal; the expansion of steam was utilized, so as to serve two cylinders instead of one, and the power applied to treating the salt water was economized. Still more substantial was the economy attained by triple-expansion engines, with a cylinder intermediate between those of the high and lower pressure. It was in the *Rattlesnake*, launched in 1886, that this type of engine was first used in the British Navy, and the saving of coal thus effected is actually from one-third to one-half of the whole consumption per horse-power per hour of the older engines. In other words, a ship with triple-expansion engines can steam double the distance without coaling that she could make with simple engines; her radius of action is doubled, and her strategical value therewith. This is a tremendous advantage. For whereas the steamer has the advantage of the sailing vessel in that she can go whither she will, fair wind or foul, she has to pay for it in the fact that without coal she cannot go anywhither at all. The number of tons she can stow in her bunkers might easily be a matter of life and death, and cannot be left out in estimating the efficiency of any warship.

In the meantime there had been introduced a very momentous innovation in the shape of forced draught. When forced draught is used the stokehold is closed, so that there is no escape for the air within it except through the furnaces and funnels. Air is then pumped into the stokehold by means of large fans; the only escape for the condensed air is through the furnaces, which consequently burn the fiercer, and quicken the generation of steam in the boilers. The action of forced draught is thus analogous on a large scale to that of the ordinary household bellows. In its early days the expedient was very freely applied. The increase in the horse-power developed was very great —for instance, 8500 under forced draught in the *Aurora*, as against 5500 under natural draught. In the six battleships of the "Admiral" class the natural draught ranged from 7733 to 8658, and the forced from 9573 to 12,567—the average being about 3000 additional horse-power. The increase in speed ran from ·8 to 2 knots an hour. Plainly this was a great economy in the space and weight of the engines and boilers, since by the aid of forced draught lighter machinery could be made to do the work of heavier. So far, therefore, forced draught, developing superior energy with less weight, ran on the general lines of naval progress, as exemplified in such inventions as Harvey armour and quick-fire guns.

Unluckily there is such a thing as false economy, and that naval engineers very soon discovered in the case of forced draught. The small boilers had to be driven at high pressure to maintain a high horse-power, and the intense heat caused the boiler-tubes to leak. The tubes became so hot, and steam was generated so rapidly, that it lifted the water away from the inner surface of the tubes; these thus came in contact only with steam or steam and water, which did not protect them from overheating. Consequently they expanded unduly, and gave way. Very soon it became almost the rule, rather than the exception, for boiler-tubes to break down in trial-trips. Even as lately as the trials of the *Royal Sovereign* in 1892 the tubes gave way because the smallness of the boilers demanded a pressure of 1½ inches in the stokehold. Ships were built, like the *Barham* and *Bellona*, in which the effort to drag high speed by means of very high pressure out of ridiculously inadequate boilers resulted in almost every tube leaking long before the estimated full horse-power was attained.

Many people consoled themselves with the reflection that a ship, having once got through her trials, would never use forced draught again. And if she spent her life in time of peace this is doubtless so. Even

ELEMENTS OF FORCE IN WARSHIPS

in war a high pressure would never be used for any length of continuous steaming. Nevertheless, the ability to add on occasion, say for an hour, a knot or two to the speed of a ship might be of vital moment in action, whether to an individual ship or to a unit in a squadron. It is rather surprising to a layman to find Mr. R. S. Oldknow, R.N., who speaks with authority about marine engines if anybody does, depreciating the value of speed in battleships. "Even in war," he says, "I do not believe that an extra speed of one knot would be likely to be of any strong advantage to a battleship. Battleships will generally be called upon to fight in company, and the speed of the squadron will necessarily be that of its slowest ship."* But surely it might make all the difference in the world whether that slowest ship could add a knot or two to her speed. The fact that the speed so attained is the speed of the whole squadron makes it not less desirable, but more. The value of speed in a fleet action appears to be one of the few questions of tactics which admit of no dispute. An extra knot an hour might make all the difference represented in old days by the weather-gage. To take a simple case, most British battleships are built to carry their four heavy guns in pairs in two barbettes, forward and aft. Most French battleships carry theirs in four barbettes, one forward, one aft, and one on each beam. Consequently the French ships can fire three heavy guns ahead, astern, or on either broadside. The British ships can only fire two ahead or astern, but four on the broadside. In an engagement between the two fleets, therefore, it would

* *The Mechanism of Men-of-War*, p. 48.

NAVAL POLICY

be of the highest importance, perhaps of decisive importance, whether the battle was fought end on or broadside on. The side that had the superiority in speed would be in a position to decide which way the action was to be fought, so that the possession of this advantage would mean (so far as heavy ordnance went) odds of three to two on the French, or four to three [*] on the British, as the case might be. To take another case, it is very possible than an admiral, whose fleet was more lightly armoured than his enemy's, but of superior speed, might circle ahead of him in such a course that all the enemy's hits on his armour would strike at a small angle to the surface, and consequently bound away without injury. For a third instance, it is hardly disputable that Admiral Ito owed his victory of the Yalu very largely to the superior speed of his squadron. If he was able to defeat the Chinese owing to the superior power of his quick-fire guns, he was no less able to withdraw his unarmoured cruisers intact because of his superiority in speed, which enabled him to select his own range, and to manœuvre in such a manner that one Chinese ship masked another. On these grounds it appears that, except on condition of increasing the natural draught speed to an extent which would have to be paid for by a sacrifice of other elements of force, it would be unwise to give up the reserve of speed ensured by the use of moderate forced draught, or some similar expedient.

A substitute for forced draught has been found in induced draught, which has been used in the *Magnificent*,

---

[*] Perhaps even two to one, since there are probably positions on the bow and quarter, where French ships could only bring two great guns to bear.

and is to be used in the *Illustrious*. The difference between the two is that, whereas, with forced draught, the air is pumped into the stokeholds, with induced draught it is sucked out by powerful fans placed at the bases of the funnels. It was objected when the system was first suggested that, in principle, induced draught was only forced draught under another name. "In both cases," says Mr. Harry Williams, R.N.,* "the object aimed at is exactly the same, viz., to cause so much difference in the air pressure in the stokeholds and funnels as to make the air rush through the line of fire in the boilers, and out through the funnels." It is claimed, on the other hand, by the advocates of induced draught that, as it acts on the top instead of the bottom of the fuel, it has the gases given off under control, so that they are developed and consumed under a constant pressure; a lower temperature in the uptakes and funnels is the result. The question, however, has yet to be solved by experience. It is to be noticed that the *Magnificent*, with induced draught, got slightly inferior results in her trials to the *Majestic*, with forced—17.6 knots to 17.9. As, however, with natural draught, the *Majestic* steamed 16.9 knots to the *Magnificent's* 16.5, the difference is, perhaps, to be attributed to other causes. In the meantime, the difficulty has been turned, rather than overcome, by the virtual abandonment of high pressure. A pressure of half-an-inch is reckoned as natural draught, and forced draught is seldom pushed much farther than this. The *Renown*, which, in her recent trials, beat all records for battleships except the Italian, steamed $19\frac{1}{4}$ knots in an hour at a pressure of only .7 of an inch.

* *The Steam Navy of England*, p. 82.

Boilers are much larger, and breakdowns on trial trips are now almost unknown.

The latest step in marine engineering is the introduction of water-tube boilers. These are now being fitted in most of the cruisers and torpedo-boat-destroyers building for the Royal Navy, and are to appear in our next series of battleships. Their use in the great cruisers *Terrible* and *Powerful* has been condemned as a rash experiment, but it must be remembered that this type of boiler has been used in the French Navy for several years, and is fitted in all new vessels, battleships, and cruisers alike. It has been taken up on a large scale by the Messageries Maritimes, and our own torpedo-boat-destroyers have given excellent testimony to more than one or two varieties of tubular boilers. The essential merit of these boilers is that they expose a far greater surface to the action of the fires than the old shell-boilers: the *Powerful* has no less than 67,803 square feet of heating surface. Attempts made to attain a high horse-power with the small heating surface of cylindrical boilers failed almost uniformly, and resulted only in burnt tubes; with the new models steam can be got up in an infinitely shorter time, and maintained at a higher pressure. Many further advantages are claimed for tubular boilers. They are composed of small parts, and it is easy to substitute a sound article for anything that may give way, without tearing up the decks. They are also lighter and compacter; stoking is easier, and their advocates claim for them a considerable economy in coal. It is not necessary here to go into any technical description of the various types of water-tube boilers, especially as there are at least a dozen of these which all claim serious attention. The boiler invented by M. Belleville, of Dieppe, is the one that is of the most practical importance to Englishmen at the present moment, as it is to supply steam to at least ten of our new cruisers. It consists of a number of what are called elements, fitted side by side above the furnace. The element is a series of straight tubes, placed one above the other; each tube is connected with the one above it by a junction-box. The shape of the element is, therefore, a flattened spiral, or, more familiarly, a zig-zag standing on end. Each element connects, at the bottom, with a feed-collector; and, at the top, with a steam-collector. Each receives its water from the feed-collector in its lowest tube; when heat is applied, the steam generated passes by the junction-box into the tube above, taking the un-evaporated water with it. More water is evaporated in the second tube, and the steam so generated, together with that from the first tube, carries itself, with the unevaporated water, by the junction-box, into the third tube; and so on to the last. Thence it passes into the steam-collector, and what water remains unevaporated passes, by tubes outside the boiler (and therefore not heated by the fires), into the feed-collector, and starts on its journey through the tubes again. As the tubes always contain water circulating through them along with the steam, they do not burn through as they would if they contained steam alone. This principle of circulation is found in all water-tube boilers.

The Yarrow boiler, a most elegant invention, has no outside tubes to carry back the unevaporated water; but this function is performed in a row of straight tubes, by those furthest from the fire, and generating less steam.*

With the aid of these, and other engineering advances, the *Esmeralda* has been able to steam $23\frac{1}{4}$ knots an hour, as against, perhaps, half-a-dozen made by the first steam paddle-boat built some seventy years ago for His Majesty's fleet. Both for larger and smaller ships there seems no limit to the advance. Twenty knots is already becoming obsolete for a cruiser. The United States have the *Columbia* and the *Minneapolis*, with top speeds of 22·8 knots; Germany, the *Kaiserin Augusta*, with nearly 22 knots; Japan, the *Yoshino*, with 23; while Chili and the Argentine have been supplied by Armstrong & Co. with quite a little fleet of cruisers, steaming from $22\frac{3}{4}$ to 23·2 knots an hour. The *Buenos-Aires*, which made the latter record, could, without doubt, steam 24 knots with forced draught. As for smaller vessels, it is difficult to say which holds the record at any moment.

With this broad sketch of recent naval progress before us, we shall be able to estimate in some degree the fitness of ships and fleets for the various operations of war. The vessel which is deficient in one or more elements of the force developed by the constant march of invention will be at a disadvantage as compared with the vessel which possesses it. The Harvey-armoured vessel is better for war purposes than the vessel which carries the same thickness of unhardened armour; the twenty-knot ship is better, so far, than the

---

* For a lucid explanation of the principle of circulation, together with a description of the Yarrow and Thorneycroft boilers, see Mr. G. R. Dunell in *Brassey's Naval Annual* for 1896. Other boilers are described and illustrated in Mr. R. S. Oldknow's *Mechanism of Men-of-War*.

ELEMENTS OF FORCE IN WARSHIPS

nineteen-knot ship. But although it is comparatively easy to compare the gun-power, or the protection, or the speed, or the coal-endurance of any ships, it is impossible to compare, for instance, speed with gun-power. England builds the *Renown* with a total energy of gun-fire equal to 251,323 foot-tons per minute, and a speed of $18\frac{3}{4}$ knots an hour. The United States build the *Kearsage* with 32,550 foot-tons more gun-power, and $2\frac{3}{4}$ knots less speed. Who is to express speed in terms of gun-power so as to demonstrate mathematically which ship is the more efficient? The two things are incommensurable. "It is distinctly absurd," says Admiral Colomb,* "to lay any stress on the bare fact that one warship has a greater sea-speed than another. . . . To make the statement mean anything, it must be added that both ships had the same displacement, the same armour, the same guns, the same ammunition, the same supply of stores, provisions, coal and water, the same torpedo armament, the same manœuvring power, the same crew, and the same cost." It would be impertinent to do anything but accept Admiral Colomb's authority. But perhaps the real significance of the quotation is in its last three words. If we find one of our ships inferior in any element of force to a foreign ship of the same class, it would probably better become the mistress of the seas, instead of falling back on our ship's superior coal or ammunition supply, to build a costlier vessel that would retain our own advantage, and equal that of the foreigner. That is to say, our ships of each class, being sea-keeping and world-traversing, will be rather larger than those of any other

* *North American Review*, January, 1896.

people, and, so far, rather more expensive. "The further we go," says Admiral Paris most truly, "the more will naval war be waged with money rather than with men." It may be deplorable, but it is inevitable. We have now to consider what value in force we have got for our money in the British fleet, and what further force, if any, it behoves us to buy.

III.

THE BRITISH NAVY

THE British Navy is pre-eminently a fighting force. It may appear a platitude to say so, for with what object except fighting, it might be asked, does any navy exist? Yet it is true that the British fleet would, in case of war, be called upon to force an action far more urgently than any other. This is plain, if only from the fact that we spend more money upon our fleet than any foreign Power, and that our fleet is consequently more powerful, while our army, if also expensive, is comparatively weak. Obviously it is our policy to use the strongest arm we possess, and our naval superiority would be wasted if a war were fought out without extensive operations at sea.

But there is also another reason why, in case of war, it would be for the British fleet to seek out the enemy at the first possible moment, and fight him wherever he might be. In a naval war England, whether apparently attacking or defending, is essentially on the defensive. To an island power, with dependencies in every part of the world, the sea is the one line of communication. This line offers itself to the attack of an enemy at every point, and must be defended on pain of the break-up of our empire. The fear of an invasion in such force as we might be unable to cope with, is

NAVAL POLICY

another imperative stimulus to this country to hold the seas in the neighbourhood of our islands. And as we must guard ourselves from invasion at home by commanding home waters, so we must guard all our colonies by commanding the seas adjacent to them. Our enormous commerce at sea presents another commodious field of attack to an enemy; on this we may depend for the bread we eat, and this also must be protected at all costs. Now a foreign power like France or Germany is vulnerable to us in none of these ways. Their transoceanic possessions are to us comparatively insignificant; their vastly superior land forces could defy any invasion by our army; their land frontiers enable them to feed themselves in comfort, and their ocean trade is the merest trifle beside ours. In a naval war, therefore, the British Empire presents many weak spots to an enemy, and the only way to keep him out is by commanding the sea.

Now how is this to be done? It is curious that it is only lately that Englishmen, even those who take a keen interest in the Navy, have come to any clear understanding of a question so vital to our national interests—even to our national existence. It is to the clear thinking and plain speaking of such recent writers as Admiral Colomb and Mr. Spenser Wilkinson that we owe the better comprehension of the subject which is beginning to filter through the British mind. The sea, to put it briefly, is to be regarded, not as a path from one country to another, but as territory. The fleet which controls the sea controls the commerce of the sea, destroys that of its antagonist, and maintains and increases that of its own country. How vital is such control to our own country needs no demonstration.

THE BRITISH NAVY

According to a recent Parliamentary paper, the total value of British sea-borne trade is to be put at £945,485,951, as against £294,753,414 French, £150,693,600 German, and £393,393,736 of the United States. Such is the vast preponderance of what we have to defend, and our possible enemies to attack.

The command of the sea, though primarily directed to the control of trade, has also a bearing on territorial invasion. The power which commands the sea can attack the enemy at what point it will, and can retreat at what moment it will. It is true there are operations, such as bombardments of sea-coast towns and descents in small force upon an enemy's country, which can possibly be undertaken without a general command of the sea. For these it is sufficient that the assailant should find no superior force in the immediate locality of his attack. But such operations can bring no substantial advantage to the attack, nor any serious damage to the defence. The bombardment of coast towns only embitters an enemy without, in most cases, impairing his ability to continue the struggle; an invasion, being liable to find its transport destroyed and its communications cut on the advent of a superior fleet, would usually result in the isolation and subsequent destruction or surrender of the invader. The Power which commands the sea, on the other hand, makes the enemy's coast-line its frontier, if so disposed, and its base for territorial attack. It disposes of the trade of the waters behind it, just as an army disposes of the resources of a conquered province, and it can proceed, if so it will, to further attacks, as an army makes one conquered province its base against the next. This

NAVAL POLICY

command can be obtained again, as in the case of warfare on land, either by destroying the enemy's fleet, or by holding it with a superior force. In the first case, it is obvious that the sea passes to the only force left on it. In the second, should the weaker fleet venture out of port for any aggressive movement, it either exposes itself, within a given time, to be attacked and crushed by the stronger enemy, or it must return again to port before it can accomplish anything decisive.

From these considerations arises the British theory of offensive defence. To secure ourselves from attack by sea, either on our commerce or our territory, we must command the sea, and this can only be done by beating the enemy at once, or by shutting him up in his ports and beating him if he ventures out. Even if we were defeated at sea again and again, this would still be our only possible method of war as long as we had a ship that could float or a gun that could be brought to bear. If we relinquish this struggle, we must lose our colonies and commerce, even if we are not overwhelmed by invasion. It is in this sense that our fleet, above all others, is a fighting fleet. It must be ready to fight any possible enemy who may show himself, at any place or time, to dispute our mastery of the sea. Consequently the first line of our Navy must be composed of ships fitted to meet any hostile ship on equal or superior terms. These must be heavily armed to crush the enemy. They must be armoured, because theory and experience alike prove that an unarmoured ship has little hope of defeating an armoured one; while a fight which leaves the enemy undefeated and at large on the seas is a British defeat, even if our own vessels escape. They must have good speed, to bring the enemy to action wherever a chance offers; and they must have good coal-carrying capacity, so as to be able to operate wherever a hostile fleet may have betaken itself. These qualities are united in the battleship, so that a superiority in this class of vessel is essential to us. We have also cruisers, faster but less heavily armed and armoured, to destroy an enemy's trade, and to defeat any of his vessels that may have eluded the armoured fleet and set out to prey on our merchantmen; we need them also to do the scouting for a fleet of battleships. After these comes the torpedo-boat flotilla, together with larger vessels to attack an enemy's torpedo-boats, and to act as a support to our own; these may be used either as auxiliaries to the battle fleet, or in isolated operations on their own account. But the battleship remains the prime factor of naval war, without which all others are as ineffective as cavalry without supporting infantry on land.

It is with the list of our battleships, therefore, that any account of the material of the British Navy must open. It will probably be found most convenient to take them in the reverse order of their chronology, beginning with the newest and most powerful. First comes a great group of nine ships, of which four— the *Majestic* and *Magnificent*, *Prince George* and *Victorious*—are completed, and the two first are at sea as flagships. Of the remaining five, the *Hannibal*, *Jupiter*, and *Mars* are to be finished next year, and the *Caesar* and *Illustrious* in 1898. These ships are probably the finest all-round fighting class in any navy. Displacing 14,900 tons, they are certainly the largest; so that if they are not also the most powerful, the designer is at fault for not making the most

NAVAL POLICY

economical use of the space at his disposal. The armament is powerful and well-protected. It consists of four 12-in. 46-ton wire guns, such as have already been described; these throw a projectile of 850 lbs. with a velocity, on leaving the muzzle, of 2700 feet, and an energy at the muzzle of 33,940 ft.-tons. These guns can be worked by hand, should the hydraulic mounting break down. They fire three rounds in four minutes. For their size they are certainly the most powerful guns afloat. They are mounted in pairs in two barbettes, fore and aft: the armour on the barbettes is 14 inches of Harveyed steel,* and the breech of the gun, when raised to the firing position, is protected by a 10-in. hood of the same material. The secondary armament consists of twelve 6-in. and sixteen 3-in. (12-pounder) quick-fire guns; all the former are protected by casemates of six inches of Harveyed steel. Bulkheads of 14 inches of the same hardened steel run across the ship fore and aft, meeting the barbettes and thus forming an armoured citadel with an extreme length of 300 feet out of the whole ship's 390 feet. The area of side armour is 220 feet long by 26 feet deep; its thickness is 9 inches, and these plates also are reinforced by the Harvey process. This is a far greater surface of side than is protected by armour in most battleships, whether English or foreign; the object of the modification is to keep out the shells of quick-firing guns, for which the thickness of metal is ample. Further protection is afforded by an arched steel deck, varying from $2\frac{1}{2}$ to 4 inches in thickness; this covers

---

* The resisting power per inch of Harveyed steel may be put roughly at the ratio of 3 to 2 as compared with compound armour, and 2 to 1 as compared with wrought-iron.

the vitals of the ship—engines, magazines, torpedo-rooms, and such like—and bends down from its highest point in the centre of the ship to meet the lower edge of the side armour. To deal the *Majestic* a mortal wound, a projectile would thus have to pierce not only the vertical nine inches, but also four inches inclined at a considerable angle, and equivalent, for purposes of penetration, to about ten inches of vertical armour. The normal amount of coal carried is 900 tons; but, if necessary, 1850 tons could be taken on board, enabling the ship to steam over 7000 miles at a speed of ten knots. This coal-capacity and endurance is greater than that of any foreign battleship afloat. The speed of the group will range between $16\frac{1}{2}$ and 17 knots with 10,000 horse-power at natural draught, and from $17\frac{1}{2}$ to 18 knots with 12,000 horse-power at forced draught.

Individual vessels, both of our own and foreign powers, may compare favourably with the *Majestics* in various respects. Several are slightly faster. Battleships building for France and Germany have a greater energy of gun-fire per minute. But, on the whole, it may be said that no ship in the world is their equal in all-round excellence. In particular, none is better protected for a close action, whether we consider the extent of side armour, the defence of the vitals of the ship, or the shelter provided for the gunners. An exception must be made as respects the 12-pounders, whose crews are wholly unprotected, and could hardly live through a single broadside of any power; on the other hand, this defect is far greater in almost every other ship in the world. If these guns' crews were ever shot down, it is fairly safe to predict that the attacking enemy would fare as badly, and probably a great deal worse. Another point in which these vessels fall short of ideal perfection is that they draw too much water to get through the Suez Canal. The only other criticism that could reasonably be passed upon the *Majestic* class is that it is half-a-knot too slow. Eighteen knots is becoming the standard speed of the new French and German battleships; and it is of great importance that our vessels should be faster, both to ensure the ability to bring an enemy to a decisive action, and to enable our admirals to choose their own tactics. For the rest, the *Majestics* are very large and very expensive, ranging in cost from £865,000 to £912,000. But if they appear to give less offensive and defensive power per ton of displacement than some foreign ships, they possess the countervailing superiority that they carry far more ammunition and more coal than any foreigner. It must also be remembered that though they are the largest fighting-ships in the world, they are not—thanks to the rapidity of their construction, and the industrial resources of this country in general—by any means the most expensive. Italy has had to pay a million apiece for more than one of her ironclads, while France is spending £1,100,770 on the *Bouvet*, and £1,100,400 on the *Masséna*—both undeniably inferior ships. On the whole, we may rest well assured that there are no more thoroughly efficient battleships afloat than these; and that, though they are expensive, we have got as good money's worth in them as have any of our rivals.

Two features of the *Majestic* class deserve a brief further discussion, since they will be found reappearing throughout the British Navy. The first of these is their homogeneity. It has been the recent policy of our Admiralty to build almost all its ships in homogeneous groups, smaller or greater. There are nine *Majestics* in the fleet, eight *Royal Sovereigns*, six "Admirals"; while there are to be five of the new *Canopus* type which Mr. Goschen is laying down this year. Very often this system of groups has gone no further than a pair of sisters, such as the *Nile* and *Trafalgar*, or the *Centurion* and *Barfleur;* but the *Renown* is the only isolated individual type laid down since 1874. Among our cruisers we find still larger families—eight *Diadems*, twelve *Eclipses*, and as many as twenty-one *Apollos*. The advantages of homogeneity, supposing the type to be a good one to begin with, are great and easily apprehensible. A man who has served on one ship knows her sister, and can fall into his work from the first moment he is ordered aboard, instead of wasting weeks in learning his way about the ship. Similarly, all sorts of apparatus—guns, mountings, spare parts of machinery, and a hundred others—can be readily transferred, in case of need, from one ship to another. Suppose the nine *Majestics* to have been in action, and one of them to be disabled from taking the sea again: she might yet conceivably be able to fit out her eight damaged sisters with the undamaged parts of her own equipment; whereas, with vessels of different types, damaged and undamaged parts would alike be unavailable for service. A further, and perhaps yet greater, advantage of this system of grouping warships is that all problems of strategy and tactics are enormously simplified thereby. Take the case of an admiral with ten battleships opposed to a force of eight, all the ships being roughly equal in fighting power. Seven of his own ships, we will imagine, can steam 14 knots an hour, and the other three but 10; the enemy's eight have a uniform speed of 12 knots. Is an admiral to leave behind his three laggards, and face eight ships with seven; or is he to maintain his superiority, and run the risk of missing the enemy altogether? With a homogeneous group these perplexities cannot arise. In battle, again, an admiral need not be always altering his plans to support any weak point in his line which might be threatened, since the line will be equally strong at all points. The battle of the Yalu—in which Admiral Ito destroyed the weak extremities of the Chinese line at his leisure, while the powerful ships in the centre actually found their fire masked by feebler comrades—proves that this is far from an imaginary danger. A squadron of ships which all turn in the same circle, again, is far superior in manœuvring power to one whose units require different times and spaces for going about. We may, then, fairly congratulate ourselves on the wisdom of our Admiralty which has given this uniformity to considerable sections of our fleet. Carried to excess, the practice would, of course, strangle all progress; but, though we have carried it further than any other Power, there is no reason to suppose that our battleships, at any rate, have not kept well abreast of the march of naval architecture.

The other feature worthy of a word of notice is a smaller structural point. The battleships of the *Majestic* class, in common with all our most recent types, have a belt of plating of a greater or less length amidships; but both bow and stern are left wholly unarmoured. The theory is that the steel deck, which runs from end to end of the ship, would protect everything beneath the water-line, while even if the

THE BRITISH NAVY

upper part were wholly shot away, the ship could still float, and fight her guns. It has been thought better, therefore, to devote the weight thus saved to other uses. This resolution to chance the ends and concentrate power amidships, is characteristic of the British constructors, though the Russians have lately favoured it, while the Italians have carried it further than the boldest of our own experiments. France, Russia (until lately), and Germany have all acted on the opposite principle. They have run a narrow belt of great thickness from stem to stern. Taking care thus of the water-line, they expect the rest of the ship to take care of itself. The rival merits of the two systems were, until lately, the subject of a standing controversy between Sir Edward Reed, who designed several completely belted ships for our own and other navies, and Sir William White, the author of the later types. Sir William White, being the man in office, has naturally backed his opinion by going on constructing vessels with unprotected ends; but the question will probably not be settled beyond doubt without a great naval war. It may be urged in favour of the complete belt that it gives more strength for ramming; but the ram, as has been already said, will in most future cases be forestalled by the torpedo. It may also be contended, and that without possibility of answer, that a ship which loses her bow, even if she does not founder, will sink lower in the water, losing much of her speed, and, therefore, of her manœuvring power and efficiency generally. On the other side, it is more conformable to the spirit and conditions of the British Navy to give our crews guns behind armour to sink the enemy rather than a ship which will float on with

NAVAL POLICY

guns out of action—unharmed, but also harmless. The invention of quick-firing guns cuts both ways. While they make it easier to destroy the British unarmoured ends, they will make fearful havoc of the great expanses of unarmoured side exposed by the French belted types. The only experience so far attainable —that of the Yalu—tells in favour of the British model. The two Chinese battleships, the *Chen Yuen* and *Ting Yuen*, had bow and stern completely unprotected, yet they came out of the battle perfectly seaworthy, and able to manœuvre together. Even their guns on the extreme forecastle and poop were still in action. It may be that the Japanese shot badly, and certainly the range was long. Yet the fact that they carried out of the fight some two hundred shot-dints apiece shows, at least, that such a partially belted ship can sustain a very fair degree of punishment without disablement.

Of the next class in order of modernity—the eight *Royal Sovereigns*, built under the Naval Defence Act— there is much the same to say as of the *Majestics*. They displace 750 tons less, and are ten feet shorter; the compound armour belt, however—8 to 18 inches thick, and 8 ft. 8 in. broad—covers 250 ft. of their length, instead of 220 in the later type. Above the belt, to a height of 9 ft. 6 in. from the water-line, is a sheath of 3- to 5-in. armour; in the *Ramillies*, *Repulse*, *Revenge*, and *Royal Oak*, this is of nickel steel, which has given such admirable results in America; in the *Royal Sovereign*, *Empress of India*, *Hood*, and *Resolution* of simple steel. The bulkheads range from 6 to 16 inches of compound armour, with 17 on the barbettes, and a 3-in. armoured deck. The *Hood* carries her heavy guns in two 18-in. turrets, instead of barbettes, but is otherwise similar. The main armament consists of four 13½-in. 67-ton guns. These, as will shortly be seen, are a trifle more powerful than the wire-wound pieces of the *Majestic*, though considerably less so in proportion to their weight. The secondary battery of 6-in. quick-firers is mounted between the barbettes as in the *Majestic;* it contains ten guns instead of twelve, and only four of these, carried on the main deck, are protected by 6-in. casemates. The others are on the upper deck, and unprotected by armour—a great defect. Equally naked are sixteen 6-pounder and twelve 3-pounder quick-firers intended to meet the attack of torpedo-boats; for their own peculiar purpose they do not, of course, need any armoured protection, but they could hardly survive a few minutes of a severe quick-fire cannonade, after which the *Royal Sovereigns* would be well-nigh helpless against torpedo-boats. With 1450 tons of coal this class is reckoned to steam 7900 knots at 10 per hour. The speed is officially quoted at 15 knots with 9000 horse-power at natural draught, and 17½ with 13,000 at forced draught. As a matter of fact several vessels of this class could probably exceed both figures, so that with clean bottoms they should be able to keep station at full-speed with the *Majestics*. If we compare the two classes, the principal difference is found in the complete recognition in the *Majestic* of the revolution effected in naval war by large calibre quick-firers. Thus, if the *Majestic's* thick armour is shorter than the *Royal Sovereign's*, it extends higher and covers a greater portion of the ship's side; and as it starts with the advantage of the Harvey process, the total of protection given is much greater. It is part of the same revolution in artillery that the *Majestic's* quick-fire armament is both stronger—containing twelve 6-in. guns instead of ten, and 12- instead of 6-pounders—and better protected. These ships cost some thousands apiece less than the *Majestics*.

There were also built under the Naval Defence Act the *Barfleur* and *Centurion*, projected as second-class battle-ships, but now described as first-class. These may be described as reductions in scale of the *Royal Sovereign* —smaller and lighter and less powerful. Of 10,500 displacement, they have on the face of it as good a right to the title of first-class as, for instance, the American *Indiana*. In armour and armament, however, these ships are much nearer the second-class, if classes there are to be, than the first. The thickest belt armour (which sheathes 200 feet out of 360) is 12 inches compound; above it is 4 of nickel steel. The bulkheads are 8 inches; the deck $2\frac{1}{2}$ inches at its thickest. The barbettes carry 9 inches compound with 6-in. shields of nickel steel protecting the breech of the gun, which in the *Royal Sovereign* is exposed in the firing position. There are 2-in. casements of the same material, arranged as in the *Royal Sovereign*, for four of the quick-firing guns. The protection is slight as compared with the *Royal Sovereign*, but complete enough as far as it goes. The main armament is four 10-in. 29-ton guns; the secondary battery, ten 4·7-in. quick-firers; the anti-torpedo armament, eight 6- and nine 3-pounders. This is certainly a very light armament to carry on 10,500 tons; the *Indiana*, which displaces over 250 tons less, and is exceptionally weak in quick-fire, works out at over 170,000 ft.-tons of gun-power per minute to the *Centurion's* 97,195; while the new German *Kaiser Friedrich III.*, of only 326 tons more, exceeds her gun-power by more than four to one. Here, then, is plainly a case where the mere setting down the two ships as first-class conceals a tremendous inequality. The compensation of the *Centurion* is found in her sea-going qualities. With a top speed of over $18\tfrac{1}{2}$ knots, she held the record among British—and, if we except the great Italian ships sometimes ranked as cruisers, among all—battleships for several years. The *Barfleur*, curiously enough, could only get within a knot of this on trial, though on paper similar in every respect. With 1240 tons of coal, these ships are reckoned capable of about 10,000 knots at an economical speed without coaling. Both on this account and that of their speed they are rather adapted to carry an Admiral's flag on a foreign station than to take their place in a fleet which would have to meet the heaviest guns and attack the heaviest armour. Thus the *Centurion* is far more in place on the China Station than is the *Barfleur* in the Mediterranean. The *Centurion*, for instance, being better protected and of equal speed, is probably the only vessel in Eastern waters that could face the Russian *Rurik*.

The *Renown* is to the *Majestic* what the *Centurion* is to the *Royal Sovereign*—much the same ship on a smaller scale. Or to complete the proportion, the *Renown* is to the *Centurion* as the *Majestic* is to the *Royal Sovereign*—a development with special reference to quick-fire. She carries the same main armament as the *Centurion*, but ten 6-inch quick-firers, all behind armour, and eight 12- and twelve 3-pounders. This gives her roughly two and a-half times the *Centurion's* volume of fire. Her armour—6 to 8-inch belt, 6 to

10-inch bulkheads, 10 inches on barbettes and 2 to 6-inch casements—is all of Harveyed steel, thinner than the *Centurion's* compound plating, but more widely extended over the side. In speed the *Renown* beat her predecessor's record and greatly exceeded expectations; she steamed very little short of 18 knots with natural draught and $18\frac{3}{4}$—at one time reaching $19\frac{1}{4}$—with a forced draught representing only ·7-inch pressure. This rate of steaming, however, is not very useful in a battle-ship, unless she is combined in a fleet with others of the same high speed, and these at present we do not possess. It is probable, therefore, that the *Renown*—which is also under-gunned, as compared with foreign ships, for her 12,350 tons—will be used like the *Centurion* as a flagship abroad. The time may come, however, when she will fall into line with the five new battleships which Mr. Goschen purposes to lay down this year. With 12,900 tons displacement, exactly the same gun-power as the *Majestic*, though lighter armour, and the same speed as the *Renown*, these should be among the most useful and powerful battle-ships the world has yet seen.

Next in the same reverse order of seniority come the twin turret-ships *Nile* and *Trafalgar*. At the date of their completion—1890—they were the heaviest vessels in the service, displacing 11,940 tons. They are 345 feet long—45 less than the *Royal Sovereign*—and 73 feet in the beam. Excellent ships in most respects, they are especially distinguished by the stoutness of the resistance they would offer to even the most power-ful attack. They carry no less than 4,230 tons of com-pound armour, disposed in the following manner. A vertical belt 230 feet long, 8 feet 6 inches wide, and

20 to 16 inches thick protects the sides of the lower citadel; transverse bulkheads 16 inches ahead and 14 inches astern close its ends, while a sloping steel deck of 3 inches prolongs the belt to strengthen the unarmoured bow and stern. Above the lower citadel is placed an upper storey as it were—the shorter upper citadel with an extreme length of 193 feet, and protected by 18 to 16 inches of compound armour. The heavy armament is two pairs of $13\frac{1}{2}$-inch guns carried by pairs in 18-inch revolving turrets at the forward and after ends of the upper citadel. Between them is the auxiliary battery of six 4·7-inch quick-fire guns; this battery is protected from splinters by 5-inch steel bulkheads which cut off the secondary armament from the turrets, thus dividing the citadel into three compartments. There are also seventeen 6- and 3-pounder quick-firers, besides machine guns. The *Nile* and *Trafalgar* each made 16·7 knots on their trials with forced draught, and are good for 15·6 nominal at natural draught, which should mean a sea-speed of thirteen to fourteen. The normal coal capacity is 900 tons, and this can be increased on occasion to 1200, giving a radius of action at 10 knots of 5000 and 6500 respectively. The weakness of these vessels is the secondary armament, which is not over-powerful, and defended by no more than an inch of steel-plating. But as they date from the infancy of quick-firing artillery this is but natural, and cannot be imputed as a fault to the design. Despite this they are a most formidable couple, and able to take their own part against any warship afloat.

The *Sans Pareil*, of 10,470 tons, is sister of the unfortunate *Victoria*. Like the *Nile* and *Trafalgar*, she is a turret-ship, but, unlike them, concentrates all the attacking power of her heavy guns in one turret, placed forward. This contains two 16¼-in. 111-ton guns, the heaviest weapons ever mounted in any navy —though Herr Krupp has turned out heavier ones, such as are mounted, for instance, on shore at Spezia— and the most powerful guns the world ever saw. The projectile of these monsters weighs 1800 lbs., and is discharged with a velocity of 2087 feet a second; the energy exerted would move 54,390 tons one foot, and is sufficient to penetrate 3 ft. 2 in. of iron at the muzzle. Since this gun puts forth so prodigious a force, it may be asked why it has not been mounted on our later ships. The answer is that, though the 111-ton gun is superior in absolute power to any other, we have many guns that in relative power—that is, in force exerted per ton of gun—far surpass it. The 13½-in. 67-ton gun has an energy of 35,230 ft.-tons, while that of the newer 12.-in. 46-ton wire gun stands at 33,940. The relative energy per ton of gun of the three is thus represented by the figures 490 for the 111-ton, 526 for the 67-ton, and 738 for the 46-ton. A further advantage of the lighter guns consists in the greater rapidity with which they can be worked. The 111-ton fires one round in two minutes, the 67-ton seven rounds in twelve minutes, and the 46-ton three rounds in 4 minutes. Thus, in twelve minutes, the number of rounds fired would be 6, 7, and 9 respectively, and the muzzle-energy, which is the real measure of the work done by the gun, would come out in the proportions of 326, 247, and 325. It is true that the 111-ton still seems the most powerful weapon, though the 46-ton runs it close. But it must be remembered that a warship cannot go on increasing the weight and number of her guns indefinitely. Only a certain proportion of the displacement can be given to heavy guns, and both the newer models do more work in proportion to their weight. The four 67-ton guns of the *Nile* weigh only 46 tons more than the *Sans Pareil's* two, and yet the destructive energy they put out in twelve minutes is as 988 to 752—a gain out of all proportion to the increased weight the designer has to find room for. Still more advantageous is the change to the four 46-ton guns of the *Majestic*. These weigh actually 38 tons less than the *Sans Pareil's* two, and their energy, in twelve minutes, is as 1500 to 752—all but double. On the other hand, the *Renown's* four 29-ton pieces would only give an energy, in the same time, of 346 to the *Sans Pareil's* 752; but then the *Renown* gives hardly half as much weight to heavy guns, so that the complaint that she is too lightly armed is certainly borne out so far. Yet, though it is possible to go too far down in the scale, the rule holds good that it is better to supply four lighter guns than two heavier. The downward limit of size is that the heaviest pieces should be able to penetrate the thickest armour of any opposing battleship, and this both the 67-ton and the 46-ton would almost certainly do. Another argument in favour of carrying lighter guns, and more of them, is that thereby a better all-round fire can be obtained, and the disablement of one gun will not go so far to disable a ship. With four heavy guns, the silencing of one piece means one quarter of the power gone; with two, it means one half. It is true that both these points depend for their application upon the system on which the guns are mounted; for instance, a pair of lighter guns, mounted together in a barbette or turret, give no wider area of fire than a heavier one, mounted alone, and are almost as likely to be put out of action by a lucky shot. In the case of the *Sans Pareil*, however, this consideration does not apply. Both the huge guns are mounted in a single turret forward, and one of them could hardly receive damage without simultaneously disabling the other. Moreover, although they can be trained through a very wide angle of fire—no less than 300°—so that they can bear not only ahead, and on either broadside, but also (at least in theory) on either quarter at an angle of only 30° to the ship's axis, they cannot attack an enemy dead astern. This leaves a very weak spot in the vessel, which is hardly made good by a 10-in. gun mounted on the poop, without any other armour protection than a mere shield. The *Sans Pareil* must thus be pronounced out of place in the British Fleet, since she is incapable of fighting stern-on with any effect, while nearly all the other ships with which she would be likely to be in line, are as well fitted for that possibility as for engaging an enemy ahead. Great indeed may be the importance of homogeneity to a squadron, and if it were necessary to fight such an action, the *Sans Pareil* would be almost useless and an encumbrance to the other vessels. For the rest, the fact that the secondary armament of twelve 6-in. guns (lately exchanged for quick-firers of the same calibre) is aft of the turret, and also wholly undefended by plating, only emphasizes the weak point in the ship, since this open battery could be raked by an enemy.

The *Sans Pareil* is protected by sixteen to eighteen inches of compound plating along only 162 of 340 feet of length; she carries 18 inches on the turret, a 6-in. bulkhead forward of the secondary battery, and sloping backward from the turret, and—true to the neglect of the stern—only a 3-in. bulkhead protecting half the 6-in. guns. The *Sans Pareil* steamed, on trial, 16 knots under natural, and 17·75 (with 14,483 horse-power) under forced draught. This was a very remarkable speed for 1888—indeed, it is a fraction more than the *Magnificent* made a few months ago. She can stow 1200 tons in her bunkers, which should take her 7000 miles at 10 knots. Her cost was £719,442—nearly £140,000 less than that of the *Trafalgar*, but it is hardly doubtful that the more expensive ship is better value for the money.

Next comes the "Admiral" class—so called because its six ships are named after Anson, Benbow, Camperdown, Collingwood, Howe, and Rodney. This type is not only important by reason of the number of vessels conforming to it, but also as marking an epoch in the history of our armoured fleet. The *Collingwood*, the earliest of the series (1886), was the first battleship in which the barbette system of mounting the heavy guns was adopted, and therewith a higher freeboard and greater seaworthiness than was possible in turret-ships. It is true that the "Admirals" themselves are low in the bow compared with later barbette-ships; but they are an improvement on the earlier turret-ships, and prepared the way for yet further advance in sea-going qualities. The *Collingwood* was also the first vessel that gave an adequate space and weight to the secondary armament. Her four 12-in. 45-ton guns were mounted by pairs in barbettes, forward and aft, 140 feet apart, whilst the six 6-in. breech-loaders were ranged in a box battery between. This disposition of the lighter guns between two pairs of heavy ones

NAVAL POLICY

reappears in every one of our later ships, except the *Sans Pareil*, so that the *Collingwood* may reasonably be called their original progenitor. The distribution of the armour also marked a sharp break with the methods of the immediate past, and, in its turn, helps to stamp the *Collingwood* as the ancestor of all our later ships. We get in the *Collingwood* the long plated citadel, with transverse bulkheads, instead of the short oblong of the turret-ships which came before her. In the *Collingwood* the belt covers only 140 feet out of 325; but in the *Colossus*, the last of our old-pattern turret-ships, it is no more than 123 on the same length. This proportion of belt to total length increases from 43 per cent. in the *Collingwood* only to 44 per cent. in the *Sans Pareil;* but in the *Nile*, by a great advance, the belt already protects two-thirds of the whole length. This proportion is maintained in the *Royal Sovereign* class; but falls off again, in consequence of the greatly increased area of side-plating, to 56 per cent. in the *Majestic*. The thickness of the *Collingwood's* compound-plating is 18 to 8 inches on the belt, 16 to 6 on the bulkhead, and 14 to 12 on the barbettes; the steel deck is 2½ inches. Her faults are many, especially in matter of armour. The unarmoured ends are very long; the secondary armament is also wholly unarmoured. Worst of all, the bases of the barbettes are similarly unprotected, so that the smallest shell might enter, and explode under them. This would certainly disable the main armament, even if it did not cause the huge iron tray, with its two heavy guns, to drop through the ship's bottom, and sink her. Another defect, as has been pointed out, is her low bow; this may not be much felt in the Mediterranean,

THE BRITISH NAVY

where most of the "Admiral" class have served for several years, but might easily handicap the ship in manœuvring and fighting her guns in any sea. But these faults have been gradually corrected in later vessels of similar type, while the distinctive arrangements of armament in the *Collingwood* have been adopted—sometimes sooner, sometimes later—in the most recent battleships of every considerable naval Power.

The other vessels of the "Admiral" type are enlargements and modifications of the *Collingwood*. The *Rodney* and *Howe* displace 10,300 instead of 9500 tons, upon which, instead of the older 12-in. gun, they mount four of the $13\frac{1}{2}$-in. guns which form the main armament of the *Nile* and *Royal Sovereign* models. The *Anson*, *Benbow*, and *Camperdown* are of 10,600 tons, and five feet longer. The first and last are armed like the *Howe*. The *Benbow* carries two $16\frac{1}{4}$-in. 111-ton guns, similar to those of the *Sans Pareil*, instead of four $13\frac{1}{2}$-in., and ten 6-in. guns instead of six. As the heavy guns are mounted one in each barbette, they are not exposed to the simultaneous disablement which is a danger to the *Sans Pareil;* the *Benbow* is also able to engage an enemy stern on, as well as to train both guns on either broadside. However, the two guns are inferior in power, as has been seen, to the four $13\frac{1}{2}$-in., which can plant more, if less crushing, blows upon an enemy, while less power is wasted in case of a miss by one of them. On the whole, therefore, it appears wise that the experiment was only tried in one ship out of six. On the other hand, the *Benbow* has an advantage in the greater number of her 6-in. guns—an advantage multiplied by the substitution of quick-firers for the slow-fire breech-loaders with which they were first equipped. The *Benbow* ought now to possess an energy of fire per minute of 233,377 ft.-tons to 189,573 ft.-tons of the *Howe* or *Anson*.* It sounds almost incredible that, although the 6-in. quick-firer has been used in the service for over five years, this substitution of quick-firing secondary armament has only been made, and that just recently, on two ships of this class—the *Collingwood* and *Benbow*. Any time these five years they have been serving—all, or most of them—on the Mediterranean Station, which is the first line of our defence. Had we come to war with France in that time—which we nearly did more than once—half of the line which would have had to fight the first action with the flower of the French fleet would have been found depending on an obsolete weapon, and deprived of half its due power. The neglect to re-arm these ships is an example of official sluggishness, which would appear impossible in a service so generally efficient, were not the retention of effete muzzle-loaders on our older battleships too deplorably exact a parallel to it. However, the *Collingwood* has at last been re-armed at Malta, and there is hope that before long the whole of the class will receive the same belated attention. This done, the "Admirals" will be serviceable ships for many years, though their ineffective protection against quick-fire shells must shortly relegate them to the second line. The trial speeds of the six ships under forced draught resulted, respectively, as follows:

---

* The shooting-power of these guns, which are the old 6-in. breech-loaders converted into quick-firers, is here and elsewhere reckoned as that of the 6-in. quick-firer proper; it is, however, in fact, slightly inferior.

Collingwood, 16·8 ; *Howe*, 16·9 ; *Rodney*, 16·9 ; *Benbow*, 17·5 ; *Camperdown*, 17·1 ; *Anson*, 17·4. Of these results that of the *Benbow* should be discounted, as she was not tried at her normal weight. The top natural draught-speed of the class is from 16 to 16½ knots an hour. All stow from 900 to 1200 tons of coal, which should enable them to steam from 5000 to 7000 knots, at 10 knots an hour—the *Collingwood* rather more, since she is smaller and lighter.

All the ships described above are officially ranked as first-class. That distinction is a convenient one, inasmuch as the "Admirals" are the beginning and pattern of our modern battle-fleet, but it is not wholly trustworthy. One class shades into another. When the vessels of a fleet represent a continuous progress, as ours do, the superiority of the best first-class ship over the worst is almost certain to be greater than the superiority of the latter over the best second-class ship. The *Majestic*, for example, exerts an energy from all her guns over 3-in. calibre, which may be roughly put at 316,000 ft.-tons per minute; the *Collingwood*, before the substitution of quick-firers for her original armament, had about 50,000 ft.-tons; and the *Colossus*, the leading vessel of the official second-class, over 45,000. In point of offensive power, it would be absurd to put the *Collingwood* in the same class as the *Majestic* and omit the *Colossus*. The disparity in protective armour is almost as great. Again, the old first-class ship will often be less powerful than the new second-class. The energy of the heavier guns on the French second-class *Bouvines* is about 160,000 ft.-tons to the *Collingwood's* 50,000; she is probably as well armoured, and a fraction of a knot faster. It is true that the substitution of quick-firers brings the *Collingwood's* energy of fire up to 130,000, while she has a great strategic superiority in stowing 900 tons of coal to the *Bouvines's* 300. Nevertheless, even if we grant that the *Collingwood* is the more desirable ship of the two in a squadron, the balance of superiority is so slight that the sharp distinction of first and second class loses nearly all its significance. It is this impossibility of drawing a hard and fast line between classes, and of putting the same value on all ships within the same class, that invalidates all estimates of relative strength based on the official denominations. Hence arise bluntly conflicting calculations of force, such as perplex Parliament and the public. Plainly it makes a vast difference, if we are basing a calculation upon first-class ships, whether the six "Admirals" are included in the British total or not. If you take them in, our position is fairly satisfactory; yet it is grossly misleading to reckon a *Collingwood* as one, and a *Majestic* as no more than one. If, on the other hand, you exclude the "Admirals," you ignore a group of ships certainly superior to most vessels usually ranked as second-class. There can be no exact measurement of force: the only possible method is to analyze the several capacities of each vessel.

The second-class is mainly made up of a series of turret-ships, built between 1870 and 1880; the type has been already sketched in the previous chapter. The turrets are not placed at either end of a long central battery, as in the *Nile*, but together amidships. In the *Nile* the guns of one turret bear ahead, and those of the other astern; in the later ships of the second-class, the turrets are placed *en échelon*—that is, obliquely: one on one beam, rather forward of the ship's centre, and the other on the other beam, rather abaft of it. With two guns in each turret, this arrangement obviously gives a great concentration of all-round fire; all four heavy guns can bear ahead, astern, on either broadside—in any direction, indeed, except on one bow and one quarter, where one turret would mask the other. With this arrangement, the natural tendency was to concentrate the armour also round the heavy guns, thus making a small citadel in the centre of the ship. The vessels built on this plan are (in order of newness) the *Colossus* and *Edinburgh*, *Agamemnon* and *Ajax*, and *Inflexible*. The two first are fairly successful ships; the three last are not. The *Colossus* and *Edinburgh* are of 9420 tons, and mailed with 14 to 16 inches of compound armour; they carry four 12-in. 45-ton guns, and five 6-in. slow-firers, as well as light quick-firers for use against torpedo-boats. Their trial speed, without forced draught, for which they are not fitted, was 16 knots, and they carry coal enough to maintain this rate for over 2000 miles, and 10 knots for 6000. It must be added that the *Edinburgh* lamentably failed in steaming powers at the 1896 manœuvres, and had great difficulty in making 11 knots. The *Agamemnon*, *Ajax*, and *Inflexible* are far less valuable; indeed, it might be doubted whether the loss of their crews, risked by sending them to sea in war-time, would not be greater than any service they would be likely to render. They are armed with obsolete muzzle-loaders, they are very slow, and they will not steer. Besides these special demerits of their own, they share with the *Colossus* the disadvantage that the greater part of the hull, and therewith the auxiliary armament, is

NAVAL POLICY

unprotected. These ships were the first to mount medium-sized guns, but the want of protection for their crews almost destroys the value of the innovation. These were also the first British ships on which compound armour was used, and the first also with the armoured deck below the water-line that has since partly superseded the belt in our battleships, and wholly in our cruisers.

The earlier turret-ships of the second-class—the *Neptune, Dreadnought, Thunderer,* and *Devastation*—are like the *Nile,* in that the turrets are not *en échelon,* but fore and aft on the centre-line of the ship. They are completely belted by thick iron plating; and having, except the *Neptune,* very low freeboards, are armoured over almost their whole surface. The *Thunderer* and *Devastation,* designed by Sir Edward Reed nearly thirty years ago, are still most efficient and valuable ships; they have been re-armed with 10-in. breech-loaders, and light quick-firers, while new machinery has given them a speed, in smooth water, of over 14 knots.

Besides the turret-ships, there are also ranked in the second-class, the *Téméraire, Superb,* and *Alexandra.* These are central battery, or casemate ships, though the *Téméraire* carries two of her heavy guns in barbettes. The central battery was an effort to secure the bow and stern fire, in which the earliest broadside ironclads were necessarily deficient. These ships are completely belted, and also armoured on the central battery; they command a good all-round fire; their speed is 13 to 14 knots.

The disabling weakness of these ships is their obsolete armament. It is no use to waste words in condemnation

THE BRITISH NAVY

of the policy which retained the slow and feeble muzzle-loader for years after every civilized nation had abandoned it. But it is perhaps worth while to insist that the mistake, once recognized, should be immediately made good. "Our available supply of heavy breech-loaders," wrote Lord Brassey in 1887, "is still lamentably insufficient. . . . The delay in adopting the breech-loading system for the British service is much to be regretted. We have to face a large expenditure to bring our store of guns to a level with our great requirements." This was in 1887; the first heavy breech-loaders had been mounted on the *Conqueror* in 1882. It is now 1896, and the work of re-armament is hardly begun. Here again is one of the extraordinary contradictions, which awake the doubt whether the British Navy is, after all, the first in the world or the last. In fourteen years we have succeeded in re-arming the *Thunderer* and *Devastation* wholly, and the *Alexandra* partially with heavy breech-loaders; while we have supplied the third-class *Sultan* and *Hercules* with ten 4·7-inch quick-firers between them. Feebler attempts to keep our ships up to the requirements of war there could not be. The result is that more than half the second-class of our battleships, and all the third-class, are unfit to send to sea except in peace time. The Admiralty is supposed to be pursuing a steady course of renovation and reconstruction with our older ships; they do indeed go into dockyard hands for months, and heavy sums are spent upon them. But when they come out again, as did the *Superb, Hercules, Sultan*, and *Monarch*, with next to nothing but their old muzzle-loaders to depend on, whose crews would likely enough be shot down to a man by quick-fire shell before their second round, then the only conclusion is that the money spent had much better have been thrown into the sea. The official defence against this charge of modernization, which is no modernization, is that, the ships being built for muzzle-loaders, it is not possible to substitute the longer breech-loaders without virtually taking the ship to pieces and putting her together again. This, it is said, would not be worth the money, which would be better spent on new ships. Very well; but if it is not worth the money to re-arm them efficiently, how much less worth it must be to spend large sums and leave them inefficient. Let us have one thing or the other. Either let us spend enough to arm our older ironclads with breech-loaders and quick-firers, well protected, and to re-furnish them with modern engines; or else let us recognize that the money will be better spent on new ships, and spend it accordingly. Only then let us quite frankly admit that more than half our second, and nearly all our third line is virtually ineffective. Or, better still, let us sell the ships to the Emperor of China, or some other innocent potentate who desires a ready-made toy fleet. But let us leave the present farce of counting the ships as efficient on the one side of the account, and crediting ourselves with the money required to make them efficient on the other.

The third-class battleships on the effective list are twenty-six in number. This includes fifteen vessels classed as coast-defence ships. The classification is misleading, in so far as it is not the custom of our country to build ships intended for coast-defence alone. Our frontier is the enemy's coast-line, and all our ships should be able to take the offensive on that frontier, leaving the sea secure in British possession behind them.

THE BRITISH NAVY

The coast defenders in our Navy are so called because improvements in shipbuilding have left them unable thus to operate against a distant enemy, either through deficiency of coal-supply, or because their low freeboard renders them incapable of contending against any sea. It is not worth while to give a detailed account either of these or of the sea-going third-class ironclads. The most efficiently armed are the *Conqueror* and *Hero* —twin turret-ships built on the model of the *Sans Pareil*, but much smaller. Each carries a pair of 12-inch breech-loaders in a single forward turret, as well as four 6-inch slow-firers as auxiliary armament, with light quick-firers. The compound armour-belt protects the whole length except 20 feet astern. They are handy ships, but so low in the bows that their speed falls to ten knots in a seaway, and on this account they would often be more of an encumbrance than a help to a sea-going squadron. Somewhat similar are the older *Rupert* and *Hotspur*. These are completely belted. The *Rupert* has had two 9·2-inch breech-loading guns substituted for the muzzle-loaders in her turret, and is so far efficient that she is now serving as guardship at Gibraltar; it is, however, instructive, as demonstrating the dependence of low-bowed ships on the weather, that she had to turn back from her first attempt to get there. The double-turreted *Monarch* has also been reconstructed, and can steam $14\frac{1}{2}$ knots nominal, but the muzzle-loaders remain. Of the other third-class ships, the *Sultan* and *Hercules* are remarkable for the stoutness of their build. They would last for years yet if they were better armed; as it is, a costly reconstruction stopped short with the provision of four 4·7-inch quick-firers for the one, and six for the other, leaving the heavy muzzle-loaders still in place. The *Bellerophon*, a central-battery ship over thirty years old, has been re-armed with 8-inch breech-loaders, and could take her place in the line of battle at a pinch. The *Magdala* and *Abyssinia*, turret-ships used for Indian defence, have been re-armed with the same guns. The rest of this class would only be used in line as a last reserve, though they might any of them be useful as depôt-ships for torpedo-boats acting as coast-defence, or to convoy merchantmen. For the same duties the Admiralty could draw on four antique broadside ironclads, officially miscalled armoured cruisers. As none of them can make more than $13\frac{1}{2}$ knots, they have little in common with such ships as the *Terrible*. All retain their pristine muzzle-loaders, but the *Minotaur* and *Northumberland* mount a few 4·7 quick-firers which, backed by their great surface of armour, would enable them to drive off any but a powerful cruiser.

The real cruiser of to-day is very different from such stout, unwieldy machines as these. With warships, as with everything else, function governs structure. So the cruiser, being, as it were, the cavalry of the sea, must be swift to move even more than strong to strike. It falls to the cruiser to discover the whereabouts, the movements, and the strength of the enemy, and thus enable the battle-fleet either to engage or avoid him. This is the function of cruisers with a fleet. Their other main duty is to act independently for the defence or attack of commerce at sea. For both purposes they clearly require a high degree of speed—speed, too, not shown in a spurt over the measured mile, with boiler-tubes just holding out unburned for the four hours, but maintained for long periods in any sort of sea. To ensure such a high sea-speed, an efficient cruiser, whether in scouting for a fleet or a long chase on her own account, must be of a certain size; otherwise her nominal speed will fall too much in contending with the waves. But besides the capacity for continuous hard steaming, she must possess also the capacities of a fighting-ship. The fastest scout might often be compelled to fight a running action with an enemy, and the inability to defend herself might result in the loss of momentous information. And though it needs no overwhelming degree of military power to capture a merchantman, isolated cruisers must always be ready for actions with the cruisers of the enemy. Especially is this so with British cruisers. On the high seas, as before an enemy's battle-fleet, we shall be on the defensive; but our defence must, in both cases, be offensive. We present to the enemy's attack a sea-borne trade greater than that of any other three nations together. We alone of all the nations of the earth might be brought to our knees by the destruction of our commerce at sea. Therefore the cruiser of an enemy would ask nothing better than to be left undisturbed in the inglorious, but most effective, occupation of destroying our merchant marine. We, on the other hand, must attack and destroy the hostile cruiser at all times and at any cost. Every hostile cruiser at large is a menace to our national existence; and every action, even though of itself indecisive, which leaves a hostile cruiser at large is essentially a British defeat. French writers have said that the commander of any French cruiser in war-time ought to be court-martialled if he engaged a British ship when he could avoid it. If so, a British officer should be court-martialled if

NAVAL POLICY

he neglects to engage a hostile cruiser when there is even the faintest hope of disabling her. Our cruisers, then, must have speed to bring them into touch with the enemy, and gun-power to enable them to defeat him.

The modern cruiser, like many of the appliances of modern naval war, is the invention of Lord Armstrong. In 1879 there had been completed at Portsmouth the *Mercury*, which, on trial, got the splendid result of 18·7 knots an hour. But the *Mercury* does not stow coal enough to be really efficient on a cruise, while the fact that her engines and boilers are above the water-line, and wholly unprotected by armour, seriously reduces her value as a fighting-ship. The latter of these disadvantages were avoided in the *Esmeralda*, which Lord Armstrong produced in 1889 for the Chilian Government. The *Esmeralda* (now sold to Japan, and renamed the *Idzumi*) is a knot slower than the *Mercury*, and is also inferior in coal endurance; but she carries two 10-in. and six 6-in. guns against thirteen 5-in. on the *Mercury*, which would give her, roughly, one-third again as much gun-power. What was far more important, she had an arched protected deck below water, which covered engines, boilers, steam-pipes, and magazines, while all the more important guns were protected by steel screens. With this *Esmeralda* began a series of cruisers combining very high speed with an enormous attacking power. The series has culminated in the second *Esmeralda*—also built for Chili—which may fairly be called the most remarkable warship in the world. She is built to steam a trifle under $23\frac{1}{2}$ knots an hour, which makes her the fastest war-vessel (other than torpedo craft) in the world. Carrying two 8-in., sixteen

THE BRITISH NAVY

6-in., and ten 6-pounder guns — all quick-firing — her energy of fire per minute comes to the enormous total of 509,091 ft.-tons, which surpasses not only all cruisers, but all battleships in the world, whether built, building, or to be built. Moreover, she is protected with a 6-in. belt over four-fifths of her length, carries 5-in. shields on her guns, and has a 2-in. steel deck. On occasion she can carry 1000 tons of coal—and all this on a displacement under 8000 tons.

In our own line of cruisers we have nothing to show of such brilliance as the *Esmeralda*. Our latest, largest, and most expensive are the *Powerful* and *Terrible*. They are of 14,200 tons, and so large (500 feet long between perpendiculars, and 538 over all), that a couple of new docks have had to be built for them at Portsmouth, since no existing one would take them. But an analysis of their offensive and defensive powers is at the first blush very disappointing. They were built as an answer to the *Rurik* and *Rossia*: compare them with these Russian cruisers and with the *Esmeralda*. They have greater tonnage—nearly double the *Esmeralda's*—and they have not only cost as much money in themselves, but have caused us to spend £375,000 more in making docks for them. What do we get in return? The *Terrible's* energy of fire per minute is 306,647 foot-tons; the *Esmeralda's* is 509,091, while the *Rossia's* is estimated at 470,000. The *Terrible* has no side armour; the *Esmeralda* and *Rossia* are belted over four-fiths of their length with six inches of steel. The *Terrible* steams 22½ knots an hour, and the *Esmeralda* over 23; the *Rossia*, it is true, but 20. Briefly, it seems that at a vast expenditure of money we have got a ship which could neither catch the cheaper *Esmeralda*, nor fight her if she did. She has indeed a couple of knots in hand of the *Rossia*, but, being weaker both in offence and defence, it looks like the advantage in running away—a position which, for a British cruiser, is neither dignified nor profitable.

But a closer examination of these ships puts a somewhat better face on the matter. The *Terrible* carries fore and aft a couple of 9·2-inch guns of greater range and penetration than anything mounted by her rivals, and this goes to neutralize their side-armour. Furthermore, although wholly unarmoured on the side, she has an arched steel deck of 4 inches over her vitals, as against less than 3 inches in the *Rossia*, and but 2 in the *Esmeralda*. Her two 9·2-inch guns are in 6-inch barbettes, and her twelve 6-inch quick-firers are protected by 6 inches of armour before and 2 inches behind; the *Esmeralda's* have 5-inch shields in front, but the crews are defenceless against shells bursting behind them. The *Rossia's* guns, too (if she is like the *Rurik*) are protected only by shields, and mostly carried in an open battery, so that one shell might put half-a-dozen of them out of action. Moreover, the very size of the *Terrible* gives her a considerable advantage. Her gun positions are more widely distributed, so that guns will be less easily put out of action. It is true that she carries four of her 6-inch pieces in casemates exactly over four others, but even so her armament would probably require more blows to silence it than that of her rivals. The *Terrible* can steam 25,000 knots at 10 knots, the *Rossia* 20,000, and the *Esmeralda* a beggarly 2000. In speed, again, the *Terrible's* size favours her; the *Esmeralda* may have done more on the trial trip, but the *Terrible's* high bow and great length and weight would probably bring her well to the front at sea. Her 22½ knots, moreover, are attained under natural draught. In ocean speed, indeed, the *Terrible* and *Powerful* are likely to prove decidedly the fastest cruisers in the world. Unlike the United States cruiser *Columbia* of 7475 tons, which in crossing the Atlantic fell four and a half knots below her trial speed, they are likely to give their form in all weathers for days together, and are probably the only cruisers afloat which could chase a liner with the least chance of overtaking her. Yet when all is said and done, it is doubtful whether it would be wise to build many *Terribles*. It is not so much that they are not good enough, but that they are too good and too expensive for the work they are likely to have to do. Assuming, as we fairly may, that they could fight a *Rossia* or a *Rurik* on equal terms, the two or four knots superiority in speed might be just as well one for all useful purposes, so that here is a certain waste of power. A coal endurance of 25,000 knots, again, is probably more than would ever be wanted in practice. As for the *Esmeralda*, she can never operate a thousand knots away from her coaling-base; so that if our probable enemies acquire any such ship it would be more economical to build ships with coal enough to bring them into her radius, and sufficient gun-power and protection to overcome her. After all there are but half-a-dozen cruisers in the world that would be worthy antagonists for the *Terrible*, and not a dozen foreign liners that would need such high speed to run them down.

So that for nearly all probable eventualities of war the new *Diadem* class will doubtless be found quite fast and powerful enough. The *Diadem* and seven sisters—

NAVAL POLICY

Andromeda, Europe, Niobe, and four as yet unnamed—will displace 11,000 tons. They are armoured on the same plan as the *Terrible,* except that the casemates are of 4½-inch steel instead of 6. Instead of the two 9·2-inch slow-firing guns in barbettes, the *Diadem* will mount on forecastle and poop two pairs of 6-inch quick-firers. This will add greatly to the energy of fire, which in the *Diadem* reaches 355,235 ft.-tons a minute as against 306,647 in the *Terrible.* It may be objected as against this that the 6-inch gun is adequate to pierce armour of any thickness, and the suggestion has several times been made that a couple of 8-inch quick-firers would have been better than either the two 9·2-inch or the four 6-inch; the rate of fire would have been far greater than that of the former, and nearly as great as the latter, with far more efficiency for the attack of armour. The *Diadem,* like the *Terrible,* is fitted with Belleville water-tube boilers. At natural draught these ships are estimated to steam 20½ knots, which estimate, following the very commendable custom of our ships, will probably be exceeded on trial. With forced draught, if it is used, they would doubtless do a knot more, but even without it the *Diadem* class will probably be able to hold their own in a sea with any cruiser of any probable enemy.

The rest of our first-class cruisers are several years older. The *Blake* and *Blenheim,* which rank next in size, power, and speed, date from 1890. Of 9000 tons, they are considerably smaller than the *Terrible* and the *Diadem,* measuring 390 feet, as against 500 and 435, and are consequently able to use many of our existing docks—a consideration not without importance. They carry forward and aft two 9·2-in. guns, of an older pattern than the *Terrible's*, which latter are of wire, and therefore strong enough to use a more powerful charge. On each broadside they carry five 6-in. quick-firers; below this calibre they have no gun larger than their sixteen 3-pounders for repelling torpedo-boats, whereas the *Terrible* mounts sixteen, and the *Diadem* fourteen 12-pounders, besides a dozen 3-pounders apiece. Nevertheless the *Blake* and the *Blenheim* are very well armed for their date. They would be well able to stand up to such first-class cruisers as the French *D'Entrecasteaux*, launched only the other day, and should make short work of anything of a lower class. They have no vertical armour, but carry 6-in. casemates for the four 6-in. guns mounted on the main deck; the others have only protective shields. This is a weakness, but it belongs to their time: the importance of shelter for guns has only been gradually realized as the tremendous destructive force of quick-fire shells has come home to naval constructors. The protective deck is from 3 to 6 inches. The engines present a novel feature, there being four distinct sets of triple-expansion engines, two on each side. The forward and after sets on each side can be coupled up together to work at high speeds, or disconnected when moderate speeds are desired by using the after engines alone. The *Blake* performed disappointingly on her earliest trials, steaming only 19 knots, against the *Blenheim's* 22, but after a commission on the North American Station, she was fitted with new boiler-tubes, and being tried again, reached $21\frac{1}{2}$ knots. These ships, with 1800 tons of coal, were intended to steam 15,000 knots, at 10 knots an hour, or 2000 knots at full speed.

It may be here remarked that the coal-endurance of

ships is apt to be exaggerated, since often no account is taken of the coal burned by the auxiliary machinery. Also, if the endurance is calculated on the basis of the fuel consumed on the trial-trip, no allowance is made for steaming against wind or sea, which is naturally more expensive of coal. All calculations of coal-endurance are, therefore, to a certain extent untrustworthy, unless arrived at by actual experiment in average conditions of weather. Nevertheless, as it is of the first importance in estimating the strategic value of a warship, and as the error is fairly uniform in all cases, the calculated endurance of any two ships may be taken as representing roughly the proportionate, if not the actual, radius of their action. Modern ships are estimated to burn approximately 2 lbs. per indicated horse-power per hour, with a daily wastage of one to six tons for auxiliary engines.

We possess nine first-class cruisers of the *Edgar* class. This group really contains two slightly different types. The *Edgar, Endymion, Grafton, Hawke,* and *Theseus* are of 7350 tons; the *Crescent, Gibraltar, Royal Arthur,* and *St. George* of 7700. With engines of the same power, the lighter type, which also has a slight advantage in the proportion of length to beam, is about half-a-knot the faster; these ships steam 19 and 20 knots with natural and forced draught respectively, the *Crescent* and her sisters $18\frac{1}{2}$ and $19\frac{1}{2}$. The coal-endurance is reckoned at 10,000 knots at 10 per hour, and 2800 at 18. The main armament (two 9·2-in. and ten 6-in. quick-firers) is the same as that of the *Blake*, with the advantage as against torpedo-boats of twelve 6-pounders and five 3-pounders, instead of sixteen 3-pounders. The *Crescent* and *Royal Arthur*, however, carry only one 9·2-in. gun and twelve 6-in. quick-firers—an arrangement which gives a greater volume of fire, though less power of penetrating armour. The steel deck has a maximum thickness of 5 inches, and there are, as in the *Blake*, four 6- to 2-in. armoured casemates. Altogether these are, perhaps, the most satisfactory cruisers we possess. They cost from £350,000 to £400,000 apiece, as against £440,000 and £425,000 for the *Blake* and *Blenheim*. They are perhaps a couple of knots slower; on the other hand, for less money and on a smaller tonnage, they are more powerfully armed, and almost as well protected, and are worked by 544 men instead of 590. Even the superiority of speed in the *Blake* is more apparent than real. She dates from the era of excessive forced draught, which could only be safely used for a short spurt, and her natural draught speed can hardly be more than 19 knots. On the other hand, to take specimen cases, the *Edgar* has run twenty-four hours on end at 19¾ knots, and the *Royal Arthur* twice as long at 17¼. In a word, there are very few cruisers abroad that these fine sea-going ships could not catch in a long chase, and fewer still that could withstand their powerful quick-firing broadside. While we have such ships there is little need to go in search of extravagant displacements, or even excessive speed.

Of what are called armoured, as opposed to deck-protected, cruisers, our constructors seem never to have had a very high opinion. There are, indeed, seven belted cruisers—*Aurora, Australia, Galatea, Immortalité, Narcissus, Orlando, Undaunted,* laid down in 1885 and 1886; and the *Impericuse* and *Warspite,* four or five years older. These ships are protected on the water-line by narrow belts of compound armour—200 feet long in the 300-ft. *Aurora*, 5½ feet broad and 10 inches thick; and 140 feet long out of the *Warspite's* 315, 8 broad, and 10 inches thick. In each ship transverse bulkheads close the ends of the belt. But a narrow strip of armour like this is rather an alternative to the protective deck than an advance upon it in resistance to projectiles. As the curved deck would, in most cases, be hit obliquely, it will be, roughly, twice as difficult to penetrate, so that a 5-in. steel deck would answer exactly the same purpose as the 10-in. side-plating. The analogy is completed by the fact that at their load-draught the *Aurora* class sink until the belt is almost entirely submerged. This is, in itself, no disadvantage; for the belt emerges if the ship rolls, and thus protects the vital parts just in the circumstances where they are exposed to most damage. But so far as protection to the hull is concerned, it is misleading to call the *Aurora* an armoured cruiser any more than the *Edgar*. To find the real armoured cruiser we must look abroad to the French *Jeanne d'Arc*, *Dupuy-de-Lôme*, and *Bruix* class. Here the hull is really armoured with a thin sheath of steel over all but its whole surface. Whether our constructors have been wise in neglecting this type of cruiser is doubtful. The *Jeanne d'Arc's* 6-in. mail will defy under any conditions the shot of all our service 6-in. quick-firers, except the wire-wound model. The 4-in. plates of the others will do as much for the 4·7-in. quick-firer, and stop even the 6-in. shot at long ranges. Oblique hits, even from most powerful guns, will glance aside off their armour; and, with a superior speed, a captain can so manœuvre that most hits will be oblique. The attack of shell will be entirely defeated, since shell will burst outside the ships. This means that until the armour is broken up the principal offensive weapons of naval war will be powerless against them. It is by no means certain that even our most formidable cruisers could meet such vessels with an even chance of success. This being so, is it wise to go on putting all our eggs in the unarmoured basket?

To come back to our belted cruisers. The *Aurora* type is of 5600 tons. They mount two 9·2-in. and ten 6-in. guns, which latter will, by the end of the year, be converted to quick-firers in all but the *Orlando* and *Undaunted*, which are serving on distant stations abroad. The *Warspite* carries four 9·2-in. breech-loaders—one ahead, one astern, and one on each beam, all in 8-in. compound-armour barbettes; also ten 6-in., four 6-pounder, and nine 3-pounder quick-firers. Both types reinforce their belt with a 3-in. steel deck. In point of protection and gun-power, therefore, both types rightly rank as cruisers of the first class. The *Aurora* displaces, for example, 5600 tons to the *Blake's* 7000, and cost £287,000 to £440,000. She is, on the whole, as efficiently protected, and her guns give out about 201,000 ft.-tons of energy per minute to about 206,000. The *Warspite*, on a displacement of 8400 tons—though at a cost, it is true, of £529,000—has better protection, and a fire-energy of over 220,000 ft.-tons. The deficiency both of the *Aurora* class and of the *Warspite* is in speed. The former ships steam from 18 to 19½ knots at top speed; the latter 17 knots. This belongs to their day, but they remain far better armed, in proportion to their tonnage, than most of our cruisers. Once they got up to an enemy they could give a very good account of themselves.

NAVAL POLICY

The modern second-class cruisers of the British Navy are all developments of one type, so that no long time need be devoted to their description. The archetype is found in the *Apollo* and twenty sisters, built under the Naval Defence Act in 1890 and 1891. To be strictly accurate, there are two divisions in this class: ten* are of 3600 tons, 300 ft. long, 43 ft. 8 in. in breadth, and 17 ft. 6 in. draught; and eleven of 3400 tons, being of the same length, but 8 inches narrower, and drawing 18 inches less water. All alike have a protective deck from 1 to 2 inches thick; all carry two 6-in. quick-firers at bow and stern, and three 4·7-in. quick-firers on either broadside. They also have eight 6-pounders. In speed the narrower and lighter class naturally have an advantage: all reached 20 knots an hour with forced draught, and the *Sappho* and *Scylla* 20½. The ten heavier boats made about 19¾.

These vessels have been severely criticized, and with good reason. They are very decidedly under-armed, and especially weak in end-on fire. If we compare them with French second-class cruisers, such as the *Chassseloup-Laubat*, it is plain that a combat could only by a miracle result in anything but disaster for our ship. Whether the *Apollo* chased or ran, she would find her single 6-in. bow or stern-chaser faced by three 6·3-in. and two 3·9-in. quick-firers. In three minutes the *Apollo* would throw sixteen shots, represented by 43,696 ft.-tons of energy, from her one gun; the *Chasseloup-Laubat* ninety-three shots, of 227,192 ft.-tons, from her five.† As it will be the object of French cruisers to keep

---

* For names, see table in Appendix.

† See a forcible article by Mr. H. Arnold Forster, in the *Pall Mall Gazette* of March 27th, 1895.

away from our ships and devote themselves to ruining our trade, and as, therefore, actions between cruisers will usually begin with a chase, this inferiority in end-on fire can only be fatal. The *Apollo* will be more than half a knot to the good each hour; but of what use will that be when she can hardly help being disabled before she can come up with the enemy? And even if we suppose her to have come up, and to use superior speed to force a broadside action, the case is hardly bettered. The *Apollo* brings to bear on the broadside two 6-in. and three 4·7-in. guns; the *Chasseloup-Laubat* four 6·3-in. and two 3·9-in.: that is, 141,143 ft.-tons in three minutes for the *Apollo*, to 227,192 for the Frenchman. The conclusion is that only by an overwhelming superiority in gunnery, such as we have no right to assume for our seamen, could one of these ships escape defeat at the hands of a typical second-class French cruiser. It may be answered that the *Apollo* is superior to her rival in coal supply, in ammunition, in the possession of a double bottom for going aground on; and that a British cruiser, having to operate in any seas, must needs possess these qualities. Possibly that is a very good reason why our second-class cruisers should have a larger displacement than any Power else's. But the fact remains that British cruisers—British cruisers, indeed, above all others—are built to fight their enemy, and that this particular type is unable to tackle an average opponent of its own class. As a fighting-ship, it may have every other merit on the face of the waters, only—it cannot fight.

The first modification of this type is seen in the *Astræa* class of eight vessels. These vessels are an improvement in that they mount a couple more 4·7-in.

quick-firers, and that two of these can fire ahead or astern as well as the 6-in. chaser. This is an undeniable gain. But even this leaves a pursuing *Astræa* at a great disadvantage against the *Chasseloup-Laubat's* stern fire, while she still remains inferior in broadside fire. Moreover, against the *Astræa's* gain in gun-power, we have to set the following points of inferiority. She is of 760 tons greater displacement than the *Apollo*, she costs £60,000 more, is half a knot slower, takes 318 men to work her instead of 273, and, having the same bunker capacity with a greater weight to propel, has but 5500 as against 7000 knots radius of action.

The next advance in the type of second-class cruiser is the *Eclipse* class, of which, complete and completing, we have nine, with three more to be laid down on the 1896 programme. These vessels are a trifle more satisfactory. The *Eclipse* brings to bear forward three 6-in. quick-firers, and two astern, with three of these guns and three 4·7-in. on each broadside; she has also 3-in. 12-pounder quick-firers instead of 6-pounders. Both ahead and broadside fire are only a trifle weaker than that of the French cruiser. As, however, the *Eclipse* is of 5600 tons—the same displacement as the far more heavily-armed and armoured *Aurora*, and more than that of many first-class cruisers of other nations—it cannot be said that she is over-gunned for her size. The work of her guns per minute comes to 162,209 ft.-tons; that of the *Chasseloup-Laubat*—nearly 1900 tons lighter—to 177,284, and that of the Elswick-built Argentine cruiser *Buenos-Aires*—1100 tons lighter —to no less than 292,340 tons. The speed of the *Eclipse* class, moreover, was estimated for at $18\frac{1}{2}$ and $19\frac{1}{2}$ knots with natural and forced draught respectively, which was progressing backwards. But as the *Eclipse* and *Talbot*—the first two tried—made over 19 and 20, the official forecast has been falsified for the better.* The protective deck is 3 to 1½ inches—half as thick again as that of the *Astræa*, and the radius of action substantially larger. The complement is 480, and the average cost will be under a quarter of a million. Yet when it is recalled that the *Buenos-Aires* aforesaid, besides her superior gun-power, is three knots faster, carries about as much coal, has a wider radius and a smaller crew, the *Eclipse*, excellent sea-boat as she turns out, seems hardly to come up to the full associations of her name.

Nor are the *Arrogant, Furious, Gladiator,* and *Vindictive*, now building, very much more likely to make good their names. Displacing 5750 tons, they mount one 6-in. gun less than the *Eclipse*. On the other hand, their deck-protection is better; in this nickel steel is used. The *Arrogant* is expected to do 19½ knots without forcing her furnaces, and on the analogy of the *Eclipse* we may hope to see her make 20. This will give her a full-power sea-speed that should make her a fairly useful scout for a squadron, and keep her out of harm's way if she is worsted by a better-armed enemy when cruising independently at sea—a contingency by no means unlikely.

Of the cruisers now ranked as third-class, the most efficient are the *Pearl* class, which in their day were accounted second-class. They carry eight 4·7-in. quick-firers—no extraordinary armament for their 2575 tons —two apiece on forecastle, poop, and either broadside.

---

* It ought to be added, however, that the *Eclipse* was tried at less than her normal draught. Since then the *Venus* has also exceeded 20 knots on trial.

The *Medea* class is larger, but carries only six slow-firing 6-in. breech-loaders. Both types nominally steam 19 knots with forced draught; they were intended to do more, and actually do less. Then there are the *Barham* and *Bellona* and the *Barracouta* class, each armed with six 4·7-in. quick-firers, which were built to act either as scouts to a squadron, or for use on distant stations. For both duties they are somewhat handicapped by their small size—1830 tons in the *Barham*, and 1580 in the *Barracouta*—which makes against high speed in bad weather. They also belong to the epoch when all things were expected of an immoderate forced draught; the *Barham* and *Bellona*, especially, never came near the expectations entertained of their speed, and broke down again and again through overheated tubes. Designed to steam 19 knots with 6000 horse-power under forced draught, they never got within a knot of it. Both ships, however, have since been in commission, and when their engineers came to know their ways were good for 18 knots at a spurt, and 15 to 16 for a long run. They are now to be fitted with water-tube boilers. Although our third-class cruisers are too small to do much in a sea—as has been found notably in the *Archer* class of 1170 tons—they are so much cheaper than the larger second-class vessels, that it has been thought well lately to lay down the *Pelorus* and seven sister ships of 2135 tons. These will doubtless be useful as scouts for a fleet in reasonably smooth waters—the Mediterranean, for instance—and should be a great deal more efficient for all services than any existing British ships of their class. The armament will be eight 4-in. quick-firers distributed as in the *Pearl*. This 4-in. gun is a new wire piece with a 25 lb. shot, a muzzle-energy of 1046 ft.-tons, and calculated to pierce 11 inches of wrought-iron at the muzzle. The top speed of the *Pelorus* is to be 20 knots, and her radius of action 7000 miles. It must be acknowledged that the *Pelorus*, like all our cruisers, compares unfavourably for gun-power and speed with the Elswick-built vessels of the same class—as for instance the Italian *Piemonte*, which carries six 6½-in. and six 4·7-in. quick-firers, and steams 21 knots. If the *Pelorus* is to fight, she is ill-equipped; if she is to be merely a scout, she is hardly fast enough: 20 knots an hour at this stage of engineering progress is becoming obsolete as the measure of high speed.

There is one very satisfactory feature, however, about the steaming of our cruisers, and, indeed, of all our ships of war, which must be borne in mind when their powers are criticised. The trial speed is obtained, as a rule, under favourable conditions of wind and sea, so that there is a general disinclination to take these performances as representative of the average working capacity of the ship. But, besides these, there are regular periodical trials during the period while a ship is in commission, and on these, when the engineers have come to know their machinery, and stokers are in good training and well up to their work, even better results are often obtained than when the ship is new. The splendid performances of the *Edgar* and *Royal Arthur* have been referred to already. The *Vulcan*, torpedo-depôt ship, with a trial speed for four hours' run of 17½ knots, last year steamed 850 miles in 48 hours— an average of 17¾ knots. The *Sirius* did 18·2 knots on her way home from a three years' commission in South America, with her bottom foul, and in much need of

NAVAL POLICY

docking. The *Camperdown* is actually said to have come into Malta, after her disastrous collision with the *Victoria*, and with several feet of her bow torn away, at 16½ knots. As long as our engine-room complements can put in splendid work like this, we can afford to see our ships a little behind on paper.

The torpedo flotilla of this country has now to be considered in its three branches of torpedo-gunboats— or catchers, as they used to be called—torpedo-boat destroyers, and torpedo-boats. Of the first there are four types—the *Rattlesnake* (four vessels), *Sharpshooter* (nine), *Alarm* (eleven), and *Dryad* (five). The tonnage rises from 525 tons in the *Rattlesnake* through 735 (*Sharpshooter*) and 810 (*Alarm*) to 1070 in the *Dryad*. Of the uses of these boats something has been said in the previous chapter. They are to sink or beat off hostile torpedo-boats, act as a support for boats of their own side, and, in case of need, torpedo any large vessel that may offer itself. For the first and second purpose they carry (all but three of them, whose armament is obsolete) one or two 4·7-in. guns, and some 6- or 3-pounders. For the latter purpose they are fitted with torpedo tubes. But, on the whole, these boats have not been successful. They are too slow to catch torpedo-boats in any weather in which torpedo-boats are likely to venture out of port. The *Speedy* (which has Thorneycroft water-tube boilers) has made 20 knots with forced draught, but none of the others go beyond 19¾, and the *Dryad* class can only make 18½. These results compare very poorly with foreign vessels of the same type, and, partly on this account, partly owing to the superior capacity of the cheaper destroyer, no torpedo-

THE BRITISH NAVY

gunboat has been laid down in England for the last three years.

The torpedo-boat destroyer, with its wonderful speed and handiness, and its almost limitless possibilities in war, is the latest, and perhaps the most striking, development of naval science. The *Havock* and *Hornet* were only launched by Messrs. Yarrow in 1893, but their steaming powers were so astonishing that we have already seventy of them, with a score more building. They are from 180 to 210 feet long, of 18 to 20 feet beam, and of 5 to 8 feet draught of water. They displace between 200 and 300 tons. The armament is, in most cases, one 12-pounder and five 6-pounders, mounted so as to command an all-round fire. In the earliest destroyers there was a bow torpedo-tube, but the speed made by these vessels is so great, that it was found that, at their fastest, they would stand to overrun the torpedo. Since then they have been fitted with only two broadside tubes. The slowest of these boats steams over 26 knots an hour; the fastest have made the wonderful speed of 31 knots, or nearly 40 miles an hour—a very respectable figure for a fast train. All but one or two have water-tube boilers, which enable them to get up full steam in a very few minutes. All can turn within their own length. At the 1895 manœuvres it was found that they make steady gun-platforms in ordinary weather, such as torpedo-boats would be abroad in.

All this being so, it is tolerably plain that no torpedo-boat could live long with the destroyer. Far faster, almost as quick in the turn, provided with powerful search-lights, and directing all round them a shower of shells, any one of which would serve to sink a torpedo-boat, these vessels should make torpedo attack impossible in their presence. For this reason they are pre-eminently the type of craft suited to the necessities and traditions of the British Navy. The torpedo-boat is, in the main, the weapon of the weaker and defensive power; the destroyer is the counter of the stronger and of the attack. The boat's small coal-capacity forbids it, as a rule, to operate before an enemy's ports; its most characteristic function is defensive — to prevent a blockade. A blockading squadron could not venture at night within a belt of from 50 to 100 miles from shore, for fear of the enemy's torpedo-boats. Thus distant, it would be obliged to extend its ships to cover the blockaded port, and it would be the easier for vessels to slip in and out — especially if accompanied by boats to fend off the enemy's attack. The blockade of a port provided with an effective flotilla of boats was, indeed, almost an impossibility until the advent of the destroyer. The destroyers with a blockading squadron would be set to dispose of any boats venturing out of port. While they patrolled the inshore waters, the heavier ships could venture nearer in than would otherwise be safe, and so maintain a more stringent blockade. Vessels running the blockade would have even more to fear from the swift, hardly-discernible destroyer, dealing blows with either gun or torpedo at will, than from the most heavily-armed battleship or cruiser.

In order to fulfil this function of neutralizing hostile boats, it is plain that the destroyers must be capable of keeping the sea for considerable periods together, and at considerable distances from any coaling and repairing base. Can they do this? As yet, perhaps, the question cannot be answered of so young a class of vessel without doing it some injustice. With a coal supply of 80 tons the *Desperate* could perhaps keep the sea with a blockading squadron for a week; also it would no doubt be possible to coal these vessels at sea. That they can ride out any but the severest storms is most probable. At any rate the *Ardent* has now served on the Mediterranean station for many months, and proved herself seaworthy; she has also run 680 miles at 19 knots without replenishing her bunkers. The worst obstacle to sea-keeping in destroyers is the danger of breakdowns in their machinery, which has to be as light as possible, and at the same time to withstand the severest strains.

It must be allowed that recent experience with this class of vessel is not calculated to give the highest estimate of their sea-keeping qualities. In the beginning of January, 1896, the Government, as everybody knows, decided to commission the Particular Service Squadron, included in which were six destroyers. At the same time six others were added to the Channel Squadron; while three apiece were commissioned at Portsmouth, Chatham, and Devonport, for the instruction of engine-room ratings. In three months these twenty-one vessels met with the following casualties. On January 16th, before the squadrons had assembled, the *Havock* ran into the *Royal Sovereign* and staved in her side, and the *Rocket* had to return to Devonport with boilers leaking. Towards the end of the month the *Sturgeon* was detained some days at Devonport to make good defects. Early in February the *Havock* and *Surly* were disabled through broken cylinders, and had to be replaced by the *Decoy* and

Sunfish. At the same time the *Daring* developed defects in a steam-pipe. On the 10th the *Starfish* collided with the *Skate* and leaked badly, while a week after, the unlucky *Daring* collided with a channel packet, and one of her engines broke down on the subsequent run to Portsmouth. On the 26th the *Dragon* cracked her low-pressure cylinder, and on March 8th the *Banshee* went into dock for strained ribs and plates, the result of a buffeting in the Irish Channel. The next day the *Skate* had to be relieved by the *Opossum*. In the meantime the *Rocket* had broken down five times, and her boilers took to priming at 14 knots speed, though on her trials she had made 27. As a result of this last, the Admiralty ordered that all destroyers should undergo a two-hours' trial, and should not be allowed to leave port unless they attained at least nine-tenths of their contract engine-power. On the 30th the *Surly* and *Havock* were tried after repairs, and could only make 22·2 and 22·3 knots respectively. In the meantime the *Handy* had sustained defects through the water running low in her boilers, and the *Opossum* had to go into dock to repair her fan-engine. On April 17th the *Handy* developed a defective steam-pipe. Next day the *Sturgeon*, just out of dockyard hands, began to leak through defective seams in her sides.

No doubt this record is not quite so bad as it looks. The men are unused to their ships, and with more experience many of the breakdowns would doubtless be avoided. At the same time the list of casualties establishes a presumption that the destroyers are fragile craft. If this fragility can be so far overcome that they can keep the sea with a fleet, there is hardly any limit to their usefulness. They could always be employed as scouts or despatch-boats, and there is no function of the torpedo-boat which they could not perform as well or better. In night attacks on fleets or ports they would present a larger mark, but, being faster, would be more difficult to hit. In a fleet action they would play an important, perhaps a decisive, part. If the enemy were accompanied by torpedo-boats, it would be for the destroyers to meet them, should they attempt a rush at the battleships before the action, and to defeat them before its close. During the fight they might shelter behind battleships, and take advantage of the enemy's pre-occupation with larger adversaries to shoot out and send home a mortal blow. But their great opportunity would come at the end of a battle, when the unprotected quick-firing guns of the enemy would be disabled. In this case the battleship would be almost helpless against their torpedoes; they could cover or retrieve a defeat, and turn a victory into a massacre. No ship could escape them, for they would have the pace even of the fastest cruiser, and only have to hang on until nightfall delivered the victim into their hands.

Of torpedo-boats we possess 43 more or less independent and sea-going, 50 ranked as first-class, and 72 as second-class, which would generally operate with a larger vessel in support. Besides their use as vedettes the torpedo-boats, as well as the destroyers, have a most important duty to perform in regard to coast-defence. No hostile ship can remain for a night without grave risk before a port garrisoned by boats or destroyers. And in case an enemy attempted a disembarkation on our coasts, the first night should expose his transports to a furious attack from every quarter. The skill and daring of our torpedo lieutenants and men form the chief defence of our shores. Relying upon them we shall do well to build no coast-defence armour-clads, but to put every shilling we can afford into the assailant, sea-going battle-fleet that is the first and best guarantee of the inviolability of our islands.

IV.

FOREIGN NAVIES

FRANCE

OF foreign navies, that of France is at once the nearest and the most important. To us, indeed, a just estimate of its strength and efficiency may truly be said to be hardly less important than of our own. It may not be necessarily with hostile intention to ourselves that France supports the double burden of an army on the largest scale of continental militarism, and a navy hardly less powerful and expensive than ours. A very plausible explanation is found in the fact that the French Navy, as it stands, is not more than equal to the strategical necessities of a war with the Triple Alliance. This theory can be supported by the circumstance that since the connexion with Russia began in 1893, and the allies found themselves in an overwhelming position of naval supremacy to the Central Powers, France (with the exception of one second-class armour-clad, not yet laid down) has projected no further addition to her battle-fleet. For a further explanation of this energy of warlike preparation by land and sea, with which no other nation, except perhaps Russia, appears willing to load itself, we may recall the facts that France has naval traditions almost as long as our own, and that, at least on paper, she has a colonial empire of considerable magnitude. But these facts are in truth only another call upon Englishmen to pay diligent heed to the naval armaments of their neighbour. The very fact that France is by her traditions a naval and a colonial Power is a potential menace to ourselves. Her colonies increase the risk of a collision between her and us; her navy forms to us the principal danger of such a collision. Neither danger is in any way mitigated by the fact that she is now allied, in some degree or other, with Russia—another Power which has both possibilities of quarrel with us and the force to make such quarrel a serious crisis for our empire. As against France we are also beset with the peril of over-confidence. In the Revolutionary and Napoleonic age we normally beat the French at sea with a good deal to spare. We have not forgotten that; but we have, until lately, forgotten how severely France was then handicapped in meeting us. Those battles were battles of professional seamen against amateurs. At the Revolution the whole French Navy went Royalist along with Brittany, from which province officers and seamen alike were mostly drawn; we were thus able to oppose experienced officers and trained gunners to the raw, if brave, nominees of doctrinaire politicians. We are not likely to start with this advantage again. French officers and bluejackets know their business to-day, none better. The fact that naval warfare has become scientific is perhaps a point rather in favour of the scientific acumen of Frenchmen. In any case we may be sure their ships will be skilfully devised and ably handled, and that science will be backed by the brilliant gallantry in which Frenchmen can never fail.

FOREIGN NAVIES

It behoves us then, it may be repeated, to analyze the resources of the French Navy no less carefully than our own.

To adopt the same order as was used with our own fleet, the latest French battleships, as has already been said, show a tendency to approximate to British models. These are the *Charlemagne, Gaulois,* and *St. Louis,* now building. But nine feet shorter than our *Majestics,* they are to displace only 11,275 tons, as against 14,900. The armour consists of a belt of hardened steel along the water-line, rising 4 feet 11 inches above, and descending 1 foot 8 inches below it. On the line itself it is $18\frac{3}{4}$ inches thick, but tapers down to 8 inches below it. Above this belt to a height of 3 feet the hull is sheathed with 3 inches of steel. There are two armoured decks—one of $3\frac{1}{2}$ inches at the upper, and one of $1\frac{1}{2}$ inches at the lower edge of the belt. So far as water-line protection goes the *Charlemagne* has thus little to complain of, although possibly the English curved deck offers a better, because an oblique, resistance to projectiles than the horizontal ones. Above the 3-in. deck, however, a larger area of side is left naked of armour than in the *Majestic.* The heavy armament is four 12-in. guns mounted in $15\frac{3}{4}$-in. steel revolving turrets; both turrets and guns can be worked either mechanically or, if the mechanism breaks down, by hand; this advantage is also found in the *Majestic.* These guns will probably be of a new pattern—now in course of construction—giving a greater velocity than our own 12-inch wire guns, but a somewhat smaller energy. The secondary armament is very numerous and powerful—ten $5\frac{1}{2}$-in. quick-firers, of which eight are protected by $2\frac{3}{4}$-in. shields of hardened steel, as well as eight 3·9-in., and twenty-six smaller quick-firers. The whole volume of fire per minute exceeds that of the *Majestic* by 25,000 ft.-tons. The forced draught speed is expected to be 18 knots—half a knot more than the *Majestic*. With this superiority of gun-fire and speed on nearly four thousand tons less displacement the French ship looks to be a much better investment than the *Majestic*. But these, though the most impressive, are not the only points of a warship. The *Majestic's* secondary battery is vastly better protected, so that a few minutes close fighting would probably put out of action more than enough of the *Charlemagne's* quick-firers to destroy her initial advantage in gun-power. As for speed, it is very possible that in any sea the *Majestic's* higher bow would change her disadvantage into a half-knot or so of superiority. Further, the *Majestic* carries more coal—1850 tons to about 1000—and ammunition than her rival, and is probably more stoutly built. The *Charlemagne* has the advantage of being worked and fought by 632 men, instead of 757 for the *Majestic*. But in cost—which after all is the real test of the value a country gets in it warships—the *Charlemagne* runs to nearly £1,100,000, while the average of the nine *Majestics* is over £200,000 less. We may be confident that we have better value for our £880,000 or so than France for her eleven hundred.

The *Bouvet* and *Masséna* are the next examples to be considered. They are not, strictly speaking, sister ships, since the *Bouvet* measures 331 feet in length and 70 in beam to the *Masséna's* 365 and 66, and displaces 12,205 metric tons to 11,924. The *Masséna's* belt of hardened steel-plating is 17¾ inches at its thickest, and the *Bouvet's* 2 inches less. The protective deck is

$3\frac{1}{2}$ inches. The heavy guns are mounted lozenge-wise, according to the usual French custom: a 12-in. gun ahead and astern, and a 10·6-in. on each beam, but firing either ahead or astern—in each case protected by 14 to 16-in. steel plates. The advantage of this arrangement in an end-on action, when these guns can be brought to bear either ahead or astern, has already been pointed out; over and above this it has the further advantage that no two heavy guns can be disabled by a single shot. On the other hand, it is not certain that in practice the beam guns could be fired dead along the ship's axis without damaging her structure, and, in a broadside action with the British type, ships thus armed would have to meet four heavy guns with three. Eight $5\frac{1}{2}$-in. quick-firers are carried by the *Bouvet* and the *Masséna;* and here again the mounting exhibits a difference from the English system. They are carried in pairs in four 4-in. turrets, one on each bow, and one on each quarter; the end-on fire is thus once more stronger than in most battleships, none of which, except the *Majestic* class, can bring as many as four heavy quick-firers to bear directly ahead or astern.

Very similar in armour and armament to these ships are the earlier *Carnot* (12,008 tons), *Jauréguiberry* (11,824), and *Charles Martel* (11,882). The belt is about the same thickness as in the *Masséna*; but above it is another belt of 4-in. plating—a feature which is not found in the later vessels. These three ships are armed and armoured exactly as the *Bouvet* and *Masséna*, so far as their main and secondary batteries go, except that in the *Carnot* each heavy quick-firer has a turret to itself. The two later ships, however, have eight 3·9-in. shielded guns on the superstructure; the three

NAVAL POLICY

earlier have only four 2½-in. guns in their place. All five are well supplied with smaller guns for repelling torpedo-boats. None of these ships are yet ready for commission, though the *Jauréguiberry* has been tried. The speed, however, will probably turn out much the same in each case—16½ to 17 knots with natural, 17½ to 18 with forced draught. The coal capacity is but 800 tons—giving about 5,000 knots at 10 per hour—in four of them, and in the *Masséna* but 630 tons, with 4000 knots radius. In spite of this weakness, which would hamper them but little as long as they operated near their own coasts, these are plainly very formidable ships. Their gravest defect is that their designers have not allowed enough for the larger quick-firer as a factor in future war, and have left great areas of side, above the belt, wholly unarmoured. All this part of the hull could be easily and speedily destroyed; and the result, even if the vitals were untouched, would be serious loss in men and horrible disorganization of the whole ship. The uptakes of the funnels would be riddled, and the speed impaired, while the whole ship would choke with poisonous fumes. Ammunition-hoists might be destroyed, and heaps of ammunition exploded. Worse still, the heavy 12-in. guns fore and aft might be disabled by shells penetrating the armoured side, and bursting underneath them. Possibly the whole turret might fall through the ship's bottom, and sink her; possibly the huge armoured military masts—top-heavy at the best of times—might go by the board, and capsize her.

The military masts have played an important part in the short life of the next ship, the *Brennus*. This system of military masts is the lineal descendant of

FOREIGN NAVIES

the practice of stationing riflemen in vessels' tops, which Nelson deprecated as causing useless waste of life, and from which he met his own death. As sails and rigging went out of use, the tops were enlarged, and on them were mounted machine guns and the smaller calibres of Hotchkiss guns. To protect these and to enable the masts to stand up against shell fire has been an aim in all modern battleships. The French in particular strengthened and thickened the mast till it became rather a turret of steel, with a spiral staircase inside it. This was, no doubt, a very fine position for quick-fire guns, which could thence make horrible havoc of an enemy's deck; but it involved the grave objection that its huge weight impaired, and, in extreme cases, destroyed the stability of the ship. It was so with the *Brennus*. When the battleship came to her trials it was found that the enormous weight was likely to be too much for her stability, and one of the armoured masts had to be removed. There were also other faults in regard to her stability, and she had some difficulty in making her estimated speed on trial. The result of these and other repairs and reconstructions was that it was no less than six years from her laying down before the *Brennus* was fit for sea. Compared with the two years which Portsmouth and Chatham required to turn out the *Majestic* and *Magnificent*, this gives some idea of the advantage conferred on Great Britain by our superior skill and resources in the matter of ship-building. On the other hand, we must remember that such comparisons, which are very often made, compare the French worst with our best; our *Renown*, to take another example, took nearly three years and a-half to prepare for sea, and the French *Charlemagne* will hardly take much longer. The *Brennus*, to go back, is of 11,395 tons. Her steel belt, 6 feet broad, tapers from 17¾ inches amidships to 10 and 12 at the ends; above this is a narrow belt of 4¾ inches; above this again a central redoubt extending over two-sevenths of the length, and protected by 4-in. plating. In this redoubt are six 6·3-in. quick-firers, while four more are mounted on the upper deck, each in a 4¾-in. turret. The heavy guns are of 16·4 inches (34 centimetres) calibre; these guns are longer, in proportion to their calibre,* than our own 13½-in. gun, and, therefore, considerably more powerful. The muzzle-energy is 42,139 to 35,230, though the projectile is smaller. The *Brennus* mounts two of her three big guns in a 17¾-in. turret forward, and one aft in a turret plated with 15¾ inches. Owing to the central redoubt this ship exposes less surface than some of her successors to quick-fire shell, but the side below both turrets is unprotected. Top speed on trial was 17·1 knots; and it is hardly doubtful that she will never attain it again. Her normal coal capacity is only 550 tons, which means a radius of about 3000 knots. The complement is 696.

The *Magenta, Marceau,* and *Neptune* are the nearest approach, among the French battleships, to a homogeneous class. Their displacement is about 10,900 tons, their legend speed 16 to 16½ knots with forced, and under 15 with natural draught. They carry 12 to 17¾-in. of compound armour on the belt, and 17¾-in., with 3-in. shields, on the barbettes. There are four

* The technical way of putting this is that the French gun is of 42 calibres, the English of 30: that is, in the one the length of the bore of the gun is 42 times its own diameter (*i.e.* 56 feet); in the other, 30 times (*i.e.* 41 feet 3 inches). This gives the powder more time to work on the projectile before it leaves the gun.

13½-in. (34 centimetre) guns, lozenge-wise, in separate barbettes—forward, aft, and on either beam. On each broadside are eight 5½-in. quick-firers—five ahead and three abaft of the midship barbettes. In consequence of the large number of quick-firers carried, the gun-power of these ships is very great, amounting to over 380,000 ft.-tons a minute, or half as much again as the *Carnot*, and very nearly as much as the *Majestic*. Very similar to these three is the *Hoche* (11,000 tons), but she is less heavily armed. Fore and aft are two 13½-in. guns, each in a 15¾-in. turret, while on each beam she carries a 10·6-in. gun in a barbette. There are only eight 5½-in. quick-firers. All four ships are deficient in armour protection for the hull, though an armoured trunk sustains the base of each barbette or turret. A very grave fault is the enormous superstructure, which disposes the ship to roll—thus impairing the gunner's aim—and is liable to be destroyed by quick-fire; even if the parts thus riddled be indifferent to the vitality of the ship their destruction cannot but demoralize the crew. To add to their top-heaviness these ships carry two singularly heavy and hideous military masts. The *Hoche* bears 630 men; the other three 660.

The *Amiral Baudin*, *Formidable*, and *Amiral Duperré* date from the early eighties, and are generally similar. They have a narrow belt of compound armour, no less than 21½ inches at its thickest, but the greater part of the hull is left naked to the smallest projectile. The first two carry three 14·5-in. 75-ton guns—short, as compared with more modern guns, and not over-powerful. The *Duperré* has four guns of the same calibre. These ships date from the days before the introduction of large quick-firers, and the *Duperré* has not yet been re-armed. She still retains her fourteen 5½-in. breech-loaders, seven on each broadside, and has no more than a couple of 3-pounder quick-firers to defend her against torpedo-boats. The other two, however, carry four 6·3-in., and eight 5½ quick-firers, as well as a fair provision of lighter guns. The *Formidable* is credited with 16½ knots an hour, the *Baudin* with 15·2, and the *Duperré* with 14·2. The first might steam 4000 miles without coaling, the other two 3000. They carry about 650 men.

Of battleships which may be ranked as first-class—though the French Navy knows no such official classification—there remain the *Courbet*, *Dévastation*, and *Redoubtable*, namesake of Nelson's prize at Trafalgar. They are heavily armed, although their guns are now a few years out of date, but indifferently protected. By an exception to the general French rule, the heavy iron belt is not quite complete, but stops short a distance from the stern. Amidships is an armoured casemate; in this are mounted four guns—12·6-in. pieces in the two first, and 10·6-in. in the last. On the upper deck all four carry four 10·6-in. guns in unarmoured barbettes—one forward, one aft, and one sponsoned on each beam. The *Redoubtable* has been re-armed with six 5½-in. quick-firers; the others retain their breech-loaders of the same calibre. These vessels steam about 14½ to 15 knots, and have a radius of 3000 knots at most. The *Redoubtable* takes 705 men, the others 680.

To compare the French battle-fleet, as a whole, with the British, is a difficult matter. Each excels the other in various abilities, but as one cannot be expressed in terms of the other, no balance can be struck between them. Broadly, the British battleships excel as ships, the French, in certain ways, as fighting-machines. In a smooth sea their generally superior gun-fire would give them an advantage, which would be doubled if they had such a superiority in speed as would enable them to take full advantage of the lozenge arrangement of their heavy guns. As a matter of fact they do not possess this superiority, but fall short, as a fleet, of the British first-class ships by about a couple of knots. Thus our system of mounting heavy guns fore and aft, in pairs, would give us an advantage if we could compel the enemy to fight broadside on. To France remains the advantage that the heavy guns are more widely distributed, and therefore less easily disabled; the British ships, on the other hand, have exactly the same advantage in the mounting of their secondary guns. Three of the French ships have not been re-armed with quick-firers, which we may set against the neglect of our own "Admirals." As for the alternative systems of armouring, it is fairly plain that the French complete belt is either a necessity or a huge waste of weight; but which, it wants the test of war to tell. The belt was probably superior in the days of the ram; the greater extent of side-armour will probably be superior as long as the reign of the quick-firer endures. Only in considering this we must remember that some of our own ships, as the "Admirals," are almost as bare in the hull as the most exposed of the Frenchmen. In both fleets the protection of the secondary guns leaves much to desire, except in the very latest models. Perhaps the question of armour will never be settled between the belt and the citadel until the dynamite gun arrives to do away with armour altogether. In a

NAVAL POLICY

high sea the superior steadiness of the British ships, and the consequent better shooting from them, would probably give them an easy victory over the French sea-castles, whose rolling would destroy the gunners' aim, but which would continue to present a fine mark for British artillery. In coal endurance the British fleet is largely superior. But we must discount this superiority by the fact that the French do not need great coal endurance. It was lately remarked, in the House of Commons, that, for want of coal, many French ships could not operate in the Eastern Mediterranean; but then they do not want to operate in the Eastern Mediterranean. If there were a British Fleet left no French squadron could go into the Eastern Mediterranean without having to fight going or returning, and it is as convenient to it to fight outside Toulon. If there were no British Fleet left, the French Fleet would be in the Channel assisting at the invasion of England. If, then, a French battleship carries coal enough to steam from Cherbourg to Toulon, and fight an action on the way, that is as much as she is likely to require.

Next come the coast-defence ships. There is nothing about the so-called defence ships, which all Powers except England build, that fits them peculiarly for coast defence, except, in some cases, a light draught, which enables them to operate in shallow waters. But for that, and the small size which light draught implies, one ship can defend a coast as well as another. All British ships are, in a very obvious sense, coast-defence ships. The only other characteristic of a coast defender is its small coal supply, and sometimes a low freeboard, which unfits her for rough water; both of which are rather defects than good qualities. Leaving out of account light draught, it is plain that a ship carrying 1000 tons of coal can, other things equal, defend a coast as well as, and better than, one with 200 tons. This is a sufficient answer to those who urge that England should build such vessels. We may have to make our ships larger, to meet any sea and carry their surplus of coal; but that is the price we pay for our insular security. The French coast defenders may, for the most part, be best described as rather small, old, and inefficient battleships. An exception must be made for the *Henri Quatre* (projected, but as yet not definitely designed) and the *Bouvines*, *Tréhouart*, *Jemappes*, and *Valmy*. Of these, the two first have been modified into small battleships by having their bows and forward turrets raised, so as to give a higher freeboard and a better field of fire. These ships are of 6610 tons; the *Jemappes* and *Valmy* of 6590. Though small, they are powerful, thoroughly modern ships. They are protected by a belt of 18 inches at thickest, tapering to 13, and by a steel deck of 4 inches extreme thickness. The two first-named ships carry a couple of 12-in. guns, each in a $12\frac{1}{2}$-in. turret, fore and aft, protected above by revolving cupolas of $14\frac{1}{2}$ inches of steel. The other two carry 13·3-in. guns, similarly mounted and protected. All four carry four 3·9-in. quick-firers on each broadside, behind $1\frac{1}{2}$-in. shields. They have one military mast. The natural draught speed is $14\frac{1}{2}$ knots, while, with forced draught, the *Tréhouart* has steamed $17\frac{1}{2}$, and the others 17 knots. As these ships draw less than 22 feet, they might be very useful, say, on the coast of Schleswig-Holstein, or in the Baltic; but their value is much impaired by the fact that they only carry 300 tons of coal. You cannot put a quart of power into a pint of displacement. These four ships, together with the *Hoche*, form the French Channel Squadron.

Particulars of the other ten coast-defence ships, so as to avoid the weariness of unending figures, are summed up on a later page. It may be said of them generally that they are of moderate dimensions—none reach 8000 tons—efficiently armoured up to the standard of their day, and carry each a pair of heavy, though somewhat obsolescent, guns, with only a few light quick-firers. This last defect would be their heaviest handicap in modern war; but, even so, they would be more than a match for such of our own second-class ships as have not even breech-loaders. The four sisters *Caiman*, *Indomptable*, *Requin*, and *Terrible*, are to be refitted, and smaller, but more powerful, pieces substituted for their huge 75-ton guns. The *Tempête* and *Vengeur*, on the other hand, will probably be struck off the effective list in a year or two. None of these ships steams more than 15 knots even in theory, or carries, normally, more than 400 tons of coal. But the *Caiman* and her sisters can fill up with 800 on emergency; and even 400 tons, or 200, is enough to cross the Channel and fight on.

The battleships also include the *Friedland*, of 8990 tons, and the *Richelieu*, *Colbert*, *Trident*, and *Suffren*. The first is lightly armoured, but heavily armed, and is quite fit to take her place in the second line; the others have wooden hulls, and must shortly be condemned. The same may be said of six ships—one of which is the *Bayard*, the French flagship in China—classed as armoured cruisers, like our own *Agincourt* and her fellows. The French appear much readier to strike their old ships off the lists as obsolete than our own Admiralty, which makes use of them as guard-ships abroad, drill-ships, recruiting-ships, and the like. Economy is a virtue, doubtless; but it might turn out even more provident, when a ship is past her work, to say so at once, than to connive at any misconceptions as to our real fighting strength.

Among French cruisers the most notable group consists of the armoured vessels, and the most notable of these is certainly the *Dupuy-de-Lôme*. The whole hull is sheathed with 4-inch mail up to the main deck, and the two heaviest guns — 7·4-in. breech-loaders — are carried in 4-in. sponsoned turrets amidships on each beam. Besides these there are six 6·3-in. quick-firers, one on the forecastle, one on the poop, and one on each bow and quarter. Thus in theory the *Dupuy-de-Lôme* can fire five of her eight guns ahead, astern, or on either beam; whether the heavy guns amidships could actually be fired dead ahead or astern without damage to the ship is somewhat doubtful. The tonnage is 6300; the speed $17\frac{1}{2}$ knots with natural, and (in theory) 20 with forced, draught; the coal-endurance 4000 miles at $12\frac{1}{2}$ knots, and the crew 521. Even if all the advantages claimed for this ship are not realizable in practice she still remains a very formidable unit—especially formidable because her armour enables her to defy shell and all but direct hits from shot. Indeed she is so much admired by Rear-Admiral Fournier, a distinguished French sailor at present in command of a group of cruisers intended as a tactical school for officers, that he proposes to replace the whole existing French fleet, battleships, coast-defenders, cruisers and all, by

117 vessels of this type.* Thickening the armour to 6 inches, and increasing the displacement to 8300 tons, Admiral Fournier expects to produce a ship which will be self-sufficing for all the various duties of war at present undertaken by ships so different as, for instance, a first-class battleship and a third-class cruiser. He demonstrates with great ingenuity that a homogeneous squadron of this type could fight a squadron of present-day battleships by using its superior speed so to manœuvre that it would receive all projectiles obliquely, and therefore, without having its armour penetrated. Without entering into details it may be said that, granting all the advantages of a completely homogeneous fleet,† Admiral Fournier's scheme may be objected to on a double ground. An 8300-ton armoured ship is too expensive, on the one hand, to be economically used for work which can be done as well or better by, say, a 5000-ton unarmoured ship. On the other hand, it is certain that a vessel so lightly armed and armoured could not meet a modern battleship in close action, and it is doubtful whether in fighting battleships but little inferior in speed and far superior in gun-power and armour Admiral Fournier's squadron could in all cases avoid coming to close quarters; it could in no case win a decisive victory in a very long range action. The French Admiralty has, however, given a kind of very tentative encouragement to the theory by laying down the *Jeanne d'Arc*. This ship is very fast, being designed to make 23 knots, and is to be powerfully armed with two $7\frac{1}{2}$-in., eight $5\frac{1}{2}$-in.,

* "La Flotte Nécessaire." Paris: Berger, Levrault et Cie. For a detailed criticism of the scheme, see "A Naval Utopia," *Blackwood's Magazine*, June, 1896.
† See page 59.

FOREIGN NAVIES

and twelve 3·9-in. guns, all quick-firing. So far she is well fitted to put Admiral Fournier's theories into practice, since no battleship could get near her, and would be bound to suffer heavily from the hail of her fire. She carries 1500 tons of coal. But she is to be of 11,270 tons, nearly twice the size of the *Dupuy-de-Lôme*, and is to cost more than double the earlier ship, £416,000. And even with this great increase of size and cost the *Jeanne d'Arc's* 6-in. belt will rise no higher than 2 feet 3 inches from the water-line, leaving nearly the whole hull vulnerable to the smallest shell. So that plainly this vessel, though a most formidable ship, and perhaps a match for the *Terrible*, will be no match for a well-protected battleship, whether at long range or short. Of somewhat similar type to the *Dupuy-de-Lôme*, again, are the four smaller cruisers of the *Bruix* class. Their armour, which is a shade thinner, covers the whole hull, and they are armed nearly in the same way, but they are at least half a knot slower, and carry less than half the coal. The *Pothuau* (5320 tons) is somewhat similar to the *Bruix*; her armour is thinner, and does not rise so high above water; her gun-power is rather greater. All these, thanks to their armour, would be very formidable customers for even our first-class cruisers to tackle, but they hardly seem destined to supersede the battleship.

The *Guichen* and *Châteaurenault*, to be completed in 1898, are corsairs or commerce destroyers, built on the model of the United States *Columbia* and *Minneapolis*. Their business is not to fight, but to destroy merchantmen. For the latter duty they are equipped with eight large and seventeen small quick-firers; to avoid the former they are given an extreme speed of 23 knots.

NAVAL POLICY

On paper we have nothing, except perhaps the *Terrible* and the *Powerful*, fast enough to overtake these ships; on the other hand, if caught going into port to coal, even a second-class cruiser of the *Eclipse* class (with a gun-power of about 160,000 ft.-tons per minute, as against about 180,000) ought to fight either of them on tolerable terms. Furthermore, if we go by the analogy of the *Columbia*, which fell four knots short of her trial-speed in crossing the Atlantic, these ships will be unable to overtake an ocean liner, which must detract seriously from their value. And if on the ocean they can make no more relatively than the *Columbia*, they might very conceivably be overhauled and demolished by such fine steamers, however inferior in measured-mile speed, as the *Edgar*.

The remaining unarmoured cruisers, as has been already mentioned, are generally a trifle slower, of smaller coal-capacity, and perhaps less seaworthy than our own cruisers of similar size, but as a rule far more heavily armed. The *D'Entrecasteaux*, to be completed next year, is the most powerful, being the French analogue to our *Edgar* class. Of rather greater displacement, she is a knot inferior, and carries less coal, but has a rather heavier armament. The *Tage*, of exactly the same size as the *Edgar*, is inferior only because her eight 6·3-in. and ten 5½-in. pieces date from before the large quick-firer. Were she re-armed she would have a great advantage over the Englishman in offensive power, but she carries less coal than the *Edgar's* extreme capacity, and is a good knot slower. The *Cécille*, of only 5766 tons, has the same armament as the *Tage*, except that it is all [quick-firing. She possesses the same speed, and but 40 tons less coal. No doubt the *Edgar* could get away from this ship, but it would be her business to fight her, and in a fight she would be at a very great disadvantage. Of second-class cruisers the *Catinat* and *Protet*, of 4113 tons, are more strongly armed than our *Eclipse*, of 5600, and *Arrogant*, of 5780; so are the *Alger, Jean Bart, Isly*, and *Sfax*, and the slightly smaller ships which bear the philosophic names of *Descartes* and *Pascal*. It is almost comforting to come on the six vessels of the *Cassard* and *Bugeaud* types, whose offensive power is only slightly greater than that of our best second-class cruisers. It must, of course, be borne in mind that this deficiency of our ships only applies to one function of a cruiser—that of independent patrol of the high seas, attacking or defending commerce. For the, if possible, more important duty of scouting for a fleet, our own ships, being generally a knot the faster, are superior. But it is certain that in war France would, very properly, deliver a most furious attack on our merchantmen at sea, and in this case the military weakness of our second-class cruisers would compel us to use large and expensive ships like the *Edgar* in their defence.

There are nine modern third-class cruisers of 1848 to 2300 tons armed with quick-firing guns, and more than twice that number of older, slower vessels with breech-loading guns. These are intended to act with squadrons as scouts, but, although they would doubtless be found generally efficient in the still waters of the Mediterranean, they are probably too small to do their work in all weathers.

The torpedo flotilla of France has always been numerous, and very efficient. There are five torpedo-cruisers over 1200 tons, and a dozen or so torpedo-gunboats, of which the *Casabianca*, *Cassini*, and *d'Iberville* are faster than any of ours. Others, still faster, are under construction. Forty-six boats are classed as sea-going; all are 138 ft. long or over, and steam from 20 knots upwards; one of them, the *Forban*, made 31·2 knots on her trial, and thus won the title of the fastest vessel in the world. These boats accompany squadrons to sea, but often have to run into port if bad weather comes on, while the delicacy of their machinery lends itself to frequent breakdowns. However, in many circumstances they might play a very important part in a fleet action, although, now that we have numerous faster destroyers of our own, we can view the contingency with an approach to equanimity. Sixty-three first-class boats—somewhat inferior in size, coal-capacity, and seaworthiness, but mostly available for raids on hostile ships or ports in favourable conditions; eighty-four second-class and thirty-six third-class for harbour defence, and fourteen vedette boats complete this formidable flotilla. To these should be added three submarine boats propelled by electricity. Their value is yet untried, though they can certainly descend considerable depths under water; the difficulty is to steer and to see the object of attack.

RUSSIA.

Whatever is to be said of the French fleet, that of Russia can only be viewed in one light. The Russian Navy is in no sense a defensive force. It is offensive, and can only be intended as an instrument of aggression upon its neighbours. The British Navy is plainly a

FOREIGN NAVIES

defensive force: it may be used for aggression, but it is plain that it must, in any case, be maintained for the defence of the country. The same may be said of the Russian and other continental armies. But the Russian Navy is essentially offensive. Russia has ample land forces to protect herself against any possible enemy; the Baltic fleet she might use, it is true, to defend herself against Germany, by making a diversion in Denmark or Pomerania, but no such explanation is possible of the powerful Black Sea squadron. It might have been lately urged that Russia needs a fleet to maintain her communications with Eastern Siberia. But if there were any sincerity in this argument, the Siberian Railway, now approaching completion, would have been attended with a diminution of naval armaments, whereas, in fact, it has been the signal for their rapid augmentation. With a small coast-line to her vast empire, and even that land-locked like the Black Sea, both land-locked and shallow like the Baltic, or invulnerable by reason of climate like the Siberian coasts, Russia is the one great European Power which could have dispensed with the costly luxury of a navy. When she builds a fleet, and strains every nerve to increase it, the conclusion is that this fleet is not intended for the superfluous defence of her own sea-board, but for the appropriation of the sea-board of her neighbours. Having no open port, she has built a fleet, and now she wants a port for her ships; if she gets it, she will next want more ships for her port, and then more ports for her more ships, and so on in an infinite series. Few people in this country appear to have noticed the recent rapid growth of the Russian Navy, or to have realized what it portends. Before this

NAVAL POLICY

year's programme was begun, Russia was building exactly the same number of battleships as ourselves, and at that rate of progress her armour-clad fleet would double itself in four or five years. A further sign of naval activity is the very remarkable progress made by Russian shipbuilders, gunmakers, and engineers. When the Russian ironclad fleet first began to come into being, from twenty to thirty years ago, Russian workmanship was helplessly incompetent to build a warship without aid from abroad. Many strange stories filtered through official discretion about warships which took the bit between their teeth and ran away. Nowadays the yards of Petersburg and Sevastopol turn out fine battleships with the aid of native heads and hands alone. In the designing and building of engines, it is true, Russian workmanship is not quite out of leading-strings; it is customary to buy a set of engines in England for one ship of a group, and copy them exactly in the rest. Armour-plates, again, are largely bought in America. In other branches of naval industry Russia is well abreast of the foremost of her rivals. Some of her experiments with capped shot and armour-plates are for the moment classical. Her guns founded on Krupp's models, as her engines are founded on Maudslay's, do not make so brave a show, in the accounts of them allowed to be published, as our own or the French. But the experiments referred to make it certain that she has pieces as powerful as any in the world. It is possible that on certain counts Russia has still some ground to make up before she equals the skill of Western Europe. But the progress already made, and being made, may be taken as an assurance that she will not long lag behind the most advanced.

FOREIGN NAVIES

Russia has at this moment four first-class battleships completing for sea—the *Tri Sviatitelia* (Three Saints) on the Black Sea, and the sisters *Petropavlovsk*, *Poltava*, and *Sevastopol* at Petersburg. The first, which is perhaps the most powerful of Russian battleships, does not differ essentially from the latest British types. She is of 12,540 tons, and 370 feet between perpendiculars. Of this only 350 feet is armoured on the water-line, leaving the ends bare as in all our later battleships; this is a noteworthy departure, since Russia had till lately followed the French system, and belted her armour-clads from end to end. The water-line armour of the *Tri Sviatitelia* is 16 to 18 inches of nickel-steel, so that it gains in resisting power what it loses in extent. This side-armour is just short of eight feet broad, more than half of which is under water at normal draught, and below it is a 3-in. nickel-steel deck. Above the water-line armour is a large surface of unplated side; above that again is a central battery, or inner citadel, protected by five inches of armour. The main armament, carried in two 16-in. nickel-steel turrets, is four 12-in. guns of Russian make. The Russian Government prudently conceals the power of these weapons. According to published statistics, all the Russian guns are far inferior in energy to those of other Powers, but the fact that in experiments with armour-plates higher velocities have been given from Russian guns than from any others on record, makes it practically certain that they are fully equal to the latest British models. The secondary armament of the *Tri Sviatitelia* consists of eight 6-in. Canet* quick-firers, mounted four on each broadside in

* French.

NAVAL POLICY

a battery between the turrets, as in the British *Nile*, and of four 4·7-in. pieces by the same maker on the superstructure; these bear directly ahead and astern. There is a full armament of 3- and 1-pounders. The *Tri Sviatitelia* is to attain 16 knots with forced draught, and steam 4000 miles without coaling. She carries 582 men. Although the speed is rather short of the standard to which our own and French battleships now conform, she is an undeniably powerful ship.

The other three ships completing, which should all be ready for trial this year or next, are somewhat smaller, being 10,950 tons, and 367 feet long; of this about 280 feet are protected by $15\frac{3}{4}$-in. armour, and there is a 3-in. steel deck. There are four 12-in. guns mounted fore and aft in 10-in. turrets of Harvey steel. The auxiliary armament, as originally designed, was eight 8-in. guns in four 5-in. turrets, two on each beam; but this is to be replaced by twelve 6-in. quick-firers, which will give the ships a vastly increased volume of fire, nearly equal to that of the *Majestic*. The speed is to be a knot and a-half greater than that of the *Tri Sviatitelia*, the coal endurance slightly less at the normal stowage. The engines of these three ships have been copied in Russia from those built by Messrs. Maudslay for the *Georgi Pobiedonosck*.

The last-named vessel (10,280 tons) is remarkable in that she carries six heavy guns instead of the usual four. There are two barbettes abreast forward, and one aft; each contains a brace of 12-in. guns. This arrangement, of course, gives a tremendous bow-fire; indeed, the shock of the discharge is probably much too great to allow all four forward guns to be fired simultaneously. There is also the danger that one or

FOREIGN NAVIES

two lucky blows might disable the four together. The *Georgi Pobiedonosek* has a complete steel belt of 8 to $18\frac{3}{4}$ inches, and 12-in. bulkheads and barbettes, with 10-in. plating on the triangular redoubt containing the barbettes. The secondary armament consists of seven 6-in. quick-firers—two on each bow and one on each quarter in recessed ports, which give an axial fire, and one astern. These guns have no armour protection. This ship went through trials in the spring with the greatest success, developing 2000 horse-power over the contract 10,600. Three older ironclads share the peculiarity of carrying six very heavy guns. These are the *Ekaterina II.*, the *Sinope*, and the *Tchesme*. Like the *Georgi Pobiedonosek*, which is practically a modernized copy of them, they belong to the Black Sea fleet. They are heavily plated with compound armour. The heavy guns are of 12-in. calibre, but shorter and less powerful than the later weapons. The secondary armament is as in the *Georgi Pobiedonosek*, but the 6-in. guns are not quick-firing.

More recent and better equipped than these, but ranked as second class by reason of their size, are the *Sissoi Veliky*, with two sisters (one for the Black Sea fleet), and the *Dvenadzat Apostoloff* (Twelve Apostles). The *Sissoi Veliky* is of 8,880 tons, and 340 feet long; of this 241 feet are protected by $11\frac{3}{4}$ to $15\frac{3}{4}$ inches of compound armour. The four heavy guns (12-in.) are carried in turrets—the forward one protected by $11\frac{3}{4}$ inches of armour, the after by two inches less. From the upper edge of the belt rises a 5-in. plating of steel, which sheathes the whole side for a length of 195 feet; behind this protection is a broadside battery of six 6-in. quick-firers. This ship is thus,

NAVAL POLICY

granting the unarmoured ends, among the best protected from quick-fire shell in Europe. The *Rostislav*, the second of this triplet, has 10-in. guns in her turrets, and eight quick-firers. The speed is 16 knots, and the utmost radius only 2000 knots, which greatly impairs the efficiency of otherwise admirable ships; here, once more, we are met with the impossibility of combining all elements of force on a small displacement. The *Rostislav*, however, also burns petroleum, which might take her further. The *Dvenadzat Apostoloff* is 800 tons smaller than this group; she also is partially belted, and has 5 inches of steel on her central battery. Her four 12-in. guns are carried in barbettes; her secondary battery is very weak, consisting only of four 6-in. slow-firers. Her radius of action is much the same as that of the *Sissoi Veliky*, but she is a knot and a-half faster. The *Navarin*, of 9476 tons, is very similarly armoured and armed, except that she has eight 6-in. breech-loaders. The *Gangoot* (6627 tons) carries one 12-in. gun in a turret forward, and four 9-in. in a central redoubt. Russia has been very sluggish in adopting the larger quick-firers, and would probably suffer heavily for it in war.

The *Oslabya* and *Peresviet* were laid down at Petersburg in November, 1895. It is said that the Russian Admiralty, greatly daring, intends to emulate Portsmouth and Chatham by getting them ready for sea in two years; but it will be very surprising if they are tried before the ice melts in the spring of 1898. Displacing 12,640 tons, they will be the largest battleships in the fleet—if, indeed, they should be called battleships at all. They are to have a belt on the water-line of not more than 5 to 7 inches, and will carry four 10-in. guns in turrets, and eight 6-in. quick-firers in casemates. This shows even less for the displacement than our own *Renown*, and rather suggests a powerful cruiser, but the speed—17½ knots an hour—is not the speed of a cruiser. The coal supply is high—1750 tons. If these particulars are correct, which is not at all certain, one rather wonders what has been done with the huge tonnage at the designer's command.

Of the Russian coast-defence ironclads, only three come up to modern requirements. The type of these is the *Admiral Oushakoff*, which completed her trials in 1895. She is of 4126 tons, well protected, and armed with four 9-in. guns in barbettes, with the same number of 6-in. quick-firers, and numerous smaller pieces. She steamed 15 knots with natural draught, and can run 2500 miles without coaling, so that she is at least as well entitled to be called sea-going as the *Sissoi Veliky*. The rest of the coast-defenders, excluding four new armoured gunboats of the *Gremiastchy* type, are from twenty to thirty years old, and of little value.

Among cruisers, the first place is claimed by the *Rossia* and *Rurik*. The latter was the beginning of the huge cruisers now coming into vogue. The early reports of her size and power made a great sensation, and impelled our Admiralty to lay down the *Powerful* and the *Terrible*. The *Rurik* is of 10,940 tons; she steams nearly 20,000 miles without coaling; she carries 5 to 10-in. armour, 7 ft. wide, over about four-fifths of her length, besides a 2¾-in. steel deck; she is armed with four 8-in. guns in sponsons, one on each bow and quarter, with sixteen 6-in. Canet quick-firers on the main deck, six 4·7-in. quick-firers on the upper deck, and Hotchkisses to boot. With an energy of fire estimated at some 470,000 ft.-tons per minute—over 50,000 tons more than that of the most powerful battleship afloat—it is not surprising that the *Rurik* awakened great apprehension in English minds; that she was conceived of as a roaring sea-lion, going up and down the world devouring British traders, and slaughtering out of hand any British cruiser that might have the temerity to withstand her. But slowly the truth came out, that the awful *Rurik*, though decidedly a most powerful ship, is not at all the invincible monster she was pictured. To begin with, she only made $18\frac{3}{4}$ knots on trial, and that though she weighed a thousand tons lighter than when she is equipped for sea. So that no liner need fear her, and most modern cruisers can get out of her way if they have had enough of her. Then she appeared at Kiel, and was found to be heavily barque-rigged—a great encumbrance in action. Moreover, none of her guns are protected, except by shields; and twelve 6-in. guns are mounted in an open battery, where two or three high explosive shells might put the whole lot out of action. In short, as Mr. Brassey shrewdly remarks, if we had seen the *Rurik* a little sooner, we might not have built the *Powerful* and *Terrible*. The *Rossia*, which is about 1300 tons heavier, carries similar armour and the same armament, though it is possible that she will substitute quick-firers for the four 8-in. guns. She is expected to steam 20 knots an hour, and have the same endurance as her prototype. It is possible that the guns may be better protected. She requires a crew of 735 men; the *Rurik* 727.

The other vessels of the Russian Navy demand little notice. The *Pamyat Azova, Admiral Nachimoff, Dmitri*

Donskoi, and *Vladimir Monomach*, are almost entirely belted cruisers, of between 5700 and 7800 tons; their principal guns are well protected with armour. Only the *Dmitri Donskoi* has been re-armed with quick-firers (four 6-in. and ten 4·7-in.); the others are heavily, but in these days ineffectively, equipped with 8-in. and 6-in. breech-loaders. The *Pamyat Azova* and *Nachimoff* steam 18·8 and 17·5 knots an hour respectively, and have a radius of 10,000 and 8000 miles. The other two are slower and of less endurance. All but the *Vladimir Monomach* are at present on the China Station. Four elderly armour-clads are also classed as cruisers. Among deck-protected cruisers the *Svietlana*, building at Havre, is the only one that carries quick-firers. Of these she has eight 6-in. and ten 3-pounders on a displacement of 3828 tons; she is to steam 20 knots, and carries 400 tons of coal, so that she should be more than a match for our *Apollos*.

The torpedo squadrons of Russia are very strong, and are said to be well exercised. There are eight fast torpedo gunboats, with fifty-five sea-going and one hundred and sixteen smaller boats. Russia has also taken up the torpedo-boat-destroyer energetically. Mr. Yarrow built her the *Sokol*, which steamed over 30 knots an hour, and made the record of the day; now thirty copies of her are to be made in Russia. With this formidable muster of torpedo-craft, Russian waters, especially the shallows round the islands and inlets of the Baltic, would be almost unapproachable to a hostile fleet.

NAVAL POLICY

GERMANY.

The German Navy is the best-kept in Europe. In the higher qualities of seamanship our own is doubtless superior, for the German is not by nature a seaman. He is not even, by nature, a fighting man, knowing little of the ferocious joy which animates the inhabitants of these islands, or of France, in the stress of battle. But the German is a quite unequalled fighting machine, and in the days of science this artificial substitute becomes more and more equal, and sometimes superior, to the original as turned out by Nature. Germany not only expects every man to do his duty, but she drills him until he forgets how to do anything else. Having no navy to speak of, and no naval traditions at all, the creators of the German Empire imported generals into the marine service, and organized it with the same minute thoroughness wherewith they organized the German Army. We may smile at the fact that a German naval officer can seldom find himself in port without succumbing to the inbred instinct, and asking leave to drill his men ashore. But it is just the fact that the navy mirrors the army that is its title to respect. Every detail of the service is planned out at headquarters, and carefully executed; everything is remembered, everything is cut and dried, everything is ready. Every man knows what to do in every emergency, and nothing but sudden death will keep the well-trained German from doing it. The German Navy is the only one in Europe that at this moment, and at every moment, is perfectly ready for war wherever and whenever it may come. The situation, when the crisis occurred in January last between Germany and ourselves about South Africa, was thoroughly characteristic on both sides. We had half-a-dozen good ships between Cape Town and Zanzibar. But at Delagoa Bay, the pivot of affairs at the moment, Germany had the *See Adler*, while we had the *Thrush;* and the *See Adler* could have burned or sunk, or at least hopelessly disabled, the *Thrush* in a matter of minutes.

It may surprise the swaggerers who proclaimed, some months ago, that the two battleships and four cruisers of the Particular Service Squadron were superior to the whole German Navy, to hear that the German battle-fleet, exclusive of cruisers and torpedo-craft, consists of twenty-two armour-clads. Of these, four are first-class— the *Brandenburg, Kurfürst-Friedrich-Wilhelm, Weissenburg,* and *Wörth*. Of 10,100 tons, these ships are considerably smaller than the largest vessels of other navies. The water-line is completely plated with $11\frac{3}{4}$ to $15\frac{3}{4}$ inches of armour—compound in the first two, hard steel in the others. They carry three barbettes along the line of the keel, as in the French *Formidable*, but each one, unlike hers, contains a couple of Krupp guns of 11 inches; those in the central barbettes are for want of space shorter and less powerful than the others. The barbettes and ammunition-hoists have $11\frac{3}{4}$-in. armour, and there is also a $2\frac{1}{2}$-in. protective deck over the engines. In a 3-in. casemate forward of the central barbette are four 4·1-in. quick-firers; there are also eight 3·4-in. quick-firers. The additional gun-power gained by the third barbette is thus to a certain extent thrown away by the weakness of the quick-firing armament. Another fault in these ships is that the hull is wholly unarmoured from the belt upward, except

NAVAL POLICY

on the barbettes and casemates, so that they would suffer very heavily from high explosive shells. All these ships could make 16·5 knots; the *Weissenburg* and *Wörth* over 17. They carry 750 tons of coal.

Completing for sea is the *Kaiser Friedrich III.*, while another new battleship is on the stocks. The *Kaiser Friedrich III.* is of 11,000 tons; and all her armour is Harveyed steel; it is not so thick as in the *Brandenburg*, the belt (which stops short some 75 feet from the stern) being 6 to 12 inches. It is interesting to see that Germany, as well as Russia, is tending to discard the complete water-line belt which a year or two ago was thought indispensable to a battleship in both countries.

The weight thus saved in the *Kaiser Friedrich III.* goes to protect the guns against quick-fire shell. The principal armament—so says the *Berliner Post*—is to be four $9\frac{1}{2}$-in. guns mounted in pairs in 10-in. barbettes, but these seem very light pieces for a ship of 11,000 tons, and it will perhaps turn out that the armament is heavier. In respect of quick-firing guns, this vessel will be the best-equipped battleship in the world. She is to carry no less than eighteen 6-in. and twelve $3\frac{1}{2}$-in. pieces; of the former six will be carried in 6-in. casemates, and twelve in 6-in. turrets. In energy of fire per minute this ship exceeds the *Charlemagne* by 50,000, and our own *Majestic* by 70,000 ft.-tons: the Kaiser, therefore, was not wrong when, in the characteristic dithyramb he delivered at her launch, he pronounced her superior to all rivals. She is, moreover, to steam 18 knots an hour, so that it will need a very powerful type indeed to cope with her. She is to carry 750 tons of coal and 590 men, to cost a little over £700,000, and to be ready for sea about the end of 1897.

The *Baden*, *Bayern*, *Sachsen*, and *Württemberg* are second-class battleships of 7400 tons. They carry a partial belt of armour, 16 inches at its thickest, which forms a central redoubt, 12 feet high; in this are four 10·2-in. guns, while in a 16-in. barbette are two more of the same calibre. There are eight $3\frac{1}{2}$-in. quick-firers. These ships only steam about 14 knots, which, as they are all nearly twenty years old, is as much as could be expected. They are all, however, either fitting, or to be fitted, with new boilers and engines, as well as two military masts and more quick-firing guns. It is, indeed, very characteristic of the thoroughness with which the German Navy is administered that the very oldest ships are kept religiously up to all the latest requirements, so far as their build allows it. For instance, the *Deutschland*, which dates from 1874, has received a full quick-firing armament and military masts; since the danger of fire was emphasized at Yalu all the wood in her has been replaced with aluminium. The *König Wilhelm*, which has had 6-in. quick-firers substituted for the eighteen $9\frac{1}{2}$-in. guns on her broadside, is nearly thirty years old. These two ships, with the *Kaiser*, *Friedrich der Grosse*, and *Preussen*, all third-class ships, and the *Oldenburg*, a smaller and less powerful copy of the *Baden* class, complete the list of the larger German battleships.

There is, however, a very interesting group of eight ships, which were originally intended to defend the mouths of the Baltic Canal, but which, being found excellently seaworthy, are now ranked as fourth-class battleships. They might, indeed, be called third-class, since, although only of 3500 tons or so, they are probably quite capable of meeting most of the older ironclads. This class, of which the *Siegfried* is the earliest, presents various modifications according as naval ship-building advanced during its construction. The earlier vessels are completely belted with 7 to $9\frac{1}{2}$ inches of compound armour: the *Odin* and *Aegir*, the latest, have partial belts, but nickel-steel armour. All carry two $9\frac{1}{2}$-in. Krupp guns forward, and one aft, behind $7\frac{3}{4}$ inches of armour. The *Siegfried* has six 3·4-in. quick-firers in sponsons, her successors eight, and the *Odin* and *Aegir* ten. The speed varies from 15 knots in the *Siegfried* to 16 in the *Odin* and *Aegir*, which have water-tube boilers. In the history of this group we see again the anxiety of the German Admiralty to secure, without delay, every advantage which the advance of science can confer on the fighting efficiency of the fleet.

The cruisers of Germany are few, but several of them are very powerful. The vessel now building to replace the obsolete *Leipzig* would, perhaps, be better classed as a battleship, since she could certainly lie in line as well as such a ship as the *Centurion*. Her belt is complete, and of 8 inches of Harvey steel; the *Centurion's* is partial, and at its thickest 12 inches of compound. Her main armament looks somewhat inferior, being four $9\frac{1}{2}$-in. guns in 8-in. barbettes: the *Centurion's* is four 10-in. guns in 10-in. barbettes. But probably, both in guns and armour, the newer ship is the equal of the older. The new *Leipzig's* quick-firers are twelve 6-in. behind steel shields, and ten $3\frac{1}{2}$-in. to the *Centurion's* ten 4·7-in. guns, of which only four are in 2-in. casemates. The German vessel will also be

FOREIGN NAVIES

half a knot the faster. She may, therefore, reasonably be borne in mind in estimating the prospective strength of the Kaiser's battle fleet; and if the unenthusiastic Reichstag will only grant the money to lay down three more, the German fleet will be very considerably strengthened. On the other hand, this class would, to a certain extent, fall between the two stools of battleship and cruiser. The new *Leipzig* will expose a great part of her hull to high-explosive shells, while even the eight inches of armour will be vulnerable to the heavy guns which would be used in a fleet action; at the same time, her armament is not extraordinary for her 10,300 tons. Moreover, her speed of 19 knots is higher than is needful if she is to manœuvre in a squadron with the *Baden*, of 14; while it is not sufficient to enable her, as a cruiser, to overtake many liners or weaker cruisers of other nations.

The *Kaiserin Augusta* is a cruiser of over 6000 tons, protected by a 3-in. steel deck, and armed with twelve 6-in. and eight 3·4-in. quick-firers. She has a good all-round fire, but the guns are almost wholly unprotected. It was hoped that she would steam $22\frac{1}{2}$ knots, but repeated trials resulted only in 21·8; and even this figure has been called in question. In any case her speed is high, but she is not over-well equipped with coal. The smaller *Gefion* (4108 tons) has also a 3-in. protective deck, and carries eight 6-in. and ten 4·1-in. quick-firers; her highest speed is 20 knots, and she carries 800 tons of coal, so that she ought, on paper, to be a more useful ship than our own second-class cruisers. Three other second-class cruisers on the stocks are remarkable for their efficient protection. There is a curved steel deck, whose maximum thickness is

4 inches. Two 8·2-in. breech-loaders and eight 6-in. quick-firers are carried behind 4 inches of armour, while the ammunition-hoists are also protected. There are also six 4-in. quick-fire guns behind shields. The normal displacement is 5650 tons, with 500 tons of coal, or 6100 tons when the coal supply is 950 tons; the estimated forced draught speed is 21 knots. In displacement, therefore, these ships are equal to our own largest second-class cruisers, while in gun-power, speed, and, above all, in protection, they are so far superior that it would probably be misleading to describe them as anything but first-class. The efficient protection of their guns, at any rate, would give our *Edgar*, for instance, a hard nut to crack, in a very literal sense, before she could defeat one of them. For service on distant stations Germany has half-a-dozen very fairly efficient ships of the *See Adler* class. The displacement is 1550 to 1650 tons; there are eight 4-in. quick-firers, an armoured deck, a top speed of about 16 knots, and coal capacity equal to 6000 miles. We have scores of better cruisers; but the *See Adler*, as has been said, could make short work of many of the obsolete sloops and gunboats we still keep on foreign stations.

Of torpedo craft Germany has eight gunboats armed with 3- or 4-in. quick-firers, and ten division boats—very much what we should call destroyers—steaming from 21 to 26 knots. Projected additions to this class will probably have considerably higher speeds. There are 64 sea-going, 61 first-class, four second-class, and sixteen vedette-boats. The whole flotilla is admirably organized in every detail, and in constant training at sea. The shallow coasts of Schleswig-Holstein and of the Baltic afford an admirable field for its operations,

FOREIGN NAVIES

and these would accordingly be very dangerous to a hostile fleet. The division boats would be equally formidable in a fleet action at sea. Their nominal strength is not overwhelming; but, as with all branches of the German Navy, their force on paper is subject to no deductions when it comes to work at sea. Whatever naval strength Germany credits herself with, that she has well ordered and in momentary readiness for war use.

ITALY.

The present state of the Italian Kingdom is the despair of its well-wishers, and the condition of the Italian Navy is not the least depressing feature of the situation. From the beginning of the last quarter of this century Italy made strong efforts to acquire a formidable fleet. Such a fleet was plainly necessary if she was to be a factor of any importance in the military system of Europe, and especially so in view of the unfriendly relations which even then were becoming traditional between herself and France. The Franco-Italian frontier is a short and mountainous one, so that, on the side of Piedmont, Italy is at the best of times difficult to invade in force. She set herself vigorously to work to make the task even more difficult than Nature had left it; and with the help of a line of strong fortifications, with admirable regiments of Alpine troops to man them, she has largely succeeded in this aim. But fortifications on the frontier of Piedmont are of very dubious value if France, being in a position to turn them at any moment by sea, can land any force of her superior army at any point she will on the long coast-line of Italy. Italy, accordingly, set herself to neutralize the French naval superiority. By the year 1886 she had, built or building, a fleet of ten huge vessels, which for displacement, weight of ordnance carried, and speed, had no equal in the world. But the effort was not maintained. With the best of fortune it was probably a mistake for a poor country to lay down huge ironclads costing from three-quarters of a million to near a million and a quarter apiece. A single lucky torpedo might destroy a tenth of the effective navy at a blow. Even if this danger were escaped it was probable that in the chances of war an *Italia* or a *Re Umberto* would have to be used on service which a smaller and less costly ship could have performed equally well; so that here was a waste of power which a poor nation should have striven to economize. The Roman Admiralty seems to have seen this, and no more enormous battleships were laid down; instead, a couple of 9,800-ton battleships, and several armoured and unarmoured cruisers, were put in hand. But meantime the finances went from bad to worse. The shipbuilding yards were starved, so that the latest of the monster battleships were ten years old from the laying of the keel-plate before they were ready for sea. The two smaller battleships have been five years on the stocks, and are not yet even launched. An armoured cruiser was recently sold to the Argentine Government, and more lately it is reported that a second has been disposed of—probably to Spain. It is not possible to see without sympathy, and even a touch of pity, a high-spirited nation thus struggling under a burden too great for its strength.

The most notable and, in many eyes, the most

FOREIGN NAVIES

dubious feature presented by the great Italian battleships is the extreme lightness of their protective armour. The *Sardegna*, of 13,860 tons, has only a 4-in. steel belt on the water-line, covering 250 out of her 430 feet, and rising to the upper deck, whereon her heavier quick-firing guns are mounted. There is hardly a gun afloat that could not break up this mail, while many could probably pierce it with shell. The *Re Umberto* and *Sicilia* (13,300 tons), and the *Italia* and *Lepanto* (15,000 and 15,400 tons), have no armour on the water-line; the two first have 4 inches over their central battery, the others no side-plating at all. The three vessels of the *Andrea Doria* class (11,000 tons) have an 18-in. belt over about half the length, with a smaller citadel of the same thickness above it; but all their quick-firing guns are exposed. The *Duilio* and *Dandolo* (11,445 tons), the oldest pair of the ten, are similarly protected by $21\frac{1}{2}$ inches of steel on the water-line, and a shorter redoubt of 17 inches; but the quick-firers are again defenceless. It is true that none of these ships is without an armoured deck, as well as strong armour on the ammunition hoists and round the bases of the funnels; and it may be also true that water-line hits in future warfare will be infrequent. Yet it is said that the *Yoshino* sank a Chinese cruiser with her quick-firers at the Yalu; and, even apart from this, the real danger of quick-fire high-explosive shells is not so much the sinking of the ship as the destruction of the whole hull, with the auxiliary armament and guns' crews, and the paralysis and demoralization that cannot but follow. It is impossible, therefore, not to fear that quick-fire has been insufficiently guarded against in Italian ships. For

NAVAL POLICY

this reason, and their high speed, many people incline to class them rather as cruisers than as battleships. Perhaps it matters little what they are called; but, seeing that they are certainly intended to fight battleships, rather than to act as scouts or ocean-patrols, it is most convenient to rank them with the type of vessel they are intended to meet.

The sacrifice of armour has, of course, been balanced by great advantages in other respects. Most of these ships have very high speeds; the *Sardegna* over 20 knots, the *Sicilia* probably much the same if pushed hard, the *Re Umberto, Italia,* and *Lepanto,* over 18. All five can stow 3000 tons of coal if necessary, which should take them at least 10,000 miles. The armaments are also heavy. The three first-named carry four $13\frac{1}{2}$-in. guns like the *Royal Sovereign's*, eight 6-in., and sixteen 4·7-in. quick-firers. The *Italia* and *Lepanto* and the *Andrea Doria* class have each four 17-in. Armstrong guns of over 100 tons weight; but they carry no more than four 4·7-in. quick-firers, though they have also some 6-in. guns, for which quick-firers are to be substituted. The *Duilio* and *Dandolo* originally carried four 100-ton muzzle-loaders in their echeloned turrets; but in place of these 10-in. breech-loaders are being mounted, along with seven 6-in. and five 4·7-in. quick-firers. Yet the value of all these heavy armaments is impaired by the want of adequate protection for the guns; and it is probable that they would be largely put out of action before they had time to silence a better-armoured enemy. An efficient battleship, it may be repeated, should develop all the elements of force in more or less equal proportion one to another. Otherwise, the want of one—as of armour in these Italian

FOREIGN NAVIES

ships—may neutralize all the superiority obtained by its sacrifice in respect of the others.

The two battleships on the stocks—*Ammiraglio di Saint Bon* and *Emanuele Filiberto*—exhibit a striking departure from previous Italian models. They have a complete, though a thin, belt of hardened steel, and almost the whole hull is sheathed in from 6 to 10 inches of the same material, which will bid defiance to all shell until the plates are broken up by heavy shot. They are fairly heavily armed for their size, carrying four 10-in. guns mounted fore and aft in barbettes, as well as eight 6-in. and eight 4·7-in. quick-firers—the last somewhat exposed. The speed is to be 18 knots, and the extreme radius over 7000 miles. When at last these ships are ready for sea, they should be useful units in any fleet.

Of armoured cruisers Italy has the *Marco Polo* ready for sea. This vessel has a partial belt, with cross bulkheads at its ends, of 4 inches, carries six 6-in. and ten 4·7-in. quick-firers, and steams 19 knots. The *Carlo Alberto* and *Vettor Pisani* (6500 tons) are enlarged and improved copies of her, and these are protected by a complete belt of nickel steel, while above it, along the midship two-fifths of the hull, rises plating of the same thickness, forming a central battery. Within this are four 6-in. quick-firers on each broadside, while above, on the upper deck, are four more, one at each corner of the battery. The sisters also carry six 4·7-in. quick-firers—one ahead, one astern, and two on each broadside on the upper deck, and these, as well as the upper deck 6-in. pieces, are protected only by shields. Nevertheless, few cruisers would come unscathed out of an action with these vessels: but for the absence of armour-piercing guns, they might almost be called light battleships. The *Garibaldi* (6840 tons) is of much the same type, with armour-piercing guns added. There are two 10-in. guns, carried in 6-in. barbettes, ahead and astern. The central main deck battery—6-in. plated, as in the *Carlo Alberto*, but occupying two-thirds instead of two-fifths of the ship's length—contains five 6-in. quick-firers on each broadside, while six shielded 4·7-in. quick-firers are mounted on the upper deck. The *Garibaldi* has a double bottom, which is expected, though on rather dubious grounds, to protect her to a certain extent against torpedoes; between the two skins liquid fuel is stored. With a speed of 20 knots, this is a most useful ship, and another of the same class is projected. Of deck-protected cruisers, Italy has eight: of these the Elswick-built *Piemonte*, of 2500 tons, is the most remarkable. She is armed with six 6-in. and six 4·7-in. quick-firers, steams nearly $22\frac{1}{2}$ knots, and has room for coal to take her 13,000 miles; she is a very admirable cruiser for work in any but rough water. The *Fieramosca* has very good gun-power for a second-class cruiser, but is slow; the others should be very efficient third-class cruisers for Mediterranean waters. Most of them could steam 10,000 knots without coaling; indeed, the coal endurance of the Italian ships generally is very high.

There are fifteen torpedo-gunboats of good speed; in other ways also Italy has paid the attention to torpedo warfare that would seem to be warranted by her exposed coast-line, and the probability that, in a naval war with France, she would have to act on the defensive. She possesses at present a hundred and

FOREIGN NAVIES

eleven sea-going boats that could act with a fleet, and seventy-one smaller and slower vessels. A 28-knot destroyer has been ordered.

UNITED STATES.

It is only of late years that the United States have aspired to become a first-class naval power. The policy of building a fleet of fast cruisers was initiated in 1883, but it was not until 1890 that the Federation began to lay down first-class battleships. In these thirteen years, however, so many ships have been built or projected, the ships themselves are so powerful, and the resolution to continue the programme is so manifest, that, in future, the United States must be reckoned with as perhaps the most dangerous of all our rivals. It is impossible to believe that this new fleet has been built for defence alone. No Power, whether naval or otherwise, wishes to commit aggression upon the United States; how far removed is the idea from the European Powers has plainly been shown by the reception in Europe of the recent insults bestowed both upon this country and upon Spain. Had any such aggressive projects been entertained by any European Power, these provocations would have been hailed as heaven-sent opportunities for going to war with a good cause; instead of this, the transatlantic menaces were received with half-amused, half-distressed stupefaction. Even were aggression intended from any quarter, the United States have no need to spend millions of dollars on battleships to meet it. They have no great carrying trade, and no dependencies over sea which they stand to lose; they do not depend on the outside for food, as we do, but could maintain themselves on their own products for ever. It is true that many of their principal towns are on the seaboard, and comparatively unprotected. But, in the first place, the destruction of these towns would do little service to an enemy, if only the United States were resolute to continue the war; in the second, it was easy to defend them with shore-batteries and torpedo-boats, as is actually being done concurrently with the building of the sea-going fleet. If one axiom of naval war is more certain than another, it is that the most powerful fleet cannot stand up for any length of time against well-constructed, well-armed, and well-served works on shore. This being so, we can only conclude that the new navy is part of the general spirit of interference and menace which, starting with mere bluff applied to electioneering purposes, is gradually becoming more and more characteristic of the foreign policy of the United States. At present the menace can be lightly regarded, for the ocean fleet is still in its infancy. But the resources, both natural and industrial, of the United States are so vast, and potentially so much vaster, that fifty years hence will tell a very different tale. By that time they will have it in their power to outbuild all the Old World, ourselves included, and once in that position it is not likely they will fail to take advantage of it. From the military point of view, therefore, it seems a great pity that Lord Salisbury did not meet Mr. Cleveland's impertinence of December, 1895, in a far firmer spirit. Had war come, we could probably have taken or destroyed most of the United States warships, and laid under contribution or destroyed New York, Philadelphia, Boston, New Orleans, and San Francisco. Conquer the United States we could not—that is an impossibility. But with a few heavy blows at the outset we might have sickened them of the war and the new fleet at the same time. In a few years, when they feel themselves militarily stronger, this also will be an impossibility; and, knowing the irresponsible nature of the Western Federation, welded together out of the malcontents of every European people, the Old World will have to stand on guard.

The latest and most powerful of United States warships are the *Kearsage* and *Kentucky*, which will probably be ready for sea towards the end of 1898. They are to be of 11,500 tons, 368 feet long and 72 feet in the beam—the proportion of beam to length being somewhat greater than in our later battleships, for reasons which will appear in a moment. These ships are very stoutly built, very strongly armoured, and very powerfully armed. Their most striking feature, which is exhibited by no other existing battleship, is the system on which the heavy guns are mounted. Four 13-in. guns are carried in turrets fore and aft. But these turrets are double, or two-storeyed, and in the upper storey of each turret, above the 13-in. guns, a couple of 8-in. breech-loaders are carried. Both upper and lower stories turn together, so that all four guns in each turret always bear in the same direction. These turrets are very heavily armoured, as, indeed, they should be, when their disablement would mean the loss of so much power. To begin with, there is the water-line belt, which extends from the stem to the after turret. This sinks with the normal stowage of

NAVAL POLICY

coal to 4 feet below the water-line, and rises $3\frac{1}{2}$ feet above it; except just at the bow it is $16\frac{1}{2}$ inches thick. The hull, from the upper edge of the belt up to the main-deck, is sheathed with 5-in. plating. The lower storeys of the turrets are armoured with 15 inches, with an additional 2 inches in front; the upper similarly with 9 and 11 inches. The gun positions are thus completely protected from below the water-line to the top of the upper turrets. The secondary battery consists of fourteen 5-in. quick-firers—mounted seven on each broadside between the turrets and behind 6 inches of armour—and twenty 6-pounders with smaller quick-firers. All the armour is of nickel steel, and its powers of resistance may be inferred from the fact that the United States are the headquarters of the most recent improvements both in steel plates and steel shot. The speed is comparatively low, being only 16 knots. The normal coal capacity is 410 tons, but 800 tons more can be stowed, giving a total radius of 6000 miles.

It is plain that these will be very formidable ships; but their most characteristic feature—the double turret—would seem to be a mistake. That it adds considerably to the all-round fire is obvious; but there are many countervailing disadvantages. If it is risky to expose two guns in a turret or barbette to simultaneous disablement, it is much more so to expose four. The risk that both big guns may miss, and two charges be wasted, owing to an oscillation of the ship, is likewise doubled. It is to minimize this chance that the *Kearsage* and *Kentucky* are being built broad in the beam. A third objection is that it is doubtful whether the stoutest ship in the world could stand without

FOREIGN NAVIES

strain the tremendous shock resultant on the firing of the four guns. And lastly, although the 8-in. guns are mounted at a very commanding height, they restrict the range of the heavier pieces below, which cannot be elevated to any considerable degree without the risk of damage to the storey above. For all these reasons it may be doubted whether the four new battleships which the Senate has authorized will carry double turrets. For the rest, it is noticeable that in spite of the great number of heavy and middle-sized guns mounted by these ships, their energy of fire is but 283,873 ft.-tons per minute, as against the *Majestic's* 393,920; this is attributable to the comparatively small power of the United States ordnance.

The *Iowa* (11,296 tons), to be completed in November, 1897, is the next battleship. She is nothing like so well protected as her successors, since she combines the British partial belt with the French unarmoured hull. The belt, which covers about 240 out of 360 feet of length, is of 14-in. plates; its ends are joined by 12-in. transverse bulkheads; both above and below it are $2\frac{3}{4}$-in. steel decks. But for this belt there is no external armour except on the guns. There are four 12-in. breech-loaders mounted fore and aft in 15-in. barbettes, and eight 8-in. guns in pairs in 8-in. barbettes, two sponsoned on each beam, so that four fire nearly ahead, astern, or on the broadside. The quick-firing armament is weak, consisting of two 4-in. guns sponsoned right ahead behind 4-in. shields, two similarly protected right abeam, and two on the unarmoured superstructure bearing astern over the main after barbette. There are twenty 6-pounders. She is to make $16\frac{1}{2}$ knots, and, with 2000 tons of coal, is expected to steam 6000 miles. The *Iowa's* fighting value is much impaired by the fewness of her quick-firers, and the ease with which shell could be lodged through the unprotected side beneath all her six barbettes.

The *Indiana, Massachusetts,* and *Oregon* are all ready for sea. Of 10,230 tons, they are, in the main, smaller prototypes of the *Iowa*. The belt of 18-in. Harveyed steel covers three-fifths of the length; the cross bulkheads are 17 inches of the same. Above the belt to the upper deck is 5-in. plating as in the *Kearsage*. Four 13-in. guns are carried in pairs in 17-in. barbettes; eight 8-in. in $8\frac{1}{2}$ to 10-inch barbettes, mounted as in the *Iowa*, except that in these earlier types they are not sponsoned on the same level as the heavier guns, but mounted on the superstructure so as to fire over them. The quick-fire armament is again very weak—six 4-in. guns and twenty 6-pounders—and the 8-in. gun barbettes are so high that they would be much exposed to shells exploding beneath them. It seems doubtful whether this whole system of providing an intermediate armament of 8-in. guns does not expose the ship more than the additional power is worth. The *Indiana* group steam from 16 to $16\frac{1}{2}$ knots, and with 1800 tons of coal —1400 more than the normal stowage—their coal endurance is put at the probably exaggerated figure of 16,000 miles.

Passing over the *Texas*—a small battleship of 6300 tons, neither better nor worse than other vessels of her size—and some seventeen coast-defence monitors, of which only the *Monterey* is recent, we come to the armoured cruisers. Of these the *Brooklyn* is the latest and largest. She is of 9153 tons, 21 knots speed, and 15,000 miles radius of action. She is protected on the

FOREIGN NAVIES

water-line by a partial 3-in. belt of steel, and a steel deck of 3 to 6 inches. She carries eight 8-in. guns by pairs in 5½ to 8-in. barbettes, mounted lozenge-wise as in French battleships, and a dozen 5-in. quick-firers behind 4-in. plating. Thus in speed, coal-endurance, gun-power, and protection for the water-line and guns, the *Brooklyn* possesses a well-proportioned, all-round power, and can challenge comparison with any first-class cruiser of her size afloat, except perhaps the *Esmeralda*. The *New York*, which is some 700 tons lighter, has the same speed, and 1500 miles less radius. In her the 4-in. armour belt runs from stem to stern with a similar steel deck. She carries only six 8-in. guns, the mid-ship barbettes containing one apiece, and her quick-firers are only of 4-in. calibre. These are protected, as in the *Brooklyn*, by four inches of steel plating; the heavier guns by 10-in. barbettes with 7-in. steel hoods. The *Maine* (6682 tons) is much smaller, and a knot slower than these; the fact that she has a partial belt of 6 to 12-in. plating, a central redoubt of ten inches and four 10-in. guns, in heavily-armoured echeloned barbettes, leaves it doubtful whether her designers intended her for cruiser or battle-ship. The *Maine* has no quick-firers larger than the 6-pounder. The *Katahdin* is a somewhat anomalous vessel, intended to be used as a ram. She is very low in the water, and armoured over the whole hull with 2½ to 6 inches of steel. Of guns she carries only four 6-pounders. She failed by three-quarters of a knot to reach her contract speed of 17 knots, but was never-theless accepted by way of emphasizing Mr. Cleveland's Venezuela message. Her price was only £186,000; but it was probably all wasted, as almost any ship under steam could easily get out of the way of a low vessel ploughing through the water at only 16 knots.

The United States fleet of fast unarmoured cruisers is a very fine one. Mention has already been made of the triple-screw commerce-destroyers *Columbia* and *Minneapolis*, which attained, on trial, the sensational speed of 22·8 and 23 knots. This must, however, be fined down to a natural-draught ocean speed of about 18½ knots—a performance that several of our own cruisers could probably equal. Being intended to run away rather than to fight, they carry one 8-in. gun and four 4-in. quick-firers astern, with two 6-in. and four 4-in. quick-firers as bow-chasers. The guns have steel shields, and there is a 2½ to 4-in. deck. Better armed, though with a trial speed of only 21·6 knots, is the *Olympia*, which carries four 8-in. guns in 4-in. hooded barbettes, and ten 5-in. quick-firers behind 4-in. shields. She would, of course, be a far more formidable fighting-ship if she mounted larger quick-firers instead of the 8-in. guns; but, as she is, she is superior to most of our first-class cruisers in respect of speed and shelter for the guns. Of the rest, the *Philadelphia* (4324 tons), *Newark*, and *San Francisco* (4083), *Baltimore* (4600), *Charleston* (4040), and *Atlanta* and *Boston* (3189), would be classed as second-class cruisers in Europe. All steam over 18 knots except the two last, which are being re-engined, and most of them over 19. Their armament would be powerful if quick-firing guns were substituted for their old pattern breech-loaders. This has been done on the *Chicago* (4500 tons), which owes her fame to having been commanded by Captain Mahan, the epoch-making naval historian. The *Cincinnati* and *Raleigh* (3183 tons) are new second-class cruisers,

FOREIGN NAVIES

steaming 19 knots, with 4500 miles radius, and armed with one 6-in. and ten 5-in. quick-firers, which means considerably more gun-power than that of British cruisers of approximate displacement. The *Marblehead* and two sister ships, of 2000 tons, are third-class cruisers; they are well armed with nine 5-in. quick-firers apiece, but only steam 17 knots. The rest of the United States Navy is, for the most part, composed of slow gunboats of little military value, or of old ships, classed as cruisers, which fought with Farragut and Dahlgren, thirty years since, in the Civil War. Among these is the *Hartford*, Farragut's flagship at New Orleans—a wooden single-screw frigate, which has been re-armed with 5-in. quick-firers. With what object good guns and valuable men should be put aboard this ship, which was already obsolete when Farragut hoisted his flag, Heaven and the Washington Navy Board alone can tell.

Torpedo-craft have received less attention in the United States than their long, exposed coast-line, with its numerous shallows and islets, would seem to demand. There are two first-class torpedo-boats—the *Cushing* and the *Ericsson*—and five second-class. Besides these, eighteen others are building and projected; but these are all large sea-going boats of $24\frac{1}{2}$ to $27\frac{1}{2}$ knots speed, armed with small quick-firers. They are rather destroyers than torpedo-boats, and are presumably intended to act with a fleet: in other words, they are not for defence, but for aggression. This, the first word to be said about the United States Navy, is also the last.

V

RELATIVE STRENGTH

WE are now in a position to sum up the results of the past chapters. Having some general idea, first, of the purpose and efficiency of the various equipments of modern warships, and, secondly, of the extent to which each of the principal navies is equipped with them, we may now attempt to discover, as exactly as possible, how we stand in relation to our rivals. Perfect mathematical exactness, it may be repeated, is not attainable in such a calculation. For this we should require a table of naval weights and measures, with such equations, for instance, as "8 inches of Harveyed steel = one 6-in. quick-firing gun." Unluckily such formulas would be almost impossible to construct, and quite impossible to apply. Supposing that the attacking power of a wire 6-in. quick-firer is just equal to the defending power of an 8-in. Harvey steel plate, we are still no nearer the practical application of the proposition than we were before. For it is quite plain that a 6-in. gun and ammunition is better to carry than the same weight of armour, which would go only the shortest way towards protecting a ship. We might, with an approach to truth, say that a gun and ammunition protected by its own weight of armour is better than either two guns and no armour, or two guns' weight of armour and no guns. But even this is

RELATIVE STRENGTH

true or not according to the particular ship to which the formula is to be applied. For instance, if there were any fresh weight to be utilized in the *Royal Sovereign*, it would go most profitably to armouring the unprotected 6-in. guns, while in the *Majestic* all such guns are armoured already, and any additional force might better be disposed otherwise. We cannot, therefore, hope to obtain any exact measurement between our own naval force and that of others such as would reduce the forecasting of naval war to a sum in arithmetic. Even if this were possible, there would still remain the chances of actual war as opposed to the mathematical certainty of the results given on the proving-ground. Then there is always the personal equation of the men who are to work the machines; coolness and resolution may make up a disadvantage, or flurry and indecision give away a superiority. The personal element in naval war must always remain to a great extent incalculable.

We can, however—and, indeed, considering the vital national importance of the subject, we must—make as exact estimates of the force possessed by us, and by others, as the nature of the subject allows. To count ships is plainly worse than inconclusive. To lump together all ships, big and little, new and old, battleships and gunboats, and call them all ships, and, as ships, all equal units in a total, is as absurd as to count up sovereigns, shillings, and pence, and say you possess so many coins. To count up first-class, second-class, third-class ships, and the like, on the basis of official classifications is similarly misleading; as well might you take a French five-franc piece and a Papal one, and reckon each at four-and-twopence. It was such misunderstandings, as revealed in recent debates in Parliament, that we set out to clear up. By going rather more into detail we can sum up roughly the relative strength of our own and other navies, first in one element of force, and then in another.

To take, first, battleships—that is, ships furnished with armour and armour-piercing guns, such as fit them to fight in line against other battleships. That ships without this equipment cannot meet battleships with any reasonable chance of success is antecedently as certain as anything can be, and is borne out by all naval experience from the *Merrimac's* first action in Hampton Roads to the battle of the Yalu. The battleship being the one type of war vessel which cannot be driven from the sea—leaving out of account such accidents as a surprise by torpedo-boats and the like—except by other battleships, it is plain that it is on battleships that naval superiority must ultimately depend. The number of such ships possessed, or shortly to be possessed, by the principal navies may thus be tabulated:

BATTLESHIPS OF THE PRINCIPAL NAVAL POWERS.

	1896 (end).	1897 (end).*	1898 (end).	1899 (end).
Britain	61	64	68	71
France	43	45	46	49
Russia	32	36	39	40
Germany	32	33	34	35
Italy	11	11	13	13
United States	10	11	13	13

* The dates assigned for the completion of ships building are, of course, more or less conjectural. The figures for 1899 take in only ships already projected; by laying down ships at the beginning of 1897, and pushing them on, it is obvious that any Power might add to its total at the beginning of the next century.

RELATIVE STRENGTH

This table includes coast-defence ships, armoured gunboats, and the like; but omits all ships classed as armoured cruisers. The mere fact of this official classification shows that such vessels as come under it are not, in the first instance, intended to fight in line. Only thirteen United States monitors, being armed only with smooth-bore cannon, which became obsolete in the early Sixties, are omitted.

This being so, it is plain that we cannot learn very much from the bare statement without discriminating somewhat. Taking guns first, we may draw a distinction between such ships as carry heavy breech-loaders and such as have only muzzle-loaders. This makes a great difference in the British figures, which come out thus:

	1896.	1897.	1898.	1899.
Britain	33	36	40	43

while the Italian total has, for the moment, to be reduced by one ship, the *Duilio*, which is, however, shortly to be re-armed. The other totals remain the same. On this showing, our strength is actually less than that of France, and barely superior to Russia's and Germany's. No doubt this does our ships some injustice, since it must not be supposed that in no circumstances could muzzle-loading guns oppose breech-loaders. Yet it is as well to show, as crudely and brutally as possible, how far behind we have allowed ourselves to fall in heavy artillery.

We may now pass to the auxiliary armament, and give the numbers of ships that carry heavy quick-firing guns: that is—to take a necessarily rather arbitrary standard—a gun of 3-in. calibre or over. A piece of this calibre might attack with effect the unarmoured

NAVAL POLICY

parts of battleships; and, if using shot, the thickness of armour usually carried on secondary guns. As a rule, the ships carrying these guns are also armed with heavy breech-loaders; the only exceptions are our own *Hercules* and *Sultan*, but their quick-firers are few, and not of the most powerful, so that they may be conveniently regarded as a supplementary class by themselves.

BATTLESHIPS ARMED WITH BREECH-LOADERS AND HEAVY QUICK-FIRERS.

	1896.	1897.	1898.	1899.
Britain	20	23	27	30
France	24	26	27	30
Russia	5	9	12	13
Germany	21	22	23	24
Italy	11	11	13	13
United States	6	7	9	9

The elimination of the slow-firing secondary armament appears to have made a vast difference in the relative strength of the various attacks. France appears still better armed than ourselves, though her superiority is far less, taking the double qualification, than it was in breech-loaders alone, and is dwindling in any case. The weakness of Russia in quick-firing guns is very marked. Germany, on the other hand, seems to have kept her artillery more modern, in proportion to the number of her ships, than any other Power. But this table, again, is somewhat misleading. Supposing a 6-in. quick-firer fires five shots a minute to a 6-in. breech-loader's one, then a ship with five of the old pattern guns is, so far, as powerful as a ship with a single quick-firer. Substitute quick-firers for the breech-loaders, and the superiority of the ship carrying the five guns be-

RELATIVE STRENGTH

comes immediately overwhelming. Now in the French total, as stated above, many ships are included on the strength of the most meagre armament of guns between 3 and 4 inches calibre. This is apparent from the fact that at present our battleships mount 260 large quick-firers to the French 165, while in three years we shall actually have 540 to 261. The fact that the pieces possessed by France are distributed over more ships is, no doubt, an advantage; but it hardly neutralizes the inferiority of their number. It is absurd to compare the *Majestic*, with her twelve 6-in. and sixteen 3-in. quick-firers, with the *Duguesclin*, which mounts a solitary $3\frac{1}{2}$-in. piece. Most of the German ships, again, have very weak secondary batteries. We may, therefore, profitably rule out all ships whose total energy of fire per minute is less—to take a relatively low figure, which will leave in all battleships seriously armed with large quick-firers—than 150,000 ft.-tons.

BATTLESHIPS WITH FIRE-ENERGY OF OVER 150,000 FT.-TONS PER MINUTE.

	1896.	1897.	1898.	1899.
Britain	15	18	22	25
France	12	14	15	18
Russia	3	6	9	10
Germany	5	5	6	7
Italy	10	10	12	12
United States	3	4	6	6

This is probably a very fairly just estimate of relative strength, so far as concerns the attack. Italy, perhaps, is somewhat favoured by the comparison, since several of her ships only just reach the standard of fire. The re-armament with quick-firers of the *Anson*, *Camperdown*, *Howe*, and *Rodney*, would add to our score; that of the *Amiral Duperré*, *Courbet*, and *Dévastation*, three to France's. On the whole, we may consider that in gun-power we are at present slightly superior to France, and gaining on her by reason of the greater number of our ships building or projected. On the other hand, Russia, at present unready, is coming up very rapidly; and in three years France, with any one European Power, will be at least equal to us, while a coalition of three ought to possess a decisive superiority. Of ships below this standard of offensive power, we have considerably more than any rival, though fewer than France and Russia together. We are most seriously weaker in heavy breech-loaders, though this is somewhat balanced by our great superiority in large calibre quick-firers.

To analyze and classify the various battleships from the point of view of the completeness of their armour protection, is not altogether simple. It is easy to say that ship A carries more armour than ship B, but ship B may carry it where the protection it gives is more effective. Six inches of armour-plating, for example, are probably better disposed to defend a quick-firing gun than piled on to an already thick belt some feet below the water-line. A rough and ready method of differentiating between ships all claiming alike to be armoured may, however, be found. We may begin by excluding all armour-clads as insufficiently protected whose armour on the whole side, or good part of it, and on the principal gun positions, is not capable of keeping out the shot of the heavy quick-firers usually mounted by the newer battleships. It is true that these guns would probably be fired with shell, at any rate early in an engagement, with the view of destroying the un-armoured parts of an enemy; but it would be always

RELATIVE STRENGTH

possible, and doubtless sometimes profitable, to use shot, or shot and shell alternately, to break up such armour as was incapable of resisting their blows. In any case, ships that do not need heavy armour-piercing guns to pierce their armour are at a disadvantage compared with those that do. The thickness of armour which can be penetrated by the heaviest quick-firers, at close range, may be put roughly at 12 inches of wrought iron, 8 of compound armour, and 6 of steel hardened by the best known processes. The number of battleships for each Power that possess this qualification is the following:

BATTLESHIPS INVULNERABLE BOTH ON SIDE AND PRINCIPAL GUN-POSITION TO LARGE QUICK-FIRERS.

	1896.	1897.	1898.	1899.
Britain	36	39	43	46
France	29	31	32	35
Russia	13	17	19	20
Germany	16	17	18	19
Italy	5	5	7	7
United States	6	7	9	9

In ships thus stoutly armoured, therefore, we have a small, but slightly increasing, superiority over France, but a combination of France with either Russia or Germany would leave us in a perilous position of inferiority. Italy, it will be noticed, the only Power which might, in conceivable circumstances, be found on our side, comes very badly out of this comparison, owing to the neglect of side armour in some of her finest ships.

It must not, of course, be supposed that ships less heavily armoured than those which appear in the table above would necessarily find their heavy guns dis-

NAVAL POLICY

mounted, or themselves sunk by quick-fire shot. The force with which a projectile would be likely to get home in war is not that which it exerts on the proving-ground. Some captains will, perhaps, be chary of firing their guns with the full charge, even in action, for fear of straining, or even bursting, the gun, or of damaging parts of their own ship by the concussion. It must also be remembered that only in case of direct hits will the full force of the projectile be realized; with an oblique hit the force will be less, and, with very oblique hits, at an angle of 45° or so, shot would probably bound off without penetrating at all. On the other hand, it is very possible that defective plates exist unsuspected in many vessels; a blow might find out the weak spot in a plate which, if sound, ought to defeat its attack.

The results given above seem to call for still further differentiation, since nobody would call, for example, the *Nile* and the *Colossus* equally well protected. An enlightening comparison of strength might be formed by counting only ships whose thickest armour is capable of defeating the most powerful gun afloat. But unfortunately no such ship exists. The *Indiana* and her two sisters of the United States Navy approach most nearly to it, having 17 inches of Harveyed steel on their barbettes, and 18 inches at thickest on the water-line. The most powerful guns are estimated to pierce nearly 39 inches of iron, which represents about half that thickness of Harveyed steel. In practice, no doubt, the *Indiana's* thickest armour is very unlikely to be penetrated, but hardly any other ships approach her in defensive strength. A more profitable basis of comparison, in view of the great part which quick-firers certainly, and high explosives possibly, will play in the next naval war, might be the armour carried on quick-firing guns, without which they could hardly hope to escape speedy disablement from the shell of the enemy. This form of protection is only of recent introduction, and consequently is found in very few ships actually ready for sea, though most Powers are recognizing its importance in their newer models.

BATTLESHIPS CARRYING THEIR LARGE QUICK-FIRERS BEHIND ARMOUR.

	1896.	1897.	1898.	1899.
Britain	5	8	12	15
France	3	5	6	9*
Russia	2	5	8	9
Germany	4	4	5	6
Italy	—	—	2	2
United States	3	4	6	6

This table tells much the same tale as the others. We are first in the list, but so poor a first that a combination of second and third would leave us behind. Italy, having laid down few ships since the importance of the quick-firer was realized, is again behind; Germany and the United States, in proportion to the number of their ships, are well forward. With regard to our own force, it may be conceded that the number of ships building of the *Majestic* and *Canopus* types brings us a trifle better out of this comparison than some of the others. We must also add to the British total the eight ships of the *Royal Sovereign* class, and the two *Centurions*, each of which carries four out of her ten 6-in. quick-firers in armoured casemates.

* In default of information it is assumed that the *Henri Quatre's* quick-firers will be protected by armour.

NAVAL POLICY

In respect of speed the construction of a comparative table is an easy matter. The present standard of speed for battleships, to judge by the ships now building, is 18 knots an hour. For ships completed it is 17, while any vessel with less than 15 knots would probably prove a serious hindrance to a squadron of modern ships. It must be remembered in this connexion that most warships never steam at their extreme forced-draught speed after the day of their trial. Some, at any rate, of our own vessels are capable of attaining or even exceeding their nominal speed for a spurt of a few hours, such as might be sufficient for the tactical necessities of a battle. But for continuous steaming most ships would probably make from three to four-fifths of their highest recorded performance.

BATTLESHIPS STEAMING 15, 17, AND 18 KNOTS AN HOUR.

	1896 Knots			1897 Knots			1898 Knots			1899 Knots		
	15	17	18	15	17	18	15	17	18	15	17	18
Britain	10	14	2	10	17	2	10	19	4	10	19	7
France	12	5	—	12	7	—	12	7	1	13	7	3
Russia	9	1	—	10	4	—	11	6	—	12	6	—
Germany	9	2	—	10	2	—	10	2	1	10	2	2
Italy	3	2	5	3	2	5	3	2	7	3	2	7
United States	3	1	—	4	1	—	6	1	—	6	1	—

On this showing we are very fairly well off, though still inferior in point of ships of good speed to the next two Powers. But our great superiority in speed at 17 knots and over would probably be of service to us, whether in a fleet action or in strategical combinations. It must, however, never be forgotten that the speed of a fleet is set by the slowest ship, not the fastest; for this reason the possession of two very fast battleships like the *Renown* and *Centurion* is of no use to us until we have others to act with them. In respect of speed Italy

RELATIVE STRENGTH

comes out far the best of the Powers, and the United States worst; the former has sacrificed protection to speed, the latter speed to protection.

To make a table on the basis of coal-endurance is not a very difficult task, but it is one of doubtful profit. The particulars vouchsafed by most Powers with reference to their warships sometimes estimate the distance they can steam at economical speed without coaling, but these estimates, as has already been pointed out, are often vitiated by the fact that they make no allowance for the coal used by such auxiliary machines as turning-engines, fresh-water engines, fire-engines, and the like. The coal consumed by these varies according to the number there may happen to be on board a vessel, and the frequency with which they are used. But leaving these out of consideration for purposes of comparison—on the assumption that the error in all calculations is much the same—we may put the radius of action of the battleships of each Power as follows. The standard—ability to steam 5000 geographical miles without coaling—is again more or less arbitrary. It has, however, for British purposes a certain appropriateness in that it would allow a ship to steam at economical speed from a Channel port to Malta and back, with a good margin for fighting an action on the way.

BATTLESHIPS WITH A RADIUS OF 5000 MILES.

	1896.	1897.	1898.	1899.
Britain	31	34	38	41
France	3	3	4	6
Russia	2	2	4	4
Germany	—	—	1	2
Italy	5	5	7	7
United States	3	4	6	6

Here, at any rate, we come out of the test with flying colours. At present we are more than double the total of the five other Powers, and though they are now building ships of better coal-endurance than hitherto, we shall enter on next century with a great superiority to them all together. Moreover the Power that comes next to ourselves is Italy, the nation whose enmity we have least reason to apprehend. French writers have very severely criticized the policy which has built their ships incapable of acting even in Egyptian waters without being driven to look for some neutral port wherein they may coal. Even if they find such a port, it is plain that the necessity of frequent coaling must involve delay, and, in future naval wars, even more than in Nelson's day, time will be an essential condition of success. Nevertheless, we must not set too much store on the superior coal-carrying of our ships. An abundant supply of coal has its off-set in the fact that it entails great size and draught of water; this cuts ships off from many of the harbours of the world, and many of the docks. However, the advantage secured by a large radius of action more than counterbalances the disadvantages for British ships. Our vessels have to go anywhere the enemy is to be found, and to go quickly before he escapes, without losing time to coal by the way. But it is not at all so certain that foreign nations need to give very much of their available displacement to coal. A certain quantity they must have; for instance, a French ship loses more than half her strategic value, if she cannot steam from Cherbourg to Toulon, with a margin for any fighting that may be necessary. But within some such limit as this the foreigner, as against England, may rest content with an inferior coal-capacity. It is our business to go to him, not his to come to us. If he beats us on his own shores he can come to us, and invade us at his leisure; if he does not, it is at least better to be beaten near his own port than to have to run home after the damage of a battle.

It is hardly necessary to carry the analysis of battle-ships further. The important point in making any such comparisons is to keep the standards and classes as elastic as possible. It may, perhaps, be claimed for the tables drawn out above that they are based on real elements of strength in a ship, and that the standards themselves, though inevitably of an arbitrary nature, are roughly representative of a real superiority of the vessels which satisfy them over those which do not. The general result of them all is that our naval position relatively to other Powers is growing worse instead of better. In attacking-power we are inferior to the two second nations, while in breech-loading artillery we are even inferior to France alone. In the protection of our ships we are already falling behind any two of the principal Powers, while even where we are strong, as in speed and coal-endurance, our rivals are reducing our lead. However, to sum up the exact amount of our deficiencies, we shall do well to wait until the next chapter, and to consider what Powers we are likely to be called on to encounter, and what force we shall need to defeat such possible attack.

To pursue the same analysis in respect of cruisers, we seem, so far as mere numbers go, to possess a considerable superiority; though even here, considering the vast volume and vital national importance of our sea-borne commerce, we have not a single ship, even on

NAVAL POLICY

paper, which we can afford to spare. The total numbers of cruisers for the principal Powers are the following:

	1896.	1897.	1898.
Britain	126	136	150
France	56	63	64
Russia	31	31	33
Germany	18	18	21
Italy	22	24	25
United States	36	36	36

No profitable distinction can be drawn between the ships represented by these figures on the basis of the official distinction into armoured, first, second, and third-class. An arrangement which puts the *Rossia* and the venerable *Black Prince* (now used as a training-ship) in the same category cannot but be worse than misleading. Proceeding, as in the case of the battleships, to analyze the figures on the basis of the various elements of force, we may first eliminate all ships unfurnished with the larger quick-firing guns, with which exclusively British cruisers have been armed for nearly ten years.

CRUISERS ARMED WITH LARGE CALIBRE QUICK-FIRE GUNS.

	1896.	1897.	1898.
Britain	74*	84	98
France	27	34	35
Russia	2	2	4
Germany	8	8	11
Italy	10	11	12
United States	14	14	14

Our own total is thus shorn away by nearly one-half,

* The *Northumberland*, *Nelson*, and *Minotaur* are omitted, their few 4·7-in. quick-firers being balanced by the fact that their principal armament is muzzle-loading.

RELATIVE STRENGTH

but those of our rivals are still further reduced. That of Russia is particularly insignificant, but it appears likely that, with the hope of maritime dependencies in Chinese waters, she will now devote herself to building new cruisers. It will be seen that both now, and for the next two years, we are superior in cruisers armed with quick-firers to the five other Powers put together. But this table somewhat overstates our strength, since although our number of ships with a modern armament is large, they are, on the whole, less heavily armed than the corresponding ships of other Powers.

If we take a higher standard—for example, a fire-energy of 150,000 ft.-tons a minute, as was done in the case of battleships—the figures come out thus:

CRUISERS WITH A FIRE-ENERGY OF OVER 150,000 FT.-TONS PER MINUTE.

	1896.	1897.	1898.
Britain	20	27	33
France	19	25	26
Russia	1	1	3
Germany	1	1	4
Italy	2	4	4
United States	4	4	4

This puts a very different face on the matter. The minor Powers are more minor than ever, but France is at the moment virtually on an equality with us as regards ships of this standard of gun-power. Suppose that a ship satisfying this standard were regarded as possessing the minimum of offensive power that would justify her for independent cruising, while weaker ones were used to scout with fleets. We should then be vastly superior to France in the number of our scouts, but should be very badly off on the high seas. Twenty ships could hardly run down and capture nineteen, until the nineteen had done considerable, perhaps mortal, injuries to our food-supply. No doubt we should send weaker vessels to cruise than are numbered in this class, which includes the *Eclipse* type among our so-called second-class cruisers, while excluding all the others. But we should do this at the manifest risk of meeting more powerful opponents. Less powerful vessels might perhaps be set to cruise in pairs; two *Apollos* could doubtless defeat a *Chasseloup Laubat* very easily. But that would mean employing £350,000-worth of ship to get rid of £250,000-worth, and—what with our present dearth of officers and seamen is far more important—550 men to neutralize 350. The conclusion wherefrom is that, with all allowance for the fact that we are now building a trifle faster than France, the list of our more powerful cruisers ought to be a good deal longer than it is.

In point of protection it has already been pointed out that armoured cruisers, in any real sense, are very rare. Our own *Aurora*, which is so classed, can hardly be called better armoured by reason of her belt than she would be by an arched deck of stout nickel-steel. The same applies to all cruisers which are merely protected by a thin armour-belt on the water-line, while among cruisers which carry real side-armour to protect them against quick-fire shell, the *Dupuy-de-Lôme* stands almost alone.

On this basis, therefore, we can hardly make any satisfactory discrimination between cruisers. To classify them according to the presence or absence of deck-protection would be similarly inconclusive, since nearly

RELATIVE STRENGTH

all vessels built since 1880 or so* have this to a greater or less degree. The most profitable way of discriminating between cruisers in matter of protection would probably be according as their guns are, or are not, protected from shell-fire. But this principle, as was remarked in dealing with battleships, is of such comparatively recent recognition that the materials for a comparison hardly exist as yet. The ships of our own *Blake* and *Edgar* classes carry each four 6-in. quick-firers in 6-in. casemates, while the *Terrible* and *Powerful* have all, and the *Diadem* class twelve, of their guns similarly protected. Several French ships carry their heaviest guns in lightly-armoured turrets. The German *Freya* and her sisters will have all their guns of 6-in. calibre and upwards, either in casemates or turrets of 4 inches greatest thickness.

In speed, which is of the utmost value to a cruiser, whether she acts as intelligencer to a squadron or independently, a tabular comparison is simple enough. The same caveat must, however, be given as in the case of battleships with regard to nominal speed and sea speed.

CRUISERS STEAMING 18, 19, 20, 21 KNOTS AN HOUR.

	1896. Knots.				1897. Knots.				1898. Knots.			
	18	19	20	21	18	19	20	21	18	19	20	21
Britain	6	33	20	4	6	33	26	4	6	33	40	8
France	3	10	9	1	3	17	10	1	3	18	10	1
Russia	2	—	—	—	2	—	—	—	2	—	2	—
Germany	1	1	1	1	1	1	1	1	1	2	1	4
Italy	2	4	—	1	2	4	2	1	2	4	2	1
United States	4	4	2	5	4	4	2	5	4	4	2	5

In very high speeds the United States are well ahead

* The first cruisers were our own *Comus* class, launched in 1878 and succeeding years.

of all competitors; but in a few years, if all our ships turn out well on trial, we shall be equal to them in the proportion of our cruisers that make high speed, and, of course, far superior in the total. With regard to European Powers our position is satisfactory in point of nominal speed, while in practice we should probably find ourselves more nearly able to realize the results gained on trial. It may be said, roughly, that our cruisers are from half a knot to a knot faster than the continental cruiser of the same class.

The coal endurance of their cruisers is of more general concern to the nations of the earth than is that of their battleships. If they are at war with us we shall, if we are wise enough and strong enough, come after their battleships; but their cruisers must be ready to go after our merchantmen. No Foreign Power is over-well equipped with coaling stations in distant seas, and such as they have it would be Britain's first business to attack. Neutral ports, which foreign cruisers would have to use largely for coaling purposes, would—again, if we were strong enough—be watched by British cruisers. The case might therefore easily arise that a cruiser, whose bunkers had run low, would be obliged to fight, because she had not coal enough to take her into any other port. It would be our business to ensure that this took place as often as possible; it would be the enemy's—whose real objective would be not our cruisers, but our merchantmen—to reduce the possibility of being brought to action for lack of coal to a bare minimum. It follows from this that foreign cruisers need a large radius of action just as much as ours do. How large, is a question that admits of more dispute. The *Rurik* is reckoned to steam 20,000 knots without coaling, and the *Terrible* 25,000—more than the earth's circumference. It is doubtful whether this would ever be necessary, especially in the case of powerful ships like these, which would have little reason to avoid a coaling station for fear of meeting an enemy in its offing. It might well be argued that it is better for a ship to have her bunkers so arranged that she can coal quickly than to carry such enormous quantities as this. By way of a standard to differentiate cruisers of a high coal capacity from the ruck, we may, perhaps, not unreasonably fix the ability to steam 10,000 miles without coaling; that is, a voyage rather longer than to the West Indies and back, and rather short of India round the Cape. The results for the various nations are the following:

CRUISERS OF 10,000 MILES RADIUS, AND OVER.

	1896.	1897.	1898.
Britain	17	17	21
France	4	4	5
Russia	2	2	3
Germany	2	2	5
Italy	1	1	1
United States	5	5	5

Once again, as whenever it is a question of sea-going qualities, we are in a highly satisfactory position, and likely to remain so. Unless the standard of 10,000 miles is far too high, it appears that foreign nations have generally under-estimated the times and distances over which their cruisers must keep the sea. An extensive radius of action, however, is only needed for independent cruising for the attack and defence of commerce. Cruisers acting with a fleet can presumably coal wherever the battleships coal, and, though they would have much more steaming than the battle-ships, might do with an endurance of considerably less than 10,000 miles.

The following table is formed by combining the previous one with the two previous to it, and represents the number of vessels possessed by each Power which have a fire-energy of 150,000 ft.-tons per minute, can steam 20 knots an hour, and go 10,000 miles without coaling—perhaps as good a qualification for the name of first-class ocean cruiser as any other.

	1896.	1897.	1898.
Britain	9	9	13
France	3	4	4
Russia	—	—	1
Germany	1	1	4
Italy	1	1	1
United States	3	3	3

Among the aristocracy of cruisers, therefore, we return to our old equality, both now and in the future, to all the other Powers together. But then our interests on the high seas are greater than that of all the other Powers together. For to them the possession of sea-trade means luxuries; to us it means our daily bread.

The torpedo flotillas may be briefly tabulated as they will stand for 1897, and need no comment.

	Britain.	France.	Russia.	Germany.	Italy.	U.S.A.
Torpedo-gunboats over 21 knots speed	—	5	6	3	3	—
Do. under 21 knots speed	29	16	2	5	14	—
Destroyers	90	—	1	11	1	—
Sea-going boats	43	46	55	64	111	20
Other boats	123	197	116	81	71	5

VI

SHIPBUILDING POLICY

WE now know roughly where we are in point of naval armaments, and with what rival forces we are confronted. Is our preparation sufficient? Can we say, with Mr. Goschen, that, with the completion of this year's building programme in 1899, "We shall have reached some point where we may stand"? It appears that the First Lord clings to this view, for, on the Budget, he acquiesced in the following statement of the Chancellor of the Exchequer:—"The increase over last year's estimate is due mainly, of course, to the vast increase of £3,122,000 in the Navy Estimates. Every Chancellor of the Exchequer for the last ten years has been burdened with the ever-increasing burden of the old man of the sea. I do not complain of it, because, in the first place, I believe the expenditure to be necessary. I know that it is far more economical that we should incur it at a time when we have leisure to think out a systematized plan on which it can be made, than to defer works which we ought to do ourselves, to be attempted some day, perhaps too late, by our successors, and to allow to be passed votes of credit amounting to enormous sums, most of which would certainly be wasted, and all of which might be too late for the object for which it would be required.

Therefore, sir, I do not grudge this increase in the Navy Estimates of the current year. I am sanguine that next year may show a decrease." It is impossible that Sir Michael Hicks-Beach should have uttered the last sentence without the consent of his colleagues, and, among them, of Mr. Goschen—who, indeed, was sitting at his side, and is stated by the newspapers to have cheered the statement. When attention was called to the matter later in the debate, Mr. Goschen said that the charge of the first year of his scheme was the heaviest—thus by implication allowing that there would be no fresh scheme next year. It is true that in the last days of the Session, replying to Sir Charles Dilke, he limited his diminution of estimates to the shipbuilding vote only, and appeared to contemplate an increase in the Estimates as a whole. On the other hand, the rest of his speech was deplorable. He alleged that this country must be limited in an increase of battleships, otherwise necessary, by the inability to provide enough guns and armour-plates. It is quite true that several of the battleships of the *Majestic* class have been delayed by the tardy supply of guns and plates. Yet that is not an excuse for a First Lord, but rather an additional condemnation. If the makers of guns and plates were guaranteed a demand for a term of years, there would be no difficulty about the supply. However, Mr. Goschen appears to have chosen the easier part, and to be disposed to do little for the battle-fleet in 1897.

Are we to agree with him that we may put our money in our purse, or devote it to teaching our agricultural population their catechism, secure in the adequacy of our Navy to meet all calls likely in

SHIPBUILDING POLICY

reason to be made upon it? Or are we to take the view of Sir Charles Dilke, Sir John Colomb, and Mr. Arnold Forster—who also have given attention to this subject — and believe that still further efforts are necessary before our safety from defeat is assured? To decide between them we must consider a wholly new series of questions. We know what our Navy is, and what proportion it bears to that of others. We have now to enquire what it needs to be, and what proportion to that of others it ought to bear. By what standard are we to measure the adequacy or inadequacy of the Navy?

What, in the first place, is the Navy for? Plainly to protect us against attack, or against such encroachment on our imperial standing, or commercial interests in any part of the world, as amounts to an indirect attack. If any such attack were made upon us by a single Power, possibly Mr. Goschen is right, and we are already—so far as ships go, and leaving the question of men for separate consideration — able to defend ourselves. We command, as has been seen, a very substantial superiority over any single Power except France, and have a tangible, though too small, margin of superiority over her. But a small, or even a handsome, superiority to any single Power is not enough. Any child can forecast the possibility that we may be assailed by two or more in concert. The limit of such a combination is a concert which would include every naval Power on earth. Such a coalition is not inconceivable, and we cannot consider ourselves absolutely and unconditionally impregnable to all possible attack, unless we have a naval superiority over the whole world put together. But that, unfortunately, is outside any immediate possibility. We must compromise the matter, and look to the nearer probabilities of the political situation. With how many, and how powerful, nations is there a reasonable possibility that we might be engaged? That is what Sir William Harcourt means when he says that policy governs estimates. The phrase is one of those half-truths, half-falsehoods, in which the party politician takes unfailing comfort. It is undoubtedly true that policy governs estimates in a sense; forward policy demands a military force to carry it through, which halting or backward policy seems able to dispense with. On the other hand, it is just as true that estimates govern policy; you cannot carry out a policy unless your estimates are heavy enough to provide the military force which is always at the back of diplomacy, and which is its only sanction. If we are to play the leading part in the world's affairs that most Britons conceive to be our right in virtue of our national character and achievements, we must have the force to make our voice respected in the councils of the world. We rule better than other nations, and therefore we ought to rule more than other nations: such is the central idea of what is called the Imperialist spirit, and, given the premises, it is difficult to deny the conclusion.

But to return to Sir William Harcourt. With Powers like France and Russia (supposing them to be united, as they presumably are, at least in a defensive alliance) it is perfectly true that for the moment policy governs estimates. There is no Power, or Powers, likely to attack them, and unless they propose to attack others they can ease off their preparations for war. But is this true of Britain? To answer the question, we need only ask why it is true of France and Russia.

First, because they are allied, and, having common interests against us, naturally allied. But we are not allied with anybody, and not likely to be. France and Russia do not need our alliance, and the only terms on which they would accept it is the surrender on our part of just those interests which our Navy exists to defend. Nobody wants to conquer and enslave Great Britain and Ireland, to govern them as satrapies from Paris or Petersburg. But both France and Russia want empire and trade where we also want it, and where at present we have it. They covet our goods much more than we covet theirs—Egypt, for example, or the trade of China. Therefore they have no use for our alliance except on terms of our giving up to them either something we already possess, or something which we have as good a claim to possess as they, and which may be used as a base to proceed to take what is actually ours. If we have to ally ourselves on these terms—and French statesmen and privileged Russian journalists avow that nothing less will content them—we may just as well sell our fleet at once for what it will fetch.

Nor does the other great European combination offer us any better prospect. Of the members of the Triple Alliance, Italy is a Platonic but feeble friend, neither able nor anxious to help us in any need; while Austria, more able but not a whit more willing, has no immediate use for any return we could pay for her friendship. Germany, the head and controlling will of the Alliance, is bitterly hostile, and certain to remain so. The personal relations of its autocrat with our monarchy, our national sports, and the like, had veneered

NAVAL POLICY

this hostility for years, but the outburst with which the whole German press and the whole German nation gave tongue, when once the Kaiser led off the chorus, can leave no doubt as to the feelings with which we are regarded in Germany. It is only fair to add that the feeling of this country towards Germany, if less ebullient, is as deeply unfriendly. Nor is it disputable that the instinct of our democracy is a true one. With France and Russia we may have more immediate causes of friction, but among European Powers Germany is our true enemy. We are commercial rivals, engaged at this very moment in a life-and-death struggle for the markets of the world. This kind of enmity makes little show at ordinary times on the surface, but it goes very deep. Moreover, it comes home to everyone, be he politician or not. You cannot go into the City without seeing before your own eyes, and hearing in your own ears, evidences of the commercial war—and what is worse, the successful war—which Germany is waging against us. Alliance with Germany is impossible; it is forbidden by the national feeling, and the competing commercial interests of either country alike.*

* As an example of a German view of our international position, and the readiness to take advantage of it, there is interest in this recent utterance of Prince Bismarck's *Hamburger Nachrichten:* "A wise policy must, therefore, take care that we hold aloof from England's conflict with France and Russia, which will not seek war with us when fighting England in three continents, and that we should reserve our strength in order to be able to throw it into the scale when things come to be rearranged.

"But the British are tormented by another anxiety. They no longer believe entirely in the unassailability of their European Island Empire, for, whereas many things have changed elsewhere in the last decade, England's system of defence is still the same as in Wellington's time. It suffices for non-European countries. In view of the world-wide extent of

SHIPBUILDING POLICY

Outside Europe the field for British alliances is hardly more promising. Recent events have shown that we cannot count on the friendship of the United States, although in a naval war between European Powers her interest in neutrality would be so great that we need not necessarily apprehend her hostility. In Asia, having made it our policy for years to sustain China against Russia, we have recently allowed her, first, to be beaten to her knees by Japan, and then saved from dismemberment by that very Russia, whose encroachment it was the one aim of our policy to forbid. Japan, it is true, offers a possibility of alliance on the basis of common rivalry to Russia. But industrially and commercially, Japan is our rival even more than she is Russia's. We have done nothing to earn her friendship; on the contrary, our recent impotent display in the Far East must have gravely depreciated the value of our alliance. It is even now possible that

her interests, she must have more ships on foreign coasts than Russia and France. But the Power or Powers which preponderate where the conflict must be decided, that is, in the Channel and the North Sea, will be victorious. But the French Channel fleet alone is already a match for the English, and its junction with the Russian Baltic fleet would put an end to England's superiority in the waters in which the conflict must be decided. Add to this that just her insular position involves the danger of England being starved out by the enemy, so that she must unconditionally surrender, if a victorious hostile fleet should succeed in cutting off her supplies. England has not ignored this danger, and is, therefore, working diligently at the task of increasing her navy to such an extent that it will be superior under all circumstances. If she maintains her superiority at sea, her antagonists must try to convert the sea war as quickly as possible into a land war, and to seek a decision where all the nerves of the World-Empire meet—that is, in London. The essay entitled 'Attempts to invade England,' by Baron Lüttwitz, a Prussian officer of the General Staff, expresses the opinion that the question of the possibility of such an invasion must be answered in the affirmative. The attempt to invade England is still, indeed, a risky, but no longer an impossible enterprise."

Japan may discreetly have come in and made her peace with Russia.

From the point of view of alliances, therefore, there is no analogy between ourselves and the Franco-Russian combination.

The second reason why they are in a position to allow their policy to govern their estimates is equally inapplicable to us. They are in a position of military superiority to any probable enemy. As against the Triple Alliance, it is almost as easy for Russia to make war on her whole Austro-German frontier as on the German frontier alone: she could bring the whole strength of her army into play almost at once, whereas this would be impossible, for reasons of transport, along the three practicable lines of advance into Prussia. France, meanwhile, could probably paralyze Italy by her superior fleet and threats of invasion at all points, while still keeping ample forces to operate on the frontiers of Piedmont and Lorraine. As against Britain the coalition is equally powerful. Locking up the best part of our troops in Afghanistan on the one hand, Russia could co-operate with France in threatening us with invasion on the other. Even if this threat were unexecuted, as it would most probably turn out, the combined fleet could challenge our supremacy at sea, and with it the supply of the food we eat. In battleships, whether we consider the total number or the powers of attack and defence, they are equal to us to-day, and in a year or two equality will have grown into preponderance. In point of cruisers they are inferior, it is true, yet not so inferior but that they might cause us the greatest embarrassment and loss, while their shores and harbours are defended by

SHIPBUILDING POLICY

torpedo flotillas far more powerful than any which could be brought against them. In this position of equality tending to superiority France and Russia might be justified by a pacific policy in reducing their naval expenditure. But we, with the equality of to-day declining inexorably to the inferiority of to-morrow, cannot be justified by any such blameless intentions in neglecting our defence. Only the stronger Power can afford to be pacific. The weaker cannot choose between war and peace — only between war and surrender. And by the end of 1897, and during the following years, we, as against France and Russia—which in their relations with us may be counted as one Power—shall be the weaker party, and exposed to all the aggression which weakness inevitably invites.

There is yet another reason why a pacific policy might permit France and Russia to reduce expenditure, which does not apply to us. The naval strength of the allies is not only sufficient to enforce their policy at the present, but yet more amply sufficient for the immediate future. The wisdom of their rulers, which led to the laying down of many ships in the years immediately precedent, permits them now to complete those ships at leisure without laying down others. France is taking this course, though Russia's procedure is exactly opposite. But our improvident rulers, who attend to the first interest of the country only by fits and starts, neglected the Navy during the years succeeding the completion of the Naval Defence Act programme. The result is that, barely equal now, we shall be behind our rivals next year, and must build for the future. The immediate future is irredeemable, but by the beginning of next century we may pull level again. If a battleship could be built in a fortnight, the policy of the future might be left to take care of its own estimates. But a battleship takes, on the average, three years to build; and who can foresee to-day the policy of 1900? We have let ourselves drop behind through exaggerated confidence in the fact that we can build warships faster than any other Power. We can; but not so much faster as a consideration of our best performances without taking into account our worst—the remembering of the *Majestic* and the forgetting of the *Renown*—would lead us to believe. Laying down five battleships in 1896, we shall perhaps have two of them ready in 1898, but hardly more. If we want ships by 1900, therefore, we must lay them down without fail in 1897.

The dictum, then, that policy governs estimates, with its implication that a policy of alliances or avoidance of aggression can justify us in reducing the amount expended in armament, turns out false and misleading at every turn. We cannot reduce our expenditure on the strength of alliances, for there are no alliances open to us, even if we desired them. Pacific intentions will not avail us, for our rivals are in a position to impose upon us either surrender or war at a disadvantage. On this view policy does, indeed, govern estimates; but exactly the wrong way about. It is their policy that governs our estimates—a position neither safe nor consistent with the dignity of a great empire. And not only our rivals' immediate policy, but their contingent future policy also. We have to make ourselves ready to-day to meet any onslaught they may choose to make in 1900.

It is the policy of our rivals, therefore, that must furnish the measure of our naval expenditure during

SHIPBUILDING POLICY

the next years; and, so far as that policy can be forecast, it affords no warrant for drawing tight the purse-strings. That there exists, in spirit if not in letter, a world-wide confederation against us has been plain to us, and to the rest of the world, any time since January, 1896. We consoled ourselves with the phrase "splendid isolation." But in the mere fact of isolation there is no more splendour than there is in that of association. The consciousness of isolation may be splendid if isolation is met with coolness and courage; but if this very courage leads to neglect of the exceptional precautions which isolation demands, then the sense of isolation is rather dismal than splendid. It is rather significant of this ostrich-headed attitude that the same Mr. Goschen who adopted the phrase was found, a few months later, acquiescing in the neglect of the very naval precautions which isolation should have enjoined. Neither he nor anyone else can be unaware of the international situation. France and Russia we had always reckoned with, though at the very time of reckoning we had been allowing our forces to decline below the level of theirs. We always knew that their interests, as against us, were identical. Now we know that they have themselves recognized this identity of interest by alliance. Germany, too, as our most dangerous commercial rival, and as intensely hostile in feeling, must in future be reckoned with— the more so as recent events in the Far East have shown that the days when France and Germany could not act in concert are either over, or very nearly so. The United States stand on much the same footing as Germany. With both there is the additional danger that intestine political enmities may drive their rulers, at almost any moment, to distract their populations by foreign war. That these four Powers should unite to crush us in the near future is not, perhaps, very probable, but it is more than possible. To be safe, we should be ready to meet them all together. But that would mean doubling our fleet, so that it is hardly to be looked for in the next year or two. That we might be confronted with three of these Powers, of which France and Russia would almost certainly be two, is less unlikely than that we should have to face all four. That before many years we may have to fight France and Russia together—unless some piece of good luck happens to disassociate them: a contingency on which the present aspect of Europe gives us no right to count—is not only not unlikely, but is affirmatively more likely than not. The only alternative is that we should resign all our interests in China—in the north to Russia, in the south to her ally—as well as a great deal of what we value in Africa; and that with supplementary concessions to Germany and the United States, who would not lose the opportunity if once they found us in a surrendering mood. Many people, both at home and abroad, think that on the consciousness of our naval weakness is already supervening the habit of surrender; and there are not wanting in the diplomatic history of the last year or two facts to confirm that view. But what may have been given up is nothing to what we shall be asked to give up. Unless we increase our strength to a point that warns off aggression, we shall have either to give up all the sources of our greatness, or fight for them on conditions that will put a premium on defeat.

What force do we need, then, to fight the possible

combinations against us? To answer the question we must consider the plan on which this country would conduct a war. This plan is deduced* by the application of the broad abstract principles of strategy to our peculiar national circumstances. Although it took Englishmen some centuries to get it formulated with clearness, it is, when once formulated, very simple. The sea, as has already been said, is our territory; and we must hold it just as if it were a province. This is to be done either by crushing the enemy at once, or by keeping a superior fleet of our own that knows where to lay its hand on him, and crush him if he shows himself out of port. Only by this method of making war can we ensure the ocean communications upon which our Imperial existence depends, and draw from the trade of the sea the supplies on which our people are to be fed. Considering this necessity, we can answer at once one of the questions with which we started at the beginning. There was a doubt, in calculations of relative force, what ships we were to count. But if we are to carry the war up to the enemy's coast-line, leaving the sea in British possession behind us, this question becomes very simple. We must count every ship of the possible enemy, whether sea-going or coast-defending; and we must only count such ships of our own as can operate on an enemy's coast. This appears to put a very heavy handicap upon us; and so, indeed, it does. But we must accept the handicap if we are to command the sea, and we must command the sea if we are to live. We cannot afford to wait in the Channel until we are attacked and threatened with

* Very ably by Mr. Spenser Wilkinson (in *The Command of the Sea* and elsewhere), following up Admiral P. H. Colomb.

invasion. Such strategy, leaving great tracts of sea at the undisputed disposal of an enemy, would mean crippling financial loss at the best, and, at the worst, starvation.

There are, indeed, some who hold that we can avoid the burden of commanding the sea by transferring our trade to neutral bottoms. But there are two serious and, it must appear, fatal objections to any such makeshift. In the first place, it is in the last degree improbable that neutrality would be respected. The Declaration of Paris provided, it is true, that a neutral flag rendered all goods inviolate, except contraband of war. But it is in the highest degree probable that the first proceeding of any Power, which engaged in war against us, would be to repudiate this Declaration. The United States, indeed, were never party to it at all. Even those Powers that were, considering it is now forty years old, would hardly consider themselves still bound by it. No treaty can in these days be counted on to last much longer than the lifetime of the generation that made it. But even if the Declaration were nominally honoured, there remains the provision excepting contraband of war. What is contraband of war? The international lawyers define it as anything that assists an enemy to carry on hostilities: arms and ammunition, for instance, have always been held contraband, and coal would certainly in future be so regarded. But would not food also be contraband of war? Indubitably it assists an enemy to carry on hostilities. In our own case it is especially vital, since we should collapse in three months without supplies from abroad. There are not wanting signs that this acceptation would be put on the words of

SHIPBUILDING POLICY

the Declaration. In 1893, when France was enforcing a "pacific blockade" of Siam, rice was declared contraband: and rice, be it remembered, not imported to feed Siam, but exported to feed Singapore. How much more would not corn and cattle be immediately declared contraband of war when shipped for a British port?

There is a second reason hardly less cogent against entrusting our carrying trade to neutrals. The war over, we should never get it back. The United States, before their Civil War, had a flourishing carrying trade. The depredations of the Confederate privateers drove it into our hands, and we have kept it ever since. Without doubt they would be glad, and most reasonably glad, to receive it back again if we were at any time desirous to relinquish the command of the sea. So that even if the Declaration of Paris were, by some impossibility, most fully observed, we should still lose one of our most important industries. It is in virtue of such industries that we are a great nation; but to us the carrying trade by sea is more than a source of wealth. Supposing that in a war it passed to a neutral—the United States, for instance, or Germany or the Scandinavian Powers, who are pressing us hard enough as it is—that neutral would henceforth have our empire largely at its mercy. It would possess the most powerful of all levers for imposing upon us any conditions it pleased. If we refused, it could cut off supplies, and leave us to starve. No doubt we could go to war, and take the trade away; but then it would only pass from the new enemy to a new neutral, and we should have the whole humiliating and expensive process to begin again.

NAVAL POLICY

Britain, in short, is so completely dependent on seaborne trade that she cannot afford to see it even in the hands of a neutral.

The conclusion stands, then, that we must be able to meet every ship of an enemy that can show its nose out of port with sea-going vessels of our own. But even that does not exhaust our disabilities. It is possible, and in many cases probable, that an enemy will not choose to fight any British squadron to which he is inferior, or even equal. Supposing he prefers to remain in port, then we must have squadrons ready to engage him as soon as he decides to come out. During the Napoleonic war we thus blockaded all the important French ports for long periods together. The effort was, to a certain extent, successful, but it was a tremendous strain on our naval resources. A blockaded fleet possesses many obvious advantages over a blockader. It lies comfortably in its own port, and if it is decided to attempt to break the blockade it knows the night and hour of the attempt, and can make it with energies fresh and alert. To the blockader one night is like another. Any moment may be the all-important one when the enemy will attempt to escape. Ceaseless wakefulness, ceaseless anxiety and strain, perpetual false alarms, and perpetual disappointments are the blockader's portion, and even muscles of iron and nerves of steel must in time break down under it.

Since our last blockades the conditions of the problem have been vastly changed by two factors—coal and the torpedo, and the change has loaded a still further burden on the blockader. In the first years of this century the necessity of fresh water and provisions,

SHIPBUILDING POLICY

as well as the even more imperative necessity of resting and refreshing the crews, compelled blockading ships to return to their own ports at frequent intervals; and unless a defeat were to be risked, the place of each ship so returning had to be filled by another. But far more urgent and more frequent than either of these calls will be the necessity of coaling. A steamer, even when cruising for the most part at her most economical speed, can only keep the sea for weeks, where a sailing ship could do so for months. Warships could possibly, in favourable circumstances of weather, be coaled at sea from specially-constructed vessels. But these would need to be very fast to elude hostile cruisers, to whom they would be the most valuable of all prizes; and, moreover, we do not possess such fast colliers. Perhaps subsidized ocean-liners, like the *Campania*, could be used for the purpose, but they would not be with our fleets from the first moment of hostilities. It is, moreover, on such fast vessels that we should have to depend for great part of our supplies and communications with the outside world. At the best, coaling at sea in this way could never be aught but uncertain by reason of weather, and especially dangerous in the vicinity of an enemy.

Of the bearing of torpedo-boats on blockade something has already been said.[*] It is no exaggerated estimate of their influence that henceforth they will render impossible a close blockade of any port defended by them. A torpedo-boat carries, on the average, one-twentieth of the crew of a large battleship, while her cost represents a still smaller proportion. The blockaded Power would, therefore, be in a position to

[*] Page 102.

lose twenty torpedo-boats in sinking a single battleship. There might be occasions—as, for instance, the reduction of the invader's fighting strength to such an extent that he could be brought to action and defeated by the blockaded fleet or by a relieving squadron, or by the two combined—which would justify even further risks. It is certain, therefore, that no effort and no risk would be spared to make torpedo attacks successful. With darkness to help them every night, and often rain or haze as well, it is hardly doubtful that a blockading squadron standing near in to shore would suffer serious losses. The only really safe position for it would be so far out at sea that a torpedo-boat could not steam to it and back between dusk and dawn. The distance would vary with the length of the night at the time of year, and with the speed of the boats; but, roughly, it may be put at anything from fifty to a hundred miles. Now what would be the effect of a blockade in these circumstances? It would mean that if the blockading battleships had to stand out fifty to a hundred miles every night, the length of the semi-circle round the blockaded port would have to be from a hundred and fifty to three hundred miles. No squadron could hope to be so powerful as to be able to establish an effective circle at night-time, when seeing is difficult and scouts must be close together, over so large an area. It would be quite impossible to prevent isolated vessels from running the blockade. It is probably a little more than doubtful whether a whole fleet could be prevented from going in and out. It would be easier for a relieving squadron to get in than for a blockaded squadron to get out. To guard against this the lookout ships must be extended over an even wider semi-circle than the natural line of the blockade, so as to give early notice to the battleships of the enemy's approach, from whatever quarter. The battleships would, doubtless, be cruising together somewhere in the centre of the line—otherwise they might easily be attacked, and beaten in detail—and it is many chances to one that they could not arrive to the attack of the enemy before he had reached safety and reinforcements in port. It was thus that in the 1896 manœuvres Admiral Seymour slipped past Lord Walter Kerr into Lough Swilly. He had a far slower squadron than his opponent, and was aided only by night, which occurs every twenty-four hours, and haze, which accompanies perhaps one dawn out of two. What happened once in these very ordinary circumstances may be expected to happen again and again, and again.

It is true that the advent of the torpedo-boat destroyer has somewhat modified these conditions. Supposing that the destroyers of a British squadron had destroyed the torpedo-boats available to a blockaded fleet, well and good. A rigorous blockade, though still difficult, would perhaps be possible. But as long as there were any hostile boats afloat an Admiral would still probably hesitate, considering the relative value of a boat and a battleship, to jeopardize his battleships within the radius of boat attack, in reliance merely on a patrol of destroyers nearer inshore. It is true that a destroyer might carry coal to cruise, say, for a week, and could use the ships of the squadron as a temporary base for coal, water, fresh crews, and so on. But in time the strain would be too great, and repairs would soon become needful. Thus it would need a very large number of destroyers to relieve each other, and maintain an effective patrol against torpedo-boats. With any port not an altogether impossible distance from a friendly base, a blockade on the old system would probably not be attempted. If an inferior squadron were lying, say, in one of the French Channel or German North Sea ports, we should doubtless keep fast destroyers and cruisers outside that port, and a line of cruisers keeping communication with an English port, in which a superior fleet of battleships would lie. On receiving information of the enemy's departure, our ships could put out at once in pursuit, and even if the enemy were not brought to action, he would probably be driven back into port before he had time to do any harm. Such temporary evasions could be viewed with equanimity as long as the enemy was not so superior in speed to our own fleet that it could join a friendly squadron, and establish a superiority in force. But there are plainly some foreign, and potentially hostile, ports to which this method of quiescent blockade is inapplicable—Toulon, for instance, which is some 800 miles from Gibraltar, our nearest base. In such cases we must either have a superior squadron cruising within moderate distance, or give up the idea of blockade, and therewith the command of the sea, which is the breath of our life.

We can now sum up the disadvantages of the blockader, and see how urgently necessary it is that he should have a superiority of force to balance them. He ought to maintain a superior force before the blockaded fleet; otherwise he will be attacked at a disadvantage, worn out with watching, and racked with nervous tension, by the fresh crews of the enemy. He

SHIPBUILDING POLICY

must be able to maintain this superiority while still sending away ships from time to time for necessary refit and repairs, for coal and provisions, and, above all, for rest. And he must be most abundantly supplied with fast cruisers to maintain the circuit of the blockade and furnish intelligence to the battleships, as well as with specially constructed craft to ward off torpedo attack; all these vessels must be even more frequently relieved than the battleships. The exact degree of superiority required it is difficult to determine — this question must be left to experts' opinion. Such expert opinion, embodied in a committee of British Admirals, has decided that the proportion of battleships blockading to battleships blockaded should be at least five to three. That means that, supposing—on a quite moderate computation—there were eighteen French battleships in Toulon and nine in Cherbourg, while Russia had a dozen in the Baltic and half-a-dozen in the Black Sea, we should require thirty battleships in the Gulf of Lions; fifteen at, say, Portland; twenty off the Sound, and ten somewhere off the mouth of the Dardanelles. In all we should thus need seventy-five battleships to meet France and Russia alone, to say nothing of any other Power. And our total strength, big and small, sea-going and coast-defending, is no more than sixty-one.

Before passing to a more minute consideration of the number of ships we require, there are one or two points to be reckoned in our favour. The first is strategical: that the forces of an opponent are not so powerful divided as they are united. Russia's twelve ships, for example, in the Baltic, and six in the Black Sea, are in a position of strategic inferiority, because a fleet of fifteen battleships might very conceivably attack and defeat each squadron in succession. As we occupy the interior line between Portland and Malta, it is obvious that if the two Russian fleets were at sea, we should be able to join our Channel and Mediterranean squadrons, if necessary, in time to fall on either Russian command in overwhelming force. If France and Russia were allied against us, there would be a line of stations—say Petersburg, Portland, Cherbourg, Gibraltar, Toulon, Malta, and Sevastopol—in which a British base would always lie between any two of the enemy's, so that we might, in some cases, prevent their junction, and thus be able to defeat them with less force. But this advantage is rigorously limited by one condition: that we should have at each of our bases a fleet strong enough in cruisers to find any hostile fleet that might seek to run past and join its friends, and strong enough in battleships of superior speed to catch it and beat it. If this were not so—if, for instance, the fleet resting on Gibraltar and Malta were only strong enough to hold the fleet resting on Toulon, we could only prevent the Russian Black Sea squadron from joining the Toulon squadron at the risk of leaving the latter free either to join the Black Sea squadron before we caught it, or had time to crush it; or else to go through the Straits of Gibraltar, to join the Cherbourg squadron, to establish a naval supremacy in the Channel, and possibly to unite with the Petersburg squadron also. In that case it is conceivable that our own Portland squadron might suffer a heavy defeat before the Mediterranean squadron could rejoin it, and that we should be reduced, on the whole balance of force, to an inferiority. The con-

SHIPBUILDING POLICY

clusion seems to be that the advantage of the inner line can be lost, if there is not a sufficiency of strength to enforce it.

The other point is that if we now set to work and build new ships to re-establish our supremacy, we need not necessarily build one new battleship for every old coast-defender that may be found on the other side. A new battleship of the *Canopus* class is worth at least a couple of *Friedlands*. But this, obviously, does not apply to the new ships that other Powers are rapidly building; these may be inferior to our own, but it would be rash to take it for granted. At present our rivals are outbuilding us, and our first business is to overtake their new vessels.

It has been said above that to blockade the French and Russian squadrons we need, on the most moderate computation, seventy-five battleships, whereas our present total cannot be swollen beyond sixty-one. The computation is called moderate, because it omits all the French armoured gunboats and several old vessels, and also fourteen elderly Russian armour-clads, while including every obsolete vessel of our own. If we include everything of our rivals, we should want, on the scale of five ships to three, a hundred and twenty armour-clads to keep them in port; while out of our present sixty-one we must deduct the *Abyssinia* and *Magdala* at Bombay, and the *Penelope* at the Cape. We should, therefore, have to build sixty-seven battleships to be fit for a successful war this year, while by 1899 the additions to our opponents' strength would make our deficiency no less than ninety.

No doubt these figures are too horribly bad to be true. We should not be likely, for fear of torpedo-boats, to send a fleet nearer Petersburg than the Sound, nor nearer Sevastopol than the Dardanelles; we may therefore knock off ten Russian coast-defence ships of low coal-capacity and of little military value in any case. From the French total we may deduct the *Triomphante*, which is at Saigon, and eight weak gunboats. But even so, the combined fleets number fifty-six ships, which we ought to oppose with eighty-four instead of our present fifty-eight. By the end of 1899 we shall want one hundred and fourteen to meet seventy, and shall have at our present rate of building sixty-eight. Now consider these from the point of view of their fighting efficiency; in point of speed we are satisfactorily superior. Of the hostile seventy, eighteen will reach the combined offensive and defensive standard of fire-energy of 150,000 ft.-tons per minute, and of armour protection for their larger quick-firers, without which they cannot be considered fully equipped for modern war. Of our sixty-eight, fifteen will satisfy this double standard, and, if we add the *Royal Sovereign* class, which protect four out of ten large quick-firers, twenty-three. We therefore need seven new ships in this count alone. With regard to the fifty-two French and Russian, and the forty-five British, which do not come up to the double standard of offence and defence, we do not need to make up our deficiency in full with new and very powerful ships. That is to say, it is unreasonable to ask our Admiralty to lay down five ships like the *Canopus*, with a fire-energy of 394,000 ft.-tons per minute, with all their twelve large quick-firers in 6-in. Harveyed casemates, and with a speed of $18\frac{3}{4}$ knots—to neutralize the three French battleships of the *Magenta* type, which have, indeed, a fire-energy per minute of 380,000 ft.-tons, but expose all their secondary guns to the smallest shell, and steam under 16½ knots. Still less is it necessary to lay down five fine new ships for every three French and Russian inferior to these, the most powerful of such as fall below the double standard. Probably it will be sufficient, in this lower class, to add enough modern ships to make our total number equal to that of the allies—that is to say, seven more. This is certainly the very lowest estimate of our needs compatible with bare safety. The conclusion is then, that to be equal, without any margin to spare, to the necessities of a war with France and Russia, we shall need at the beginning of the century at least fourteen more battleships than we shall possess.

It is in this state of things that Mr. Goschen proposes to reduce the shipbuilding vote for 1897. Of what precise type the warships ought to be may be left to experts to decide, and we may have confidence that Sir William White will give us a good article for our money. But that an article for our money we must have, and that we must be ready to pay the money is most certain, and needs no expert opinion to confirm it. Experts have told us that France and Russia are allied, and that their policy is directed against us. Experts have told us on what principle a war with them should be fought, if this country is to come through it without vital hurt. Experts have told us what proportion our ships must bear to theirs, if that principle is to be put in practice. It needs no expert to draw the inevitable conclusion from the present state of the facts: it is merely a question of common-sense and simple arithmetic. To deny that on the data provided for us we shall be unequal to the bare necessities of war three years hence is to deny that two and two make four. To deny that a battleship takes, on the average, three years to build, is to contradict all experience. And yet it appears that Mr. Goschen is disposed to refuse to take in 1897 the precautions which he well knows must be taken then or never to meet the deficiencies of 1900. Fortunately ministers have always proved themselves obedient on this matter of the Navy to public opinion, if only public opinion speaks loud enough. Fourteen new and powerful battleships would cost, roughly, ten million pounds, to be spread over the four years from 1897 to 1901. Ten millions in four years is not much to pay for the security and immunity from war of a rich country—a country enriched, moreover, by peace and by the traffic of the sea.

A fortunate people should we be if only ten millions were the total price of security. We have allowed our older ships to count one for one with those of our opponents, but, to be able to do this without imperilling our safety, they must be brought and kept as far up to date as their construction will allow. Breech-loaders must take the place of muzzle-loaders, quick-firers of slow-firers, new machinery of old. Ships which are incapable of renovation ought to be replaced by new ones. This is of the very first importance. If all this were done by 1901, we should be ready to take the sea against France and Russia with eighty-two battleships against seventy. That would probably serve, though without very much to spare. After that we should need only to lay down five new ships for every three of theirs to maintain a satisfactory position.

SHIPBUILDING POLICY

We must now consider—still in relation to France and Russia—our needs in respect of cruisers. It is not quite so easy to reckon these up, since we have no guiding proportion of five to three, as in battleships. It is to be feared that five to three will not suffice us: the truth is, indeed, that we cannot possibly have too many cruisers. Their function as the eyes of our battleships is clearly of more vital importance to us than to our opponents. Since our part in war must be to fight the enemy whenever he puts to sea, even at the risk of heavy losses to ourselves, to miss the chance of engaging him would be almost as bad as a defeat. We can only hope to bring an enemy to battle by the help of fast cruisers so numerous that, as they spread out fanwise from their supporting battleships, it would be impossible for him to elude their notice. There should then be a chain of fast scouts from our own battle-squadrons to the outposts of those of our enemy in such a way that, once in touch with him, they would not lose him again until he had been either brought to action or driven into port. It must be remembered that cruisers, being liable to become foul and lose speed, need relieving as much as battleships. There is no recognized standard for determining the number of cruisers required for the efficient performance of the scouting-work for a fleet. The lowest estimate places it at one cruiser for each battleship, but many authorities—including our own admirals—are inclined to put it as high as two. Bearing in mind, however, the fact that in light weather torpedo-gunboats and destroyers could take their part of the work, we may again take the lowest possible figure and say that a modern fleet should have one cruiser to every battleship. That is to say, that by 1900 we ought to possess eighty-two cruisers capable of acting as scouts for a squadron. These should be of a displacement sufficient to make them independent of the state of the sea, and capable of maintaining a high speed for long periods continuously. They should also be sufficiently armed with quick-firing guns to beat off hostile cruisers, or destroy them in case they have important information for their own admirals, and capable of a spurt at very high speed to bring them out of imminent danger, or assist them to defeat a scout of the enemy. Such a type is furnished by our *Eclipse* class, supposing them on service to come fairly well up to their trial speed of 19 knots with natural, and 20 with forced draught. As the standard of high speed perpetually increases, it will be well to add at least a knot an hour to the pace of future vessels of this class.

But these eighty-two look-out ships by no means exhaust our requirements. There are also the independent cruisers, who are to patrol the sea, destroying the enemy's commerce and defending our own by destroying his cruisers. Vessels intended for this work plainly need more fighting power than the scouts, who would only come into action accidentally and occasionally; whereas these others are specifically meant to fight. How much offensive and defensive force they are to have depends on the military value of the cruiser with which they are likely to be found in action. Their proper number, on the other hand, cannot be fixed on this scale. It is of no use to us to have a powerful cruiser at Sierra Leone if the hostile cruiser she is intended to counteract is making prize of British steamers in the West Indies. It is useless—as was

SHIPBUILDING POLICY

abundantly shown by the long immunity of the *Alabama*—for a cruiser to follow her enemy round and round the world. There must be cruisers waiting for her wherever there is trade to be plundered. All the principal trade-routes of the world, in short, must be held by our cruisers in force, and as it will be impossible to say at what exact point the attack of an enemy's cruiser will be made, we should have several ships for his one. How many to one, is most reasonably estimated on the basis of the sea-borne trade of ourselves and other nations. We have nine hundred and fifty millions of trade to defend, France and Russia together but three hundred and sixty millions. On this showing we ought to have eight equally powerful cruisers for every three of theirs. France and Russia possess twenty cruisers exerting over 150,000 ft.-tons of energy from one minute's fire of their guns; we have exactly the same number. In 1899 we shall have gone ahead, and shall dispose of thirty-three to their twenty-nine. But if their twenty-nine had got out to sea—and it has been seen that no blockade could hope to prevent this—our thirty-nine could never run them down until they had done enormous damage. On the basis of eight to three, we want seventy-seven cruisers of the same gun-power—some with a bare 150,000 ft.-tons, others with far more, according to the respective powers of our antagonists. Some of them ought to be sheathed with side-armour to meet such antagonists as the *Dupuy-de-Lôme* on equal terms. They should all be superior also in speed, but this superiority, on the whole, we already possess.

We want, therefore, forty-four more powerful cruisers by 1900, and to them must be added the eighty-two scouts. Of these we shall have, in 1899, fifty-six of over nineteen knots speed, exclusive of the better-armed vessels that have been set aside for ocean patrols. This leaves twenty-six more to be supplied, or a grand total of seventy more fast cruisers of one sort and another. A cruiser very often takes almost as long to build as a battleship, and hardly ever less than two years. Therefore, if we are to reach our proper standard in 1901, we ought to begin laying down at once. The whole seventy ought not to cost much over twenty-three millions or so, and we have four years in which to pay for them. If this is too short a time, considering that battleships ought also to be built concurrently, cheaper vessels, such as torpedo-gunboats and destroyers, might be built instead. But it ought to be recognized that such are but a temporary makeshift, and that we ought not to relax our efforts till we have enough cruisers to supply every battle-fleet amply, and hold every ocean highway against all marauders.

Of torpedo-boat destroyers, again, we can hardly have too many. For work with our fleets, we ought to have at least one to every sea-going torpedo-boat of France and Russia, for Russia has already begun to send her boats into the Mediterranean. This comes to forty-three for France, and fifty-four for Russia. That means, already, seven above our present ninety. We might say, roughly, that our present force would be enough to accompany our fleets to battle or to blockade, since considerations of distance and coal would prevent an enemy from attacking a blockading squadron with all his torpedo flotilla at once. Then, we want a large, but indeterminate, number either of

SHIPBUILDING POLICY

destroyers or first-class boats, to protect our shores against raiding cruisers and our harbours against raiding torpedo-boats, to destroy hostile transports in case of an attempted landing, to protect our coaling-stations and colonial harbours all over the world as local defence, and to patrol such important strategic points as the Straits of Gibraltar, the Sound, or the Dardanelles. No doubt we could also do with a largely increased force of small vedette boats, such as are carried on the depôt-ship *Vulcan*, and can use the ship as their base. It is impossible to determine how many of such craft we should need, and this task is the less urgent in that more could easily be built within a few weeks of the outbreak of war.

Even so, we are left face to face with the fact that, in addition to our ships building, we must have fourteen more battleships, seventy more cruising vessels of one sort and another, and, say, a hundred destroyers and torpedo-boats, before our Navy will be equal to the necessities of a war with France and Russia, as their fleets will stand in 1899. We know that these Powers are closely associated, and we know that they have temptations to quarrel with us. We shall not seek war, and that for the best of reasons—weakness; but, unfortunately, that is also the best of reasons for fearing that we may have war thrust upon us. That, having these facts in view, Mr. Goschen should propose to diminish shipbuilding expenditure next year, would be incredible, did not his own words testify against him. A man who has come to such a decision, with the responsibility for his country's safety resting on his head, must be either much to be envied for his coolness, or much to be reprobated for his indifference.

NAVAL POLICY

Of Germany and the United States—both more than possible enemies—nothing has yet been said. Singly we could certainly deal with either, but one of them allied with France or Russia, or both, would be redoubtable enemies. Germany has the great strategic advantage that the Baltic Canal would give us two outlets to watch and blockade instead of one, which would materially add to the strength of the force required to cope with her. The same may be said of the United States, since their chief positions are far from Halifax and Bermuda, our nearest naval bases. To meet either of these Powers we ought to have at least five battleships to their every three, probably two cruisers to their one, and destroyers and torpedo-boats on rather a larger scale than as against France and Russia. For use against either we might do far worse than build a number of powerful, but small, armour-clads of light draught. These could do work, alike in the shoal waters of Schleswig-Holstein or the estuaries of the American coast, which our latest big ships could not get near enough to attempt. But for the moment, perhaps, it would be as well to concentrate attention on the reinforcements required to bring us up to the calls of a struggle with France and Russia. If we get that deficiency remedied in five years, we must then prepare ourselves for Germany also. The year 1902 will probably see France drawn nearer to Germany and Germany nearer to France, while the hostility of Germany to ourselves can only be embittered by five years of even tenser commercial rivalry. It is not a task of to-day or to-morrow, but a continuous, steady preparation. If, in two or three years more, we can draw level with the three Powers

SHIPBUILDING POLICY

together, we shall have good cause to be thankful. To be thankful—but not to rest. For it is resting after a brisk effort that has brought us to our present pass, and robbed us of that confidence in our security, without which one necessity a nation cannot take breath to enjoy a thousand blessings.

VII

OFFICERS AND MEN

So far we have only been concerned with the machinery of naval war, without any consideration of the men who put it in motion. That the machines are nothing without the men is very obvious; and it is further obvious, from what has already been said, that there never was a period in which naval war demanded higher qualities of head and heart than it does to-day. The navigation of the sea is a profession in itself, calling for a considerable technical education, as well as the moral qualities of patience, endurance, discipline, and imperturbable presence of mind. The naval officer, and even the higher ratings among bluejackets, must add to all this a high degree of attainment in more than one science, besides an acquaintance with the general principles of war.

Further, the height of disciplined courage that will be demanded by the next great naval war almost transcends imagination. To suffer punishment without either running away, and, worse still, without running at the punisher, is justly regarded as the highest test of human bravery. And in the naval battle of to-morrow this is the only kind of courage that will avail. There is no longer even the blood-heating excitement of boarding. Admiral and stoker will alike be called upon to conduct operations taxing

OFFICERS AND MEN

their whole energies, while, at the same time, the target of all the deadliest weapons of destruction that man has yet been able to devise. In a system of delicate and elaborate machinery like the modern battleship, a moment's flurry may mean the dislocation of the whole. To work without a moment's flurry when shot is screaming through the ship, when shell is tearing the steel monster to pieces and flinging the fragments abroad, when poisonous fumes are spreading suffocation around them—such is the pitch of cool heroism which will be demanded of those who make war on the sea in future. To enable any man so thoroughly to quell his natural fear of death as to come unruffled through this ordeal, it is not possible to exaggerate the degree of discipline, comradeship, and devotion that will be required. Yet, lofty and difficult of attainment as are these qualities, it is plain that without them no sailors in our day can ever hope to make a fight against those who possess them. In a word, knowledge, training, discipline, and devotion are even as indispensable to a navy as the best equipment which science has devised.

If it were possible to tabulate, to add and subtract the attributes of a good officer or a good bluejacket—even imperfectly, as was done in the case of material—the problem of naval war would be solved at once. But unfortunately you cannot make a table of weights and measures to deal with the moral qualities of various sailors. There was an old nucleus of such a table which declared one jolly Englishman equal to two Frenchmen and a Portugee; but this hardly seems to afford any basis for an exact comparison. The truth is that if much of the apparatus of naval war

NAVAL POLICY

is untried hitherto, and might give results quite opposite to expectation, the men—the soul of the apparatus—are still more completely untried. There exists no method of determining how an average British lieutenant, or an average French bluejacket, or an average Russian stoker, would behave in the bewildering stress of battle. Courage may be, indeed, confidently claimed for the officers and men of most navies. But it is the peculiar courage that consists of keeping a clear head in the midst of awful peril that will be required for a modern action at sea, and it is impossible to predict that even a brave man may not be found wanting in this when the moment of tension comes.

It is, however, possible to predict that training in time of peace will go very far to produce the desired state of mind in the crisis of war. If a man knows his ship and his work, if he knows his superior officers, his comrades and his subordinates, and knows that they also know their work and him, then the almost superhuman degree of courage required will be appreciably nearer of attainment. To this extent efficiency in peace is the measure of probable efficiency in war. Even so, it is not possible to make any exact comparison between one navy and another. Our own, it is superfluous to say, has nothing to fear from any such comparison. Professional and unprofessional testimony is unanimous that there was never a time when the Navy, in every branch, knew its business better than to-day. Officers and men are assiduously exercised, and show a keen devotion to the service without expectation—and usually without realization—of reward. Nobody can call the Navy a pampered force, unless the applause and affection of a people is pamper-

OFFICERS AND MEN

ing. They take their ships without pilots into waters where no others would venture themselves; they execute manœuvres which no others dare to risk. Their seamanship is the admiration and envy of the world, and their discipline and devotion are proved —now by such magnificent steadiness as the *Victoria's* crew displayed in going down, now by the self-sacrifice of a lieutenant in the attempt to save a comrade—one way or another almost every day.

Of other navies it is only possible to speak in generalities. Probably all are our equals in bravery—it would, at least, be discourteous and unwarrantable to presume otherwise—almost certainly all are our inferiors in seamanship. Nowadays, however, the French are probably beginning to approach us in the assiduous training of at least a portion of their numbers. The Active Mediterranean Squadron is kept in full commission all the year round, providing constant exercise for about 9000 officers and men. The Reserve Squadron in the same waters takes its full complement only during the summer manœuvres, but the ships are in commission all the year, with some 2500 officers and men. The Channel Squadron furnishes six months' training for over 3600, while the foreign squadrons keep some 3000 officers and men all their time aboard ship; these, however, are not so perpetually at sea as our own crews on foreign stations. Altogether, the French may be said to have some 12,000 men in constant, and nearly 7000 more in intermittent, training. This number, it is true, compares disadvantageously with our own. Our Mediterranean Squadron alone furnishes continuous exercise for over 10,000 officers and men, or, with recent additions from the Particular Service Squadron,

NAVAL POLICY

nearly 13,000. The Channel Squadron numbers some 8000 more. On the coastguard and portguard-ships we have, at ordinary times, say, 5000 men; but these receive comparatively little sea-training. Our distant squadrons exercise well over 12,000. We may be confident, then, that so far as training goes—and it goes very far—we are as ready to enter upon war as France.

The number of men whom Russia keeps in constant training is necessarily limited by her climate. The greater part of the Baltic and Black Sea Fleets is commissioned each summer; but the ships have to lie up in the winter by reason of the ice, and this has a bad effect on the efficiency of the crews. The Russian seamen are well disciplined, and of good physique; and they ask no better than to die for the Little Father. But intelligence is not their strong point, and modern war needs a high degree of intelligence among the superior ratings even of bluejackets. The officers —at any rate of the Black Sea Fleet—are probably, on the whole, less accomplished than those of Western nations; the engine-room complements also fall below the highest standard. Probably the ice-bound condition of the Russian ports in winter will always keep her officers and men a little worse than the best. Even the China Squadron, with a complement of over 4000, lies up in the winter, while the new Mediterranean and Atlantic Squadrons only exercise some 2000 men at most.

Germany has nearly all her effective fleet in commission in the summer months. In general the men are assiduously and admirably drilled, though perhaps too much on shore. Italy, on the other hand, though she has a large seafaring population to draw on, keeps but a small squadron in commission. Not more than 3000 or 4000 men are exercised for a year together. There seems some reason to doubt whether the want of training might not once again bring disaster to Italy, as it did thirty years ago at Lissa. As for the United States, the British bluejacket has a parable that they have but one effective ship, and that there is a mutiny aboard that. The statement is true only in so far that a most rigorous discipline is maintained on a few ships, and that there is reason to believe that the picked crews which appear in European ports are more than fairly representative of the men left behind. Probably the personal branch is the weak point of the United States' Navy, though there is no reason to suppose that it could not, and will not, be worked up to the same level of efficiency as the best of Western examples.

On this brief and inevitably vague survey we need be under no apprehension of any want of quality in our officers and men. But when we come to their number, there is a very different tale to tell. Our deficiency in this respect constitutes an even graver and more immediate danger than our shortness of ships. We have not enough ships for the necessities of possible war; but we have not even men enough to fight the ships we have. On paper we have a total of 93,750 of all ranks against France's 70,935, and Russia's 40,000. But to wage a war in a manner which shall not be ruinous to us, as an island people depending for our food on the command of the sea, we need, as has already been seen, considerably more ships than our rivals, and, by consequence, many more men. Now the total number required to take all our present ships to sea is, according to Lord Charles Beresford,

NAVAL POLICY

backed by no less an authority than Mr. Goschen himself, 99,232. Of the 93,750 nominally available by April 1st, 1897, some 7500 must be taken off for clerks ashore, cadets, boys, and the like, and a further 3000 or so for wastage from sickness and other causes. The total number ready to go to sea (again on the high authority of Lord Charles Beresford) will be 82,870, whereas we shall want 99,232. This means that before a shot had been fired, before a life had been lost, we should only have, roughly, four men to do the work of five. This being so, what is the use of counting our ships, and comparing them with the resources of others? One-fifth of the fleet would be without the men to take it to sea and fight.

It must be allowed that there is a consideration to put on the other side. A certain number of our ships are not in a condition to be risked with good men at sea in war time, and we may subtract, perhaps, 5000 men from the number required on this account. We have on foreign stations alone a number of slow, ill-armed sloops and gunboats, locking up perhaps 3000 men, which could not venture out of port in war without the most imminent risk of destruction by the first modern enemy that came their way. But we must remember that these men—some of our most efficient and seasoned—will not be at home to put on board the fresh ships we should have to commission for war. They would be scattered all over the world, and though many of them would, no doubt, be useful as reserves abroad, it would be more or less a matter of chance how soon and to what good purpose they could be employed.

But if we may subtract a little from our deficiency

OFFICERS AND MEN

on this head, there is another fact which cancels all we gain thus, and leaves us still further behind. There are projected on the 1896 programme, and to be completed by April 1st, 1899, forty-six new vessels, requiring 11,200 men. This, added to our existing deficiency, makes us no less than 27,000 short, or—crediting ourselves with the crews available from obsolete ships— over 22,000. In 1899 we shall have 82,870 men to do the work of 105,432. It may be said—and Mr. Goschen has said—that large additions can be made before 1899. That is true, but the additions will not be ready for their work until 1902 at earliest. The least possible time in which an able seaman can be turned out is five years. Knowing this, and knowing that three years on the average is the longest time that a ship takes to build, whereas many classes take far less, it seems incredible that at the same time new ships are laid down provision should not be made for manning them. Yet Mr. Goschen in 1896, though bringing forward proposals for new ships, which in three years must have 11,200 men to take them to sea, made an addition to the numbers of the fleet at sea of no more than 4310. Which can only mean that—bringing in again the deduction of 5000 on account of obsolete ships— he deliberately set himself to make the fleet less efficient by 1890 men in 1899 than it was in 1896.

In respect of officers, our position is so much worse that it can only be called desperate. For 1896 our number of lieutenants and sub-lieutenants is actually less than that of France—1221 to 1232. Counting the new ships to be laid down, we need 1900 at the very least. To train a lieutenant takes longer than to train an able seaman, and he is less easily replaced. When

NAVAL POLICY

we consider the awful demands that war would make on naval officers—the physical strain, the wearing sense of responsibility the necessity in action of keeping every faculty alert, while at the same time animating their men to endure an ordeal of courage as fearful as any man has yet been called on to face—we can hardly find words strong enough to condemn the neglect that has left us so terribly unprovided. One man can only do one man's work, and physical breakdowns, as well as losses in action, would presently throw us back on the alternatives of sending ships to sea practically un-officered or giving up the sea altogether. However, the mischief has been done, and nobody has been hanged; and it is useless to say more about it. We must do Mr. Goschen's administration the justice of saying that the problem has been squarely, if tardily, faced, and that the deficiency is now in a fair way to be made up. Completely made up it cannot be for many years. The replacement of the overcrowded *Britannia* by a college on shore, and the raising of the age for cadets so as to attract boys from public schools, ought to have a further effect in making up lost ground. But the college will not be completed till 1900, and in the meantime it is idle to shut our eyes to our weakness in point of officers.

Neither in officers nor in men are we adequately prepared for war. But preparation for war, in the sense of being able to send all our ships to sea with their full complements, and preparation in the sense of having men to fall back on to make up the wastage of war, are two very different things. That this wastage would be enormous may be taken as certain, whether we look to the probabilities of the future or the experience of the past. Before the Seven Years' War our seamen did not exceed 12,000.* During the war they ran up, including marines, to 70,000. During the Napoleonic War we had, at one time, no less than 144,000 men voted for the Navy, as against less than 19,000 in the preceding peace. Even in the Crimean War, when we had the help of France, and only Russia to meet at sea, we were obliged to raise our numbers from 43,000 —the maximum during the previous years of peace— to 76,000. These figures speak for themselves; but there is an important comment to be made upon them. In the last century it was comparatively easy to make a naval seaman. A merchant sailor, or even a pressed landsman, became fully equal to his duties in a few months. In a war under modern conditions we might easily find ourselves in want of 150,000 men, many of them needing years of training before they could be efficient. Whence should we get them?

We have, as all the world knows, a Naval Reserve. It consists for 1897 of 1600 officers and 24,200 men— a total of 25,800 to fill up deficiencies amounting to some 16,000 before a man has been lost. This Reserve —excluding 2000 stokers—is divided into two classes. The first is drawn mainly from the Mercantile Marine, the second from the fishermen of our coasts. They are inured to the sea, hardy, and, as a body, intelligent; but for the work of naval battle the Reserve, as at present organized, is very far indeed from ideal fitness. It would be vain repetition to enlarge on the complication of the machinery of modern warships, and the necessity that men should have had time to acquaint themselves

* These figures are taken from the chapter on "Manning," by Mr. T. A. Brassey, in the *Naval Annual* for 1896 (page 210).

with it. Hurriedly embarked in a strange ship on the outbreak of war, the Reserve-man would take time even to learn the passages and the internal economy of the vessel; he might actually be called upon to bear his part in an important action without so much as knowing his way about his ship. Even if he knew the ship he could not possibly know his comrades, and this is almost as important a matter as the other. A naval action under modern conditions, it has already been suggested, will be a terrific strain even on the coolest and bravest. To come through it without panic, men will need a more magnificently perfect discipline than is often found in the merchant service, and an inbred confidence in both officers and comrades. So complete a confidence is impossible to the newly-joined Reserve-man; and even if we assume that this recruit will be a prodigy of cool valour—and even a very brave man is not necessarily that without the needful experience—he will in most cases have been most inefficiently trained to the work of war. Training in batteries ashore is not at all the same thing as training afloat; shooting from a rolling ship, for example, is not an art possessed by the first comer. A stationary drill-ship is little better. Further, most of the batteries and hulks used for drilling the reserves are utterly inadequate to give any training for modern war. Seventeen batteries out of thirty-six have not even a breech-loading gun to practise the men at; only two have quick-firers, and those not larger than the 6-pounder. The Admiralty have lately made a step in the right direction by posting the cruisers *Medea* and *Medusa* as drill-ships at Southampton and Shields. But even these cruisers, though comparatively modern, are not modern enough, since their 6-in. guns are old-

OFFICERS AND MEN

pattern breech-loaders, and not quick-firers. A few of the men serve through the naval manœuvres—in 1895 575 were embarked—but the time occupied in this training is so short that the reserves are disbanded as soon as they are beginning to learn.

The further disadvantage attaches to our present Reserve that many of the first-class men would be scattered all over the world in the merchantmen on which they serve, and would not be able to join their ships for weeks, or even months. It is said, indeed, that three-fourths of them are employed at home or in home waters. But even this computation would draw at least 2000 men from a force already so slender that it cannot afford to lose one. Moreover, the Navy exists not to drain the merchant service of its best men on the outbreak of war, but to enable them, so far at least as steamers go, to pursue their necessary vocation in war as in peace.

Two other points in connexion with the Reserve make the case even worse. The nominal strength of its executive officers is 1300, and it has been seen that, for many years to come, it is almost impossible that we could fight a serious war without drawing upon it to supplement the jejune list of our lieutenants. What sort of material is it likely to supply? Of the whole 1300 — on the showing of the First Lord's own memorandum for 1896—only 158 have been, or are being, trained for twelve months on warships. The rest have received virtually no training at all. They may be, and mostly are, excellent navigating officers, and brave, intelligent men. But the complication of modern warships demands more than skill in navigation, bravery, and intelligence; and how is it possible

NAVAL POLICY

that these untrained officers should be equal to the demands that war would make upon them?

The other point concerns the engineers. The total number of engineers in the Reserve is, on paper, 200. They have not served in the Navy at all, so that in the event of war they would be new, not only to their engines, but to the whole organization of the Service. But this is not all. The deficiency of engineers in the fleet is 237. Supposing, therefore, that all the 200 of the Reserve were available, we should still be 37 short of the engineers required to drive our ships. This deficiency, therefore, could not possibly be made up, and Mr. Goschen's statement that we could man every ship by taking 11,000 men from the Reserve, turns out fallacious and misleading. We might take 11,000, but what is the use of taking an able seaman when an engineer is what is wanted? The Reserve, then, is not only no true Reserve, since it is wanted to complete our crews in the first instance, but it is not even sufficient for this.

Very different, both as to quality and quantity, are the Reserves of other naval Powers. France has a form of conscription called the Inscription Maritime, to which the whole seafaring population is liable. The inscripts are entered at the age of eighteen, and at twenty are sent to a naval port. They are bound for a service of seven years, of which five years are supposed to be spent in the fleet, and two in reserve. In practice, the term of service with the fleet has been fixed at only forty months. While in reserve these men may be called out for the manœuvres, but large numbers are not often summoned. The inscripts remain liable to be called out by a Presidential decree

OFFICERS AND MEN

at any time between the end of their seven years and the day they reach the age of fifty-five. In return for this they have a monopoly of the seaman's and fisherman's trades, and receive a pension after a certain length of sea-service, whether in the Navy or on board a merchantman. Their orphans are provided for by the State. It may be that the inscript, serving at sea only from the age of twenty to twenty-three and a-half, is less efficient than the British bluejacket, who is bred to the Navy from boyhood, and serves aboard ship for twelve years. On the other hand, there can be no doubt that he is immensely superior to our own Reserve-man, who may never have helped handle a modern gun in his life. Moreover, the Inscription Maritime furnishes no less than 135,000 men liable to service. Even if it be conceded that only 40,000 men* would be effective and available for war—surely a very modest estimate—France still has a great advantage over us, both in numbers and training. The proportional advantage is even greater than the actual, for France needs fewer men to fight all her ships than we do; moreover war would find all her ships fully manned to begin with. The French Reserve is a real one, to replace the waste of war; ours is a sham. All other continental nations obtain the material of their sailors by conscription, and pass the men through the Navy before they are relegated to the Reserve. The period of active service is usually three years; in Italy and Austria it is four. Russia and Italy both have reserves of 100,000 men. The value of the Italian Reserve, however, is discounted by the fact that the whole numbers have not

* This is the minimum figure quoted by M. Weyl in *Brassey's Naval Annual*, 1896.

received naval training. All men of twenty, who have served at least eighteen months at sea, are available. The conscripts thus usually exceed the number required for the small fleet kept in commission, and the balance are passed into the Reserve without training.

To come back to our own position, it is briefly this. Our present force of both officers and men is inadequate to supply even the ships we have at present; when the fleet is increased in accordance with the 1896 programme it will be still more inadequate. It is impossible that the deficiency can be made up with fully-trained officers and men until 1902 at the earliest. In the meantime we can fill up the complements, so far as seamen are concerned, by drafts from the Reserve. But the officers we can draw from the Reserve are almost completely untrained, while even by wholly depleting the Reserve of engineers we shall still fall short of our requirements. In fine, we cannot in any case send the whole of our fleet to sea, and can only send a large part of it on condition that we half empty the Reserve before hostilities begin, leaving ourselves next to nothing to fall back on. How is this deplorable state of things to be remedied? Five possibilities suggest themselves, which may be briefly considered in order: first, the maintenance of the fleet continually on a war-footing, by keeping up enough officers and men to take the whole fleet to sea; second, the establishment of a Reserve on the continental system by passing men through a short service in the Navy; third, the increase and better organization of the existing Reserve; fourth, the adaptation of the Marines to modern conditions; fifth, the re-institution

OFFICERS AND MEN

of the disbanded Naval Volunteers, so as to form a Volunteer Reserve.

Unquestionably the first plan supplies the most direct and the simplest solution of the difficulty. We want now, according to Lord Charles Beresford's calculations, 99,232 men for the fighting-ships built or projected before 1896, and shall want 110,432 in 1899. If we deduct 5000, as has been suggested, for ships which in three years' time will be too old to be safely sent to sea, we shall want, in round numbers, 105,500 effectives. The present force available for sea is 81,500, which, with 4310 men to be added by April 1st, 1897, makes 85,810. Therefore we have to add 19,690 men to complete the crews of the ships we shall have in 1899. Even this leaves no margin for men non-effective through sickness or other causes. It is plain that the 19,690 should be added at the earliest possible moment, since in any case they cannot be fully trained for war until at least two years after the ships are ready. On this plan we ought to add at least 15,000 men by the end of next financial year on March 31st, 1898. More ships will be required, as has been shown, and for them yet more men.

There are, no doubt, grave objections to this plan, as to any other that may be suggested. In the first place there is no end to its operation. Ships grow obsolete very fast nowadays, but yet we build new ones faster than the old ones become ineffective. Or perhaps a more correct way of putting it is that it is continually necessary to add ships with every latest improvement to our first fighting line, while still retaining the older ones as effective—not to meet the new ships of an enemy, but as a second or third line against the time when the newer ships shall have mutually disabled each other. We should thus continually be wanting more and more officers and men for the active service. This would be exceedingly expensive in two ways. First, we should have to lay out very large sums in pay, pensions, rations, and the like; Mr. Brassey puts the expense at £100 per head per annum. Secondly, it is of no use adding men to the fleet if they are to be left idle ashore; we might almost as well depend on raw levies at once. To keep our full force in constant exercise at sea will mean, virtually, keeping our whole fleet constantly in full commission. Without doubt this would be an enormous tax on the country. On the other hand, it would give the country a service probably unmatched for readiness and efficiency in the whole history of the world.

The second expedient would be less expensive. Two classes of bluejackets and stokers would be formed—long-service men, who would serve twelve years, as at present; and short-service men, who would spend from three to five years with the fleet, as might be deemed desirable. They would then pass into the Reserve, being liable to be called out for the annual manœuvres for, say, five years more. After this they would be placed in a second-class Reserve for, say, fifteen years, and only be called out in the event of war. This is, of course, only one possible outline scheme out of many. Lord Charles Beresford has proposed to supplement some such plan as this by a temporary second-class Reserve, who would be trained during two months of the year. He would stop adding to the second-class Reserve after seven years, by which time there would

OFFICERS AND MEN

be 35,000 second-class men, with 15,000 first-class men who had passed through the fleet, and 20,000 more in course of serving their five years. In eleven years there would be 35,000 of each class available. The total cost during these years he reckons at £3,740,000, while the completed Reserve could be maintained for £1,440,000 a year. As this is not so much as we annually pay for the less necessary Army Reserve, there should be no grumbling at this on the score of expense.

A short-service scheme on these or similar lines would have one great merit. It would form a valuable recruiting ground for the merchant service, which is gradually coming to employ fewer and fewer men of British nationality. On the figures quoted by Sir Charles Dilke in the debate on the 1896 estimates, the British Mercantile Marine contains 63,000 able seamen. Of these, 9000 are fishermen or yachtsmen, classed as A.B.; 7000 are Lascars, and 13,000 are foreigners. This leaves only 34,000 men of British nationality in our merchant service proper—not quite 54 per cent. Without doubt this is a very grave state of things, seeing that it is on these crews that we depend, not only for a large part of our present revenue, but for our food supplies in war time. Many of the foreigners might be removed by conscription if they belonged to a nationality engaged in any war we might undertake. Even if they were not it would be a very easy matter, with the British part of the crew withdrawn, to transfer the vessel and its trade to a neutral flag. The proportion of foreigners threatens our shipping interest with an even completer collapse in war time than it would otherwise suffer. The evil is growing worse;

why, it is not here pertinent to inquire, but probably neither the British shipowner nor the Plimsoll Acts can be held altogether guiltless. In any case the plan of forming a reserve by short-service would tend to remedy just the evil which is now rapidly reducing our present Reserve to inefficiency. It would, no doubt, be necessary to hold out inducements to merchant shipowners to employ Reserve-men. But some sort of connexion on the lines of the fatherly care shown by France for the Inscripts Maritimes—not of necessity quite so fatherly—would be far from an unmixed evil.

The objection to this method of manning the fleet is partly its expense, and partly its inconvenience. It would be highly inconvenient, it is said, to have the long-service men and the short-service men serving on the same ship. Vessels of our navy are usually commissioned for four years. It would, therefore, be necessary to send the five-year man, who would presumably have served at least his first six months in a training-ship, on a four-years' commission by the end of his first year. Otherwise his time would expire in the middle of a commission, which would involve trouble and expense in relieving him, and would be perpetually breaking up ships' crews. It is also thought by some that this would lead to the shortening of the long-service term, which would certainly be a great misfortune. Mr. Brassey also urges that the men would take very unkindly to the merchant service after the Navy. But, perhaps, this objection cuts both ways, and might work for the amelioration of the merchant service. As regards the former objections they do not seem insuperable. They would in any case be met by shorter commissions—say, for two years, which would give each short-service man two commissions in his five years.

The re-constitution of the existing Reserve presents in itself no insuperable difficulties. The first step would doubtless be the abolition of the present distinction between first and second-class Reserve. The latter consists of fishermen, all of whom should be available for immediate service. From the nature of their daily avocations they should be especially fitted for torpedo-boat operations, and boat work generally. It must be owned, however, that the contemplation of the ordinary fisherman does not instil the fullest confidence in his quickness and activity. Boat work, too, for which his calling seems especially to point him out, involves some of the most highly-specialized operations of war—as the laying and exploding of mines—to which he would go quite untrained. On the other hand, his local knowledge would make him the very man for torpedo coast-defence in his own part. He would at all events be a very fairly useful recruit, if he had first served, say, a year in the fleet, which should be the qualification for the first-class Reserve. It is probable that by throwing open the first-class Reserve, with an annual pay of, say, £8 to £10 a year, to men who had served a year, we could get a great many more fishermen than we have at present—perhaps a total of 30,000 in all. At the same time all batteries and drill-ships would doubtless be modernized and used for the training of the second-class reserve, who should also be embarked for the manœuvres.

This scheme would undoubtedly be the most economical. But with a service on which the existence of a nation depends, economy, though never to be forgotten, should be the last advantage to be remembered. The objection to this scheme is the objection that applies to the Reserve at present — that it would not produce efficient men. It is not easy to see how the Reserves could always be got on board ship for their twelve months' training; yet without it they would be all but useless. It would be as difficult to get fishermen to join for the manœuvres, which usually come on simultaneously with the herring fishery, on which they largely depend for their year's living. And even when the first-class Reserve-man had served his year, and the second-class man had had his drill and his manœuvres, they would even so not be equal to the more specialized duties of the seaman. It is answered, plausibly enough, that they do not need to be. There are many functions in war which need no great technical skill, and it is urged that if three-quarters of a ship's crew were highly-trained bluejackets, the other quarter might be half-trained Reserves. That may be. But in practice it would be quite impossible to distribute the Reserves in this proportion on the outbreak of war. Would its advocates propose to ship off quarter-crews of Reserves to China on the outbreak of war, and bring back the same number of bluejackets for the ships to be newly commissioned? Even nearer home, the Channel Squadron would probably have to go off in hot haste to the Mediterranean. As a matter of practice it would be found that the new men must be confined to the newly-commissioned ships. The proportion of untrained or half-trained, instead of being a quarter, would then probably be over half,

OFFICERS AND MEN

and the ships would be quite unfit for immediate action of a serious kind. Even on ships where the scheme could be realized, every fourth man would be an unknown quantity. At the risk of tediousness, it may be repeated that such a half-trained Reserve as is contemplated by this plan ought to be a real Reserve—to fill up gaps, and not to constitute the first fighting line.

As for the Marines, they doubtless occupy an anomalous position at present. Boarding is obsolete, and rifle-fire will no more play any part in deciding the issue of a naval action. The Marines have, indeed, their own guns which they work on board ship, and they work them very well. But it is plain that even so splendid a force, as the Marines undoubtedly are, is handicapped for sea service by the fact that it alternates between sea and land. And after all it is impossible to count on the Marines to fill up the vacancies in the fleet, for the very sufficient reason that they are counted already. The 15,861 are all included in our deficient total. To re-organize and increase the force is doubtless a measure much to be welcomed, but it is not in itself sufficient to complete our crews for all the ships available.

The Naval Volunteers were instituted during Mr. Goschen's former tenure of office at the Admiralty, and disbanded some five years ago. If re-constituted, they could be drawn from yachts' crews as well as from landsmen. They would offer the great advantage that their training, if less continuous than that of Reserve-men who put in a year on board ship, would be more constant. The Volunteers would not give all their time for any long period, but they would give part of their time every week, and thus would not be likely to grow rusty. Admiral Sir George Elliot has made the fruitful suggestion that mechanics from shipbuilding and engineering firms would constitute a very valuable section of such a body. The whole force would probably be found very useful for river and harbour defence. The permanent staff would consist of retired naval officers, though probably the supply of efficient junior officers would present the same difficulties as it does with the Rifle Volunteers. Such a corps, again, having no sea-service to speak of, could in no case be considered as a substitute for professional seamen, though it might prove in war time a valuable support for them.

It is plain there is no scheme which is not open to objection. But then there is no scheme for anything on earth that is not open to objection, and that should be no bar to the adoption of one or another. Certainly something must be done, if our expensive Navy is not to prove a worthless and delusive sham. It is also plain that all, or any, of the schemes stated above, could be used in combination; none is exclusive of the other. From remarks of Mr. Goschen in the House of Commons, it appears likely that he intends to combine the first, third, and fifth expedients; and probably this will be as good a solution as any other. The first is, of course, the best. However expensive, it is essential to the efficiency of the Navy as a fighting force that we should have trained seamen, knowing their work and knowing their officers and each other, to man all our ships in the first instance. It is, no doubt, expensive to keep ships in commission to train all the men we have; but that again has its advantages.

OFFICERS AND MEN

Ships that have long lain up in reserve have a way of developing unexpected defects, which would cause great, and perhaps disastrous delay, if they were hurriedly commissioned, in the event of war. If they are kept in commission, their crews get to know not only each other, but the ways of their ships; and the Admiralty knows exactly for what qualities it can depend upon each vessel.

It would, however, be putting too great a strain on the purse even of the richest nation in the world, to keep more active-service men than will suffice for the first fighting line. For the second, the Admiralty appears to have rejected the short-service scheme, which is probably the only one which can give a really efficient Reserve. Supposing, however, that Mr. Goschen adds to the long-service men enough to man all the effective ships, there is no more to be said about short-service; if the bluejackets fill up all the available ships, what room would be left to train the short-service Reserve? In that case, no doubt, the best course will be to develop the Reserve of fishermen, whose especial fitness for coast-defence by torpedo-craft, in the waters they have known from infancy, might be profitably made the most of.

Only a considerable addition to the mere numbers of the Reserve does not necessarily mean any increase of real power. In judging Mr. Goschen's proposals, when he brings them forward, it must be remembered that a man is next to useless, even to fill up blanks, unless he has served a year—or, at the very inside, six months—with the fleet, and is drilled every year and embarked for the manœuvres. For such men the country ought to be ready to pay a tangible retainer;

but it is simply waste of money to pay the smallest sum to an uneffective man.

It is not at all impossible that the Naval Volunteers will be revived; and they should, if too much is not expected from them, prove a cheap force—useful in time of peace as a link between the service and civilians, and far from unhandy in time of war. But it must always be remembered that the regular active-service sailor is the backbone of our defence; and no fancy scheme of Reserve can fill the place of a very substantial addition to the number of men voted for the sea service. If Mr. Goschen will supply crews to man the fighting-ships, then the country can afford to regard any proposals he may make as to the Reserve with prejudice in their favour. If he does not—unless he adds, say, 15,000 men, or 10,000 at the very least—then it will be the duty of the country to take the business into its own hands, and put its Navy in order for itself, as it has so often done before. After all, it is the Queen's and the taxpayers' Navy, not the Admiralty officials'.

VIII

COLONIES AND COALING STATIONS

IT will be apparent from what has already been said that the first and most potent defence of the distant portions of our empire is the fighting-fleet in European waters. So long as we pin down the battle-fleets of our enemies to their own coast-line they are not likely to find opportunity for any attack in force upon the colonies. None of these, except India and Canada, is exposed to land attack from a first-class Power. It follows that if we are superior in the enemy's home waters, we shall be able to prevent him from doing any great harm over-sea. To despatch a powerful expedition against, let us say, Australia, would be quite impossible. It would be, to begin with, almost impossible for any nation except ourselves to find steamers enough to transport a large army, such as would be needed, over several thousand miles of ocean. A crowded troopship is almost in worse condition to defend herself than a merchantman, and an attack by even small cruisers or torpedo-craft would very easily become a massacre. It may quite safely be said that no Power would expose valuable troops to such overwhelming chances against them, so long as we had a superior fleet posted on their coasts and fast cruisers on the high seas.

NAVAL POLICY

While we are able to do this—which, let it be always remembered, at present we are not—our insular or peninsular colonies need have no fear of subjugation. If we were not strong enough to intercept and destroy the transports of an invader, we should not be strong enough to keep him out of our own islands, and he would certainly rather strike at the heart than the extremities. Yet while most of our colonies have no need to anticipate the gravest danger, they could hardly hope not to receive occasional reminders that they were living in a state of war. We ought to be able to destroy transports and defeat any convoying fleet that might hamper itself with them, but it is tolerably obvious that no superiority in the world could guarantee our whole empire against raids by hostile cruisers. A fast cruiser could break the closest blockade possible in the days of torpedo-boats, and though she would stand to meet and be engaged by a cruiser or cruisers of our own, she would also stand to elude them. She might then shell or lay under contribution unprotected coast towns, destroy shipping lying in them, or making for and from them, besides landing small forces to do serious, if not vital, damage.

A further danger for the colonies in a naval war is constituted by the presence of military establishments of our possible enemies at a short distance from their shores. Invasion in force from Europe we could prevent, but there would still remain the troops maintained by hostile Powers abroad. Thus Australia, British Columbia, Hong Kong, and the Straits are all threatened in greater or less degree by the existence of powerful bodies of Russian troops at Vladivostock. When the Siberian Railway is completed the menace

COLONIES AND COALING STATIONS

will be emphasized tenfold, since then Vladivostock will connect with its European base by land, and not, as at present, by sea. Australia is similarly threatened by France from New Caledonia and, just possibly, from Madagascar;* Mauritius and South Africa similarly, but more nearly, from Madagascar; the West Indies from Martinique. Such attacks would be effective only according to the strength of the permanent garrisons maintained in the respective foreign stations, since a superior fleet should prevent any considerable reinforcement finding its way thither in war time. Nevertheless they might be very awkward if the enemy seized important points on trade-lines, like Port Darwin at the northern extremity of Australia, or Singapore, or Esquimault, which commands the western terminus of the Canadian Pacific Railway. A force strong enough to hold Esquimault also commands the coal-fields of Vancouver Island, while those of Westport, in New Zealand, and of Tasmania would be similarly liable to seizure. Even a small hostile force might seriously annoy our colonies in ways like these.

How, then, are such perils to be forestalled? Firstly, and principally, by the command of the sea. As the general command of the sea, if we are disposed to make an effort to secure it, will protect both our own islands and our colonies from invasion in force, so the local command of the sea will prevent invasion by any garrison which an enemy may maintain nearer at hand. If our squadron in the neighbourhood of any colony is

* France has, at present, no force in Madagascar available for purposes of offence—much less, indeed, than she needs to hold the natives. But when the present troubles are past, it is hardly doubtful that she means to establish herself there in such a way as to threaten at least our trade in the event of war.

decisively stronger than that of the enemy, then that colony has little to fear from the enemy's garrison. The British Squadron must, of course, act towards the ports of these garrisons as the main British Fleet would act towards an enemy's naval ports at home. British Columbia and Australia would be defended off Vladivostock, Australia off New Caledonia, the Cape Colony off Diego Suarez, and so on. The enemy must be beaten at sea if he offers himself, and blockaded, or kept under close observation, if he does not. With a superior squadron in the same waters, he will not be likely to risk his garrisons in attacks which may fail to reach their objective, and must in any case be sooner or later isolated. The Governor of New Caledonia, for instance, would be mad to throw any troops at his disposal into Australian territory, so long as the British Squadron was supreme in Australian waters. The only possible result would be that the invading French would find their transports destroyed or driven into port, and themselves, however valiant and well trained, overwhelmed in time by the Australians. New Caledonia, meanwhile, denuded of its garrison, would fall an easy prey to the British Squadron, and French military power in Australian waters would be annihilated. Thus a superior squadron would not merely furnish the means to defeat any such assault as this, but would almost inevitably forbid the very project of it.

Now to what extent are our foreign squadrons in a position to play this part? Equality, it must be premised, is not sufficient: what is wanted for the protection of colonies, as well as of trade, is such a superiority as will drive the enemy off to sea. We may take, first, the China Squadron—the most powerful

COLONIES AND COALING STATIONS

of those we maintain on distant stations; to this force it would fall to operate against Vladivostock. It consists of the battleship *Centurion*, one cruiser of the *Edgar* type, three so-called armoured cruisers of the *Aurora* type (one without large quick-firers), four second-class cruisers of the *Apollo* type, and two third-class. There is also a despatch-vessel, of little value for hard fighting, eleven obsolete sloops and gunboats, and the *Wivern*, an obsolete ironclad, as guardship at Hong Kong. To meet these, Russia has one elderly battleship (the *Nicolai I.*), four armoured cruisers, including the formidable *Rurik*, two armoured and seven unarmoured gunboats, a second-class cruiser, and twelve torpedo-boats. In numbers, omitting the torpedo-boats, we have twenty-four to fifteen, which is very nearly the orthodox five to three. But then we ought not to omit the torpedo-boats—the less so as four of them are very fine, new, sea-going boats, two of 22, and two of $26\frac{1}{2}$ knots speed. In an action these four sea-going boats might be present, and decide the issue against us; in any case, the twelve would prevent us from blockading Vladivostock. Moreover, if we subtract obsolete vessels, the despatch-boat and the *Wivern*, which could hardly leave Hong Kong, we have only eleven sea-going battle-worthy vessels to eight. We dispose, it is true, of a considerable superiority in artillery, our squadron mounting thirty-eight 6-in., and thirty-four 4·7-in. quick-firers, to the Russians twenty 6-in., and sixteen 4·7-in. pieces. On the other hand, five of the Russians are armoured, and only four of ours. Nevertheless we may fairly say that, considering the present force of the China Squadron, the Governor of Vladivostock would not

NAVAL POLICY

care, even if he had the troopships, to send very many of the vast force he is rumoured to command on a long sea-voyage. Even if we add the French China Squadron—an old ironclad, a powerful modern cruiser, an older cruiser, and gunboats—we might just hold our own in an action. Unless we were beaten it would be madness on the part of the Allies to attempt any operation in force against Australia, British Columbia, or even Hong Kong. It is now announced that the Admiralty mean to send a couple of destroyers to strengthen the squadron.* This is a most admirable decision, in view of the torpedo flotillas of Vladivostock and Saigon; when we are stronger in this type of vessel, it is to be hoped that the two may become half-a-dozen.

Supposing, then, that we keep the vessels of the China Squadron up to date, we are fairly well prepared in far Eastern waters, though certainly not in a position to blockade Vladivostock from the base of Hong Kong, over 1600 miles away. On the other hand, we have the Australian and Pacific Squadrons, which could possibly, in case of real need, afford the China station some reinforcement. The Australian colonists have had the good sense and patriotism to provide themselves with a small squadron of five cruisers of the *Pearl* type, and two torpedo-gunboats. It is quite conceivable that these—though, by the original understanding with our Government, limited to Australian waters—might best be in position to protect Australian trade, and even Australian territory, off Vladivostock; they almost certainly would off New Caledonia. In addition to these, the Australian Squadron comprises the *Orlando* (of the

---

* Also the first-class *Aurora* to relieve the third-class *Porpoise*.

COLONIES AND COALING STATIONS

Aurora class, but without large quick-firers), three effete third-class cruisers, and three next to useless gunboats. The Pacific Squadron, which might in some eventualities act with either of these, has the *Impérieuse* for its flagship, two obsolete cruisers, and three obsolete gunboats. The French Pacific Squadron, which has to serve for Australia as well, numbers only two elderly cruisers and a gunboat, so that their weakness is greater than ours. As things stand at present, France and Russia combined would make little head against us east of the Indian Ocean.

It must be owned, however, that this is rather because they are weak than because we are strong. On the China station we have, indeed, a number of modern ships. Yet even here nearly half the fleet is obsolete, whilst the Australian and Pacific Squadrons are admirable examples of the kind of vessel which has up to now been thought good enough to carry our flag on distant seas. Between them all they have seventeen such craft as the *Daphne*, which carries eight 5-in. breech-loaders, with machine guns, and 120 men, and is supposed to steam $14\frac{1}{2}$ knots at top speed; the *Goldfinch*, which has six 4-in. breech-loaders, 100 men, and 13 knots extreme speed; the *Partridge*, with a similar armament and speed, but only 73 men; the *Linnet*, with two 7-in. muzzle-loaders and four 6-pounder Hotchkisses, 82 men, and $11\frac{3}{4}$ knots speed; and the *Esk*, with three 6·3-in. muzzle-loaders, 46 men, and a possible $9\frac{1}{2}$ knots an hour. Now these ships are not only useless in themselves, but they are a grave source of weakness to the fleet by reason of the men they lock up. None of them have large quick-firers, and some of them not even breech-loaders. It is fairly plain that they could not fight even a small cruiser or gunboat armed with modern artillery, and it is equally plain that, with a speed of 14½ knots for the swiftest and 9½ for the slowest, they would be incapable of running away. Even if they could run away it would be little use enough. British cruisers, to be valuable, must have power to fight, and speed to overhaul the enemy; if there is only speed to get out of his way, while the power to fight is wanting, the vessel is as valueless as if she had neither the one nor the other. The sloops and gunboats under consideration have neither the one nor the other, and it would be the height of temerity to let them go to sea in war time. They could hardly catch the slowest tramp steamer, while they would themselves be in imminent danger of capture or destruction. The loss of the ships we could bear with some equanimity; but the seventeen craft in question carry between them some 1600 men, and it must be remembered that the sailors who are sent on distant service are the most seasoned in the fleet. What, therefore, would happen to these squadrons on the outbreak of war? The ships must scuttle back to port in all haste, and lie up for the whole of the war. Meanwhile the crews must rust ashore, and, while we have the greatest difficulty to man even a part of our ships at home, 1600 of our best men are useless in Hong Kong, Esquimault and Sydney. Why should we go out of our way to thus waste our strength?

This method of constituting squadrons has, no doubt, something to say for itself; every abuse has something to say for itself. The reasons for its persistence are briefly these. We must have a certain force in peacetime for the police of the seas, which duty we have

COLONIES AND COALING STATIONS

undertaken for the benefit of the whole world. If a small, slow, ill-armed vessel is strong enough and fast enough to destroy a pirate junk, or rescue a missionary in the South Seas, it would be waste of power and of men to use a large, fast, well-armed cruiser for the same purpose. Another advantage of the system is that the sloops and gunboats furnish independent commands for officers under the rank of captain: the sooner commanders and lieutenants are put on their own responsibility, the better for the service. Thirdly, there are duties, as in the rivers of China, for which large cruisers, drawing sixteen feet of water or more, are physically incapable.

Of these arguments none ought to be held valid but the last. The others rest on the thoroughly vicious theory that it is possible to have a peace fleet in time of peace, and change it for a war fleet in time of war. It is impossible to change a peace squadron ten thousand miles from home into a war squadron in less than many weeks, and in the meantime there might easily be no peace squadron left to change. We must seek in other ways the advantages gained by squadrons of these unwarlike warships. For the police of the seas a smaller number of new ships would probably be as efficient as a greater number of old. To prevent waste of force the number of ships could be reduced in proportion as their size was increased; there would thus be much the same number of men employed on each station. To display the flag abroad we might supplement the reduced squadrons by sending a fleet of fine cruisers from time to time on long voyages about the world; this would also furnish an opportunity of training Reserve-men on the high seas. As for the junior officers, they will henceforth have excellent opportunities of developing initiative and responsibility in command of torpedo-craft. Certainly no commander or lieutenant would pay very highly for the chance of finding himself a prisoner, whether in an enemy's port or his own, in the first week of war.

There still remains the fact that light-draught vessels are needed for river work. But, in many cases, a destroyer would be at least as serviceable as a gunboat with muzzle-loaders for her principal arm. Our torpedo-gunboats again are fairly fast, carry quick-fire guns, and in no case draw ten feet of water. Where these are not powerful enough, we should have specially-built ships, like the new *Alert* and her fellows, for service in shallow water; they are painfully slow, it is true, but with six new 4-in. quick-firers and Hotchkisses, they could at least make a fight for their lives.

If these suggestions should be found impracticable, it would at least be possible to keep modern cruisers in reserve at Hong Kong, Esquimault, and other headquarters of foreign stations. On the outbreak of war the crews of obsolete vessels should be immediately transferred to these. An *Apollo* would take the crews of three sloops or gunboats; an *Eclipse* of some five. We have always plenty of new cruisers lying idle in our dockyards, and they would be as well posted to open a war at Hong Kong as at Chatham. In this connexion it may be remarked that the Admiralty has of late years introduced the admirable practice of conveying new crews to distant stations in modern fast cruisers, which then bring home the relieved ones. Thus the men are habituated to the new ships and guns, while any sudden war would find relieving and relieved crews

COLONIES AND COALING STATIONS

ready to defend themselves. Would it not be possible to lay up these ships—each of which takes the crew of several smaller vessels—at the headquarters of the station to which they were sent, until the crews which brought them out were ready to return home again? They could have small skeleton crews on board, while it would be possible from time to time to freshen up the men's knowledge of the ship and the machines they would have to man in time of war. Whether this be possible or not, it is sufficiently plain that the organization of our foreign squadrons ought, in some way, to be more adapted to the exigencies of war.

Turning westwards to the Indian Ocean, we find a second-class cruiser of the *Astrea* class as flagship, with three small fairly-modern and fairly-fast cruisers, which, however, carry no large quick-firers. There are also three gunboats—mainly for the police of the Persian Gulf—and two torpedo-gunboats belonging to the Indian Government. It is not an ideal squadron, but it is far more powerful than the two old cruisers and four sloops which represent the French naval force off Madagascar. On the African station—whose sphere of influence extends, roughly, from the Gambia River to the Straits of Bab-el-Mandeb—we have the *St. George* (*Edgar* type) as flagship, the *Fox*, of the *Astrea* type, four fast and handy third-class cruisers armed with the 4·7-in. quick-firer, and half-a-dozen gunboats for river service. For North and South America (which are separate commands) we have also fairly-efficient squadrons, consisting of one first-class and three or four second-class cruisers, with more or less obsolete third-class cruisers and gunboats. These would, it is true, be quite insufficient for war with the United

NAVAL POLICY

States. It is, indeed, a real danger to keep slow and ill-armed vessels on this station, which at the first alarm of war must either take refuge at Halifax or Bermuda, or else be run down and overwhelmed by the fast Yankee cruisers. As against any other Power, however, the present force is amply sufficient. No Power is very likely to attack Canada from the sea, while in the West Indies the French naval force is so small—only two cruisers and a sloop, without a heavy quick-firer between them—that the garrison of Martinique should prove very little of an annoyance to its British neighbours.

We may, therefore, make fairly sure that, with the present distribution of strength on foreign stations, the colonies are safe. No serious violation of their territory would be attempted in face of the everywhere superior forces of this empire. But we must remember that these considerations apply only to the peace-footing of foreign establishments. At the first moment of war fast cruisers would begin to slip out of hostile ports, to prey on our commerce and the outlying portions of our empire. No blockade could be stringent enough to keep them in. They might in time—again, if we had a sufficiency of powerful cruisers, which at present we have not—be hunted down one by one, and cleared off the sea; but, at the very best, this would be the work of months. Meanwhile detached cruisers might concentrate at such points abroad as to establish a local superiority and threaten the colonies with attack. But to meet this we also could, in almost any case, concentrate our cruisers in time to checkmate any elaborate scheme of invasion, and should be only too glad to find the

COLONIES AND COALING STATIONS

enemy's cruisers collected where they could be attacked. On the other hand, it is not probable that any vigilance could prevent raids by stray cruisers on the coasts of the colonies, or on the coaling stations. A small and weak station might even be overpowered and destroyed, while considerable damage to property might always be the result. How are we to guard against this?

In the opinion of those best qualified to judge, the defence should be two-fold. In the first place, shore batteries of quick-firing guns should protect all important centres, and especially all ports in which any quantity of merchant shipping might be found. Such batteries, well protected and well served from a steady gun-platform, should render impossible a bombardment by any cruiser, which must, in the daytime, be thoroughly exposed, and the accuracy of whose fire must be affected by any sea that may be running. To prevent a hostile cruiser from hanging about the port out of range to make prize of merchantmen coming in, or from attempting any kind of night attack, defences on shore ought to be supplemented by torpedo-craft. Even a couple of torpedo-boats would probably be enough to drive off any isolated cruiser.

Now, how far are the principal mercantile centres of our empire prepared to meet such an attack? Beginning again with Australia, we find that the same intelligent patriotism which maintains a fleet of five third-class cruisers, and two torpedo-gunboats, has partially solved the further problem of local defence. Besides these vessels (which were built, armed, and equipped by the Imperial Government, and are kept up by the Colonies) Victoria possesses, as a local marine,

NAVAL POLICY

the old turret-ship *Cerberus*, two gunboats, *Victoria* and *Albert*, each carrying a 10-in. breech-loader, and four torpedo-boats. These are probably sufficient for the mobile defence of Melbourne; though the *Cerberus* might profitably be re-armed with breech-loaders, as the *Abyssinia* and *Magdala* have been at Bombay. As to shore defence, the harbour of Melbourne is at the best very difficult of attack. It is defended by heavy batteries and submarine mines. Any raiding vessel would have to run the gauntlet of these before penetrating to the capital, which lies at the extremity of the landlocked harbour. The forts are manned by a small permanent force of garrison artillery and engineers. Besides these there are some 5000 men of the colonial forces ready for service, and commanded by officers of the British Army. These, with mounted police, militia, and volunteers, could make any landing from isolated cruisers impossible; while Australia, as has been seen, has little cause to fear an invasion in force.

New South Wales is not so well equipped, having only a couple of torpedo-boats to protect the port of Sydney, and no depôt-ship like the *Cerberus* to furnish their base and their support. With regard to defences ashore, the magnificent harbour of Sydney requires very little to make it impracticable of entry to any but the most heavily armoured ships. A battery of large quick-firers, on either side of the harbour, would probably serve the turn. Half-a-dozen modern torpedo-boats might be stationed in the harbour, instead of the two old 16-knot boats that are at present all the Colony commands. Sydney is exposed to bombardment not only from its own harbour of Port Jackson, but from Botany Bay to the south; but it is very

COLONIES AND COALING STATIONS

doubtful whether it would be wise to spend money on batteries here. The best defence is a mobile defence, and this is afforded by torpedo-boats afloat, and troops ashore. The easy capture of Port Arthur and Wei-hai-Wei, in the Chino-Japanese War, proves how futile in themselves are forts on the sea-front, where the defender has command neither of the sea nor of the land. For Sydney, as for Melbourne, the local levies are more than adequate to deal with any force which a stray cruiser or two would be able to land. The provision of more torpedo-boats would make the neighbourhood impossible for such cruisers after the fall of the first night. Ships and men have the great advantage that they can go to the enemy, whereas batteries can do nothing to defeat him unless he comes to them.

For the other principal sea-coast towns, neither Adelaide nor Brisbane is well protected. The first has no torpedo-boats, and would be difficult to fortify; probably one old ironclad and a couple of torpedo-boats would be the most practicable form of defence. We possess a number of old ironclad ships at home, which would be virtually useless to us in war, since their want of sea-going power would put them out of the question for offensive purposes. Of these, three, as has been stated, have been made over to India and Victoria; a fourth, the *Wivern*, is guardship at Hong Kong; while a fifth, the *Penelope*, is at the Cape. There are at least half-a-dozen more, which might profitably be re-armed with breech-loaders, and sent as guardships abroad. Queensland owns a couple of torpedo-boats, which would doubtless be employed for the defence of Brisbane.

NAVAL POLICY

Tasmania and New Zealand must depend primarily for their safety upon the fleet. The former might conceivably serve as a base for an enemy acting against the mainland of Australia, but of course only in the event that we lost the local command of the sea. This is not, on the face of it, probable. Even if it were, it is plainly wiser to put any money that may be spent into ships to ensure the necessary command of the sea, than into filling Tasmania with forts and garrisons which might be locked up quite fruitlessly throughout a long war. For troops, Tasmania must depend on its own resources, with perhaps a light battery at Hobart; against such attack as these could not cope with, the fleet is her true defence. The same is true of New Zealand. Her very long coast-line, the fact that the railways mostly run along the shore, and the fact that in the mines of Westport she possesses the best coal in the Antipodes—all point her out as a happy hunting-ground for the raider. But it is plainly as impossible to fortify the whole coast of New Zealand as it is to do the like for the British Isles; the New Zealanders, like ourselves, must take the chance of such casual assailants as the sea may bring them. To defend the harbours of Auckland, Wellington, and Port Lyttleton, the port of Christchurch, light batteries of quick-firing guns should be sufficient. For coast-defence in general New Zealand might profitably organize a torpedo flotilla by districts; the four existing boats would form the nucleus of such a force. It may here be noticed that, with the exception of Victoria, none of the Australian colonies has added to its torpedo-boats since 1884, and that their vessels are consequently of comparatively low speed, as well as small. This is a

COLONIES AND COALING STATIONS

pity, as modern boats should be very fast to give them the best possible chance of avoiding hits by quick-firing guns; small size again makes boats dependent on the state of the sea to realize even the power they are credited with. To meet any more serious attack than could be dealt with by torpedo-boats and works at the chief ports, New Zealand has to rely on the fleet and her land forces. Two vessels of the Australian Squadron are generally in New Zealand waters. There is also the Imperial Australian Squadron. For mobile defence on land there is, as in Australia, an athletic population largely accustomed to the use of the rifle. It would further, perhaps, be possible to employ the fine fighting qualities of the Maoris.

Two spots in Australia demand a brief notice, not so much for the importance of the local population, as for their strategical position. In the south-west, at King George Sound, the trade-routes to Melbourne and Adelaide converge. It is therefore important that cruisers should patrol the adjacent waters in war time, to drive off any hostile cruisers who might there be expecting a valuable booty. For the support of these cruisers the town of Albany, which lies on the Sound, should be well supplied with coal, stores, apparatus for refitting, and the like. And as such a depôt would be a valuable prize to an enemy, as well as a proportionately serious loss to ourselves and Australia, King George Sound requires a battery commanding its entrance as well as two or three torpedo-boats. Forts have now been completed and manned by a small permanent force of artillery, which could doubtless be slightly reinforced on occasion from the population of Albany. As Australian trade is mainly the gainer by

NAVAL POLICY

such a port of supply, and the patrol which in war time would draw upon it, Australia, as a whole, has reasonably consented to share the expenses of fortification and maintenance with the Imperial Government. The cruisers of the Australasian squadron might fitly be employed to patrol these waters in time of war, especially that second-class vessels of the *Apollo* type are now to relieve the third-class *Katoombas*. This will go far to bring up the squadron to the requirements of modern war.

The other strategical point is Port Darwin, in the extreme north of Queensland. Here the ocean cable lands, and here converge the trade-routes from Hong Kong, the Straits and Eastern Asia generally to Sydney and the Queensland ports. Port Darwin, like King George Sound, has been fortified to form a base for cruisers, and to prevent it being seized and put to the same use by an enemy. The danger of this is not so imaginary as in the case of large towns like Melbourne or Sydney, since the local population is relatively sparse. There ought besides the forts to be at least a couple of torpedo-boats. This would, doubtless, be sufficient for local defence; any attack by an armed fleet ought to bring our own Australian squadron hot upon its trail to defeat it. The defences of Port Darwin are maintained by the Home and Australian Governments in conjunction. Queensland is the trustee in the one case, as is Western Australia in the other.

Stepping over the East Indian islands, we find our chief mercantile centres in Eastern Asia, Hong Kong, and Singapore powerfully armed and fairly garrisoned. But it must be remembered that the enormous distri-

COLONIES AND COALING STATIONS

buting trade of both places, which are the mercantile clearing-houses of all the commerce of Eastern Asia, would be the richest of prizes for an assailant, and that both ought therefore to be ready for serious attack. Hong Kong is defended by our powerful China squadron, and by modern works, but it is doubtful if its garrison is sufficient. In a war with Russia we should now have China passively, if not actively, against us, and it must be remembered that part of Hong Kong lies on the mainland. In these circumstances it would perhaps be as well to recruit the garrison, like the local military police, from India. Indeed there is much to say for the proposal to make Hong Kong and Singapore dependent on India for purposes of defence, as Aden is at present. Both ports had to wait years and years for modern guns, which they would not have had to do if it had lain with the Indian Government to arm them. Before this is done, however, India ought to be supplied with factories and arsenals capable of turning out all kinds of munitions of war, without waiting upon the tardy convenience of Woolwich and Whitehall. Both ports lack torpedo-boats, which would give the most effective form of protection to the merchantmen in and near them. Hong Kong already has the *Wivern* to act as their parent ship, though she is not in commission; Singapore might receive a similar vessel.

The naval defence of India is no direct concern of the taxpayer at home. The Imperial squadron on the station is superior, as has been already shown, to any foreign force in the Indian Ocean. The Indian Government possesses two old ironclad turret-ships, two torpedo-gunboats, and seven modern torpedo-boats. These are not, of course, sufficient for coast-defence in

NAVAL POLICY

any ambitious sense of the phrase, but the finances of India are not equal to such a defence, nor is there any especial necessity for it. The chief ports are fortified and garrisoned, and it is not needful to do more. Invasion of India by sea in any force is impossible while this country remains a sea-power.

In South Africa much remains to be done, but the inquiries which Admiral Rawson and General Goodenough have recently made have resulted in strong recommendations, and an apparent determination to act. East London and Port Elizabeth are to be fortified. Each of these ports has some value as the terminus of a railway, but it is to be hoped that no more than one small battery of quick-firing guns will be mounted at each place. To do more would be to waste money which might more profitably be spent, partly on a couple of torpedo-boats, and as to the balance in sea-going ships on the Australian plan. Cape Town itself has fortifications, but wants search-lights and position-finders. South Africa in general is in little need of defences on shore. The garrison, though not perhaps strong enough to hold the Boers and the vast native population, is sufficient in the absence of other calls upon it to prevent any likely invasion. Moreover, the Burgher Law of universal military service still exists, though it has not lately been used, and British South Africa is full of excellent fighting stuff. There is, however, a very grave deficiency in garrison artillery. This is to be strengthened by the enlistment of "partially paid" troops on the model of the armies of Victoria and New South Wales. They cannot be raised too soon.

The position of Canada, from the point of view of

COLONIES AND COALING STATIONS

Imperial defence, is hardly satisfactory. In this respect, indeed, the Dominion is only a weakness to the Empire, and an embarrassment to this country in diplomatic dealings with the United States. The case might easily be reversed, since the militia of the United States, though admirable raw material, is very far from well trained. A thoroughly well-equipped, well-officered, and well-drilled Canadian force might, by striking hard at the outset of a war, reap very considerable successes before the machinery of the United States Army had got into motion. The truth is, however, that the Canadian militia is not more completely trained and equipped than the force over the border, while it is heavily outnumbered. The land defences of Canada, however, only concern the present discussion indirectly. But for naval defence also Canada pays not a cent. Our own North American squadron, though stronger than it was a year ago, is not fit to meet that of the United States, and in the event of war would have to be largely reinforced from home. There are no torpedo-boats on either the Atlantic or Pacific coasts. Halifax, however, is rather overdone with fortifications than otherwise. It is defended by Imperial troops, and would not be easily captured, unless by a Power with an uncontested supremacy, both on sea and land. The cities on the St. Lawrence are all but wholly bare to attack.

On the Pacific coast the important point is the south end of Vancouver Island, and Vancouver City on the mainland. The first possesses the station of the fleet at Esquimault, and the coal-fields of Nanaimo are on the island; the latter is the terminus of the Canadian Pacific Railway. After years of negotiation between the Home and the Canadian Governments with reference to the fortification of this position, a task which the growing importance of the Pacific rendered daily more imperative, the question has been settled. Vancouver is a vital point in the new route to Japan, China, and Australia, afforded by the Canadian Pacific Railway—a route shorter than the old, and one which crosses none but British territory. As such, it would be almost certainly attacked by either the United States or Russia. The delay in fortifying this spot was due, not to any lack of urgency, but to disputes between the Dominion and Home Governments as to the proper site for the works. The former contends that a station on the island is of no value to Canada, and that any fortifications should be on the mainland. These, with an adequate force, would defend the railway terminus from land attack. The Home Government, on the other hand, was naturally unwilling to abandon the dock which had been built at Esquimault, and preferred to have its naval stations in a spot that is not threatened by land attack. The Home Government was probably in the right; and accordingly Esquimault has been fortified and garrisoned by a force of marines. It seems very unlikely that British Columbia could, in the long run, defend herself against an organized invasion from the United States, and any garrison which our army could spare for Vancouver City—even if it were disposed to spare any at all—would be too small to affect this result. The railway terminus must then go in any case; and indeed the connexion with the East is liable to be interrupted from the neighbouring United States frontier over almost its whole length. That being so, it is better to retain at least the naval station, which can only be

COLONIES AND COALING STATIONS

captured from the sea. So far as naval attack goes it matters little, provided we are superior in the Northern Pacific, whether the fortifications are on the island or the mainland. But fortifications on one spot or the other, or both, there had to be beyond question, and to these should now be added torpedo-boats with a parent ironclad. At present, as has been said, Canada has not seen fit to furnish herself with so much as a single boat of any military value, although she has borne her fair share in the defences of Esquimault.

Most of the prosperity of the West Indies has passed from them since the days when Rodney and De Grasse battled among them for the naval supremacy of the world. But if their commercial riches are largely of the past, there may come a day, and that not very remote, when they will be once more the scene of important and decisive naval action. The growing weight of the Pacific in the world's balance has been touched upon already, and when the Nicaraguan Canal is cut, this will be the main highway of traffic between the Pacific and the Atlantic basins. Opposite the Atlantic end of the canal stands Jamaica, whose strategic position may thus one day be as dominating as that of Egypt. Against this day it is important that we be prepared. At present Jamaica has at Port Royal a fine harbour and dockyard, fairly defended. In view of the canal, and the engagements which might be fought off it, a dock ought certainly to be added for the reception of cripples; France has already a fine dock at Martinique. An ironclad guardship again ought to replace the obsolete *Urgent*, with half-a-dozen torpedo-boats for the defence of Port Royal Harbour. As for garrison, one of the battalions of the West India

Regiment is usually maintained at Jamaica. The uplands of the island are healthy, and this battalion, with the present battery of garrison artillery, might suitably be reinforced. St. Lucia is at present our most important coaling station in the West Indies. Here also it is doubtful whether, considering the troops maintained by France at Martinique, the garrison is sufficient. The capture by a sudden attack of this station would be a disaster, though not an irreparable one. But, considering the strategic importance of Jamaica, we might probably do well to concentrate our West Indian strength there.

The momentous bearing of coal-supplies on the next world-wide naval war it is not possible to exaggerate. Coal will be as necessary to warships as food to armies, and the difference between good coal and bad coal is even more important than that between good and bad food. A coal which betrays the presence of a fleet an hour before the fleet itself comes in sight is a most valuable aid to the enemy's intelligence department. Happily in the coal of South Wales we possess a material which is almost smokeless, while that of Westport, in New Zealand, is hardly inferior. Thus we start well; but how is our coal distributed? To cruisers on the ocean it is essential that they should be able to replenish their bunkers frequently and in safety. It must be remembered that the coal they would burn in war time is by no means to be estimated on the radius of action at 10 knots or so, with which they are credited in the tables. These give only the distance they can traverse at their most economical rate of steaming; at full speed, escaping or pursuing, they burn coal far faster. A 27-knot destroyer, for example,

COLONIES AND COALING STATIONS

burns, per knot, ten times as much coal at full speed as she does at 10 knots an hour.

Coaling stations should be well protected, as well as numerous. Coal will be the most precious of all prizes. Coaling stations will be the objects of resolute and repeated attack; their capture will mean that the victor will take away all the coal he can carry, while what he cannot carry he will sooner burn than allow to be re-taken. Off coaling stations, again, will presumably be fought many actions between cruisers, as there vessels will endeavour to catch an enemy as he goes in or out. A coaling station should, therefore, if possible, be in a position to give help to its friends, as well as to bid defiance to its foes — should be equipped with torpedo-boats to help in a fight, with docks and repairing apparatus to salve its damages, as well as with forts and garrisons. Docks, indeed, we must have in all parts of the world, and docks must be protected against capture and destruction.

It may appear that the question of garrisons, concerning rather the Army than the Navy, is not germane to the subject of this discussion. But it does affect the Navy in a very real, if indirect, manner. Supposing war breaks out, our coaling stations must be garrisoned. If they were not garrisoned already in peace time, garrisons must be sent out for them, and who is to take them? They cannot go in any ordinary mail-boat or merchant steamer. Such a course, unless the transports were exceedingly fast, would mean capture by the first hostile cruiser that sighted them. It is manifest that these garrisons must be either transported or convoyed by the Navy. And that being so, it is further manifest that the garrisons ought not to be transported at all, but to be on the spot at the outbreak of war. The Navy will be terribly overworked from the first moment of war, and it would be as unjust as impolitic to throw any further burdens upon it. Quite apart from this, to leave coaling stations to be garrisoned only after declaration of war would in many cases be only meeting the possibility half-way that the garrison might arrive and find that its first duty was to recapture a coaling station with all its coal destroyed.

Of our principal coaling stations, most have been spoken of in the preceding consideration of colonial defences. Of those which remain, none are important except just as coaling stations, repairing bases, and ports of supply; the amount of protection they are to receive must, therefore, be estimated according to their importance in this respect alone. For instance, the islands of St. Helena and Ascension are not important. So long as we have coaling stations at the Cape, and at Sierra Leone, neither of these is essential. Both being islands, and largely depending on the sea for supplies of various kinds, must fall to the power that commands the sea. To place garrisons of any strength on these rocks would be to waste force which is urgently needed elsewhere. Sierra Leone is in a very different case. It was reported by the Royal Commission of 1878 that Sierra Leone, lying mid-way between Gibraltar and the Cape, and also near the junction of several important trade lines, ought to be retained as a coaling station. Forts were accordingly constructed, but neither guns were sent out to arm the forts nor men to fight the guns. It possesses as garrison a battalion of the West India Regiment, which might easily happen to be in

COLONIES AND COALING STATIONS

Ashanti when they were wanted, and a battery of Garrison Artillery, who live at Devonport for their health. Now Sierra Leone differs vitally from Ascension and St. Helena in that it is not an island. Freetown is not many days' march from Dakar, the headquarters of the vast empire which for many years the French have been assiduously pegging out for themselves in West Africa. With white and native troops, and sailors from the fleet, France could probably put 5000 men in the field against the colony with great ease, and it is hardly possible that they would be baulked of so easy a capture. Supremacy at sea could be relied upon in no case to prevent this. To supply bluejackets and marines enough to defend Freetown against the Senegalese forces would deplete the whole African squadron, which, for the rest, would have plenty of work ready to hand elsewhere. It is difficult to see what our Government means by building fortifications, and then refusing to arm or man them. The ways of governments are dark at the best of times, but a blacker mystery than this it never propounded to the ingenuity of the world. Either Sierra Leone ought to be frankly abandoned in a military sense, or else guns and gunners should be sent out. White troops might live in as healthy an up-country station as can be found, and connected by rail with the coast. Besides these a strong native force should be organized. The Haussas would probably be found excellent material for this purpose.

Until lately Mauritius was more or less in the position of Ascension and St. Helena, although there was no Sierra Leone between the Cape and India. But with the French occupation of Madagascar the situation is changed. Diego Suarez, in war, would become a nest of commerce-destroyers, and we ought to have a station near at hand whence we can smoke them out. For this purpose it is well to hear that a survey is to be made for a dock, though it would be better to know the date by which the dock is to be completed. As for defence, it is physically as easy to attack Port Louis from Diego Suarez, as to attack Diego Suarez from Port Louis. Both fortifications and local militia have been allowed to fall into decay. There is a volunteer torpedo corps, and it would not be inappropriate to present the island with torpedo-boats, to which an ironclad might profitably be added. The garrison should be reinforced, or at least an efficient local militia be organized. Mauritius, like Singapore, might be made dependent on India for guns and stores, were India first made sufficient for herself.

Jumping to the Western Hemisphere, Bermuda need cause us no anxiety, being well defended, and possessing a floating dock. The Falkland Islands possess an admirable situation on the line of the trade waters round Cape Horn, but they are not likely to be seriously attacked by any enemy whom a few quick-firing guns could not scare away. Fiji, again, is in a good position to break the journey between Vancouver and Sydney, though Honolulu would have been better. A little attention—not too much—to the defences of Fiji would not be thrown away.

There remain Gibraltar and Malta — incomparably the most important of all. They are invaluable, not merely as coaling stations, but as the bases of our first fighting-fleet. That being so, they should not only be impregnable to an enemy, but amply supplied with docks, a dockyard, and every kind of provisions and

COLONIES AND COALING STATIONS

stores. Malta is, on the whole, in good case, but the garrison is a weakness. It is said that the Duke of Saxe-Coburg, when in command of the Mediterranean Fleet, amply demonstrated in a sham-fight that Valetta is not impregnable. Apparently Malta could not resist an attack in force by both land and sea; but, on the other hand, it would not be exposed to such an attack until our fleet had been beaten out of the Mediterranean. Then it would be useless in any case and impossible in the long run to defend. What is more serious is the fact that there are not troops enough to man the existing works and guns against even a light attack. A force of volunteer artillery might serve as a useful reinforcement to the regulars and local militia.

Gibraltar is even more important than Malta. Defeated in the Mediterranean, we might be driven to abandon the latter, but we shall only evacuate Gibraltar when we evacuate the sea. Gibraltar is marked out by its geographical position for a most important torpedo station. It is little less than a public scandal that measures to put Gibraltar in a proper state of equipment as a naval base were only taken by our Government after years of persistent pressure from a private committee, with which the name of Mr. Arnold Forster is prominently and honourably associated. Thanks to him and others, the necessary steps are at last being taken to render the anchorage inaccessible to torpedo-boat attack. Until this is done, no fleet could lie in safety for a night, as long as an enemy had a torpedo-boat on the water. Lord Spencer's Naval Works Bill provided for the extension of the present mole, and for a detached mole parallel

NAVAL POLICY

with the shore, while the fourth side of the parallelogram thus formed will probably be filled in with a commercial mole. A single dock was also to be built, which dock Mr. Goschen has wisely multiplied by three. The value of these docks can scarcely be overestimated. If a battle were fought at Gibraltar, than which nothing would be more probable in a war between ourselves and France, to send damaged ships home, or to Malta, might easily mean sending them to founder on the way. These works will be finished in 1900, after which Gibraltar will labour only under the disadvantage that ships in its harbour can be shelled from the heights known as the King of Spain's Chair, and from the Spanish town of Algeciras. But, as we cannot move Gibraltar to any other position—as, indeed, its principal value consists in being where it is—we must make the best of this. We are not likely to be at war with Spain. And, if we ever are, Algeciras, after all, is a good deal easier to take and dismantle than Gibraltar.

IX

ARE WE READY FOR WAR?

To ask at this stage of the inquiry whether we are ready for war is truly somewhat superfluous. We are most unready. We have not the ships; we have not the men; we have not the guns. Our ships are inadequate to meet the two Powers with which we might most easily become embroiled, to say nothing of a possible three. Our men are insufficient to man even the ships we have. The chief links that hold together our empire over-sea are partly unarmed and partly ungarrisoned. This being so, it is absurd to ask in a broad sense if we are ready. The question may, however, be put in a limited form. Are we in a position to make at any moment the most of the resources we possess? It is generally held—though why, it is not altogether easy to see—that this country will never declare war, but will wait to be attacked. If that is so, the attack may come at any moment without warning. Nations sometimes fall into war, as it were, by accident—by some chance spark kindling stored-up ill-will: this was within measurable distance of happening when the Kaiser sent his telegram to President Kruger, in January, 1896. At other times war comes at the end of long years of premeditation and preparation, any trifle being seized upon to furnish the

NAVAL POLICY

occasion: this was the case with Japan and China. But whether war come the one way or the other, it is likely to find one party, at least, unexpecting and possibly unready. There are, no doubt, some nations—Germany is one—which may be taken unawares, but yet never taken at a disadvantage. The plans and the organization are there for any emergency. Whether there is the momentary expectation of using them matters nothing; there is always the possibility of using them. Are we in the same position?

Supposing that war were to be declared to-morrow, our most powerful squadron in commission would be found in the Mediterranean—ten battleships, or twelve with the Particular Service Squadron, and rather more than the same number of cruisers and gunboats, with one destroyer. It would be a chance if more than eight or nine battleships were together between Gibraltar and Malta, leaving three or four in the Levant. If our enemy were Germany or the United States, this squadron, containing some of our best ships and crews, would be out of the game, and in no position to strike an early and crushing blow such as would have great effect on the progress of the war. If, on the other hand, the enemy were France, or France and Russia, the position would be yet more unfavourable. Assuming France to be the aggressor, she would presumably have concentrated her force at Toulon ready to hit us hard and instantly. Sixteen battleships,* thirteen cruisers, five torpedo-gunboats, and at least seven sea-

---

* This number is made up of the vessels at present in the Active and Reserve Mediterranean Squadrons, together with the *Jauréguiberry*, *Charles Martel*, and *Carnot*, which should be complete for sea by the end of 1896.

ARE WE READY FOR WAR?

going torpedo-boats* would put out at once to take our squadron unprepared and unconcentrated. Even if it were concentrated, it would be a tremendous responsibility for an admiral to risk the country's finest fleet against odds of four to three. He might win : British fleets have won against greater odds than four to three times enough. But in the uncertainty attending on the untried possibilities of modern naval war the risk would be a very grave one. Even if he won his action there would still be the problem how to get his crippled ships back to port. In any case the admiral would see himself reduced in the first days of war to the uncomfortable alternative of either running from the enemy or jeopardizing our strongest fleet, and therewith the whole war, against heavy odds. It is, indeed, quite truly pointed out by apologists of the present distribution of our fleets that the Mediterranean Squadron is excellently equipped for running away, having about two knots an hour in hand of the French. But the comfort derived from this reflection is discounted by the facts that we should thus begin the war with the evacuation of the Mediterranean, which could hardly have a salutary moral effect, and that we should have been forced to forego an opportunity of fighting a decisive action which might not readily occur again.

In the meantime, what would be happening in the Channel? In the Channel Squadron, we have two battleships of the *Majestic* and four of the *Royal Sovereign* class, which, with cruisers, gunboats, and half-a-dozen torpedo-boat destroyers, make up a squadron, not perhaps very large, but more powerful

---

* It must not be forgotten that there is also a Russian Mediterranean Squadron—*Navarin*, *Alexander II.*, *Posadnik*, and two torpedo-boats.

for its size than any in the world. France has the *Hoche*, and four smaller battleships, with the armoured cruiser *Dupuy-de-Lôme*, cruisers, gunboats, and sea-going torpedo-boats. Our own squadron is the stronger, and if it caught the French would make short work of it. But would it catch the French? Until last year it probably would have done so easily enough, as their Channel Squadron was then composed of slow and antiquated ships. But now the sea-speed is little inferior to that of our own Channel Fleet. If France were the aggressor, as we are assuming would be the case, she would doubtless have her plan of action ready, and could get some start towards its execution before we could move to check it. In all probability the French Channel Squadron would set off at once towards Gibraltar, masking the operation by a torpedo-boat attack on our Channel Fleet and naval ports. Cherbourg is nearer to Gibraltar than Portsmouth, and Brest than Plymouth; with this advantage, and several hours' start, the French would probably be in the neighbourhood of the Straits before they were overtaken. In the meantime it would be for the Toulon Squadron to run past the Rock—a task presenting no difficulty in the absence of a hostile fleet by day, or of torpedo-boats by night—and unite with the Channel Squadron somewhere off Trafalgar or thereabouts. The combined French would thus be between the British fleets with a squadron superior in number to both combined—much more so to either singly—and could attack and annihilate them both in succession.

Of course this plan might miscarry; though, if the opening of hostilities found our Mediterranean

ARE WE READY FOR WAR?

Squadron so far east as Malta, it is difficult to see what could prevent at least the junction of the two French squadrons. Whether they would then bring one or both of our squadrons to action is another matter, which would depend partly upon the efficiency of the scouts on either side, and partly upon such accidents as weather and the like. Probable or not, the suggested French strategy is plainly more than possible, and it is questionable whether we ought to run such a risk as the present disposition of our forces involves. The situation is fairly simple, and its analogue was rehearsed in our own 1894 manœuvres. The French Mediterranean Squadron is superior to either of ours, the French Channel Squadron inferior to either of ours. Our two combined are inferior in number to their two combined, but perhaps equal in power. It would, of course, be easy for us, on the outbreak of war, to strengthen the Channel Fleet to a numerical equality with both French squadrons combined; but that would take time, and meanwhile our Mediterranean force would stand to be destroyed. Even without any such delay, France, as the aggressor, would have some hours in hand to begin with. It would be almost impossible to prevent her combining both squadrons between ours, and accident might easily enable her to defeat them separately. In the 1894 manœuvres the fleet which represented France was held to have thus beaten the two squadrons singly off Belfast, which stood, in the scheme, for Gibraltar. It might chance, doubtless, that either of our squadrons got warning of the enemy's neighbourhood, and made off. But, even so, the preponderant French would still be between them, and

NAVAL POLICY

it might be found difficult exactly to time a joint attack.

This strategical situation would not be necessarily disastrous; but, on the whole, it rather invites disaster than not. It has completely changed since the French Admiralty substituted a 16-knot for a 12¾-knot Channel Squadron. The question arises, therefore, whether we should not also re-adjust our dispositions to meet the new situation.

There is an influential school of writers and thinkers who would re-adjust our dispositions very thoroughly indeed by abandoning the Mediterranean altogether. This radical scheme was elaborated a year or two ago, with great ability and imagination, by an anonymous correspondent in the *Pall Mall Gazette*, under the name of "An Impossible Programme." It has been reinforced since, with the authority of Sir George Clark and Mr. Laird Clowes, and there is no inconsiderable body of naval opinion in its favour. It would be idle to deny that there is a good deal to be said for the idea, both on political and strategical grounds. Its advocates urge that the retention of a fleet in the Mediterranean is a relic of the days when we were an European Power, instead of a world-wide Empire standing outside the alliances of the Continent, as at present. The abandonment of the Mediterranean would mean the evacuation of Egypt, which would conciliate France; of Cyprus, which would conciliate Turkey; and of Malta, which the author of the "Impossible Programme" ingeniously proposed to sell to the Pope, and then to apply the proceeds to a Catholic University for Ireland. A further disembarrassment would be that we should in future have no excuse for hampering our diplomacy

ARE WE READY FOR WAR?

with Armenians and other more or less Christian subjects of the Porte. The surrender in war of the control of the Suez Canal, which evacuation would entail, is defended on the ground that the Canal would be almost certainly blocked or destroyed in any case.

Strategically, this policy has in its favour the unquestionable fact that France must always have the advantage of the interior line in the Mediterranean; it would be different if we had never lost Minorca. It is proposed, in the event of evacuation, that we should gain the consent of the delighted Continental Powers to establishing ourselves on the south side of the Straits, as well as at Gibraltar, so as to be able more effectively to seal this outlet of the Mediterranean. We should then repeat the process at Aden.

These are all advantages which it would be futile to disregard, and which it is not altogether easy to depreciate. On the other hand, there are grave countervailing disadvantages in such a scheme, and, on the whole—though the balance of reason is fairly level on either side—the disadvantage perhaps outweighs the gain. So far as the political argument goes, the first effect of it would be to throw Italy into the arms of any combination against us. It is doubtful whether, as against this, we should reap very much good-will by abandoning Egypt, Cyprus, and Malta. In morals it may be more blessed to give; but in international policy it is distinctly preferable to receive. To give means not only to lose what is given, but to lose caste and credit as well, while there is no such thing as gratitude in dealings between nations. France would thank us for leaving

Egypt by taking it for herself; such, at any rate, is the opinion of a prominent French Parliamentarian. Nor is it likely that the Sultan would forget his ill-will towards us in the joy of receiving Cyprus. Moreover, it may plausibly be suggested that, in giving up parts of our Empire to facilitate the work of our fleet, we are putting the cart before the horse. The fleet was made for the Empire, not the Empire for the fleet.

It may further be doubted whether the strategical advantages of abandoning the Mediterranean would be, in fact, as great as they are made out to be. Is it suggested that in war we should enter the Mediterranean or not? If yes, why give up Malta, with its docks and dockyard, when Malta might easily prove an invaluable coaling and repairing base, to say nothing of an admirable station whence to prevent a junction between the French and the Russian Black Sea Fleet? If no, where is the strategic gain? To prevent the French Fleet from breaking out of the Mediterranean, we must keep a superior fleet at both ends—in plain language, we shall want two ships, where now we want one. In reply, it is urged that we shall need no great force at Aden—that it is as easy for us to block or destroy the Suez Canal as for our enemies. So no doubt it is. But, with a French military occupation of Egypt, Canal and all, the blocking of it could never be depended on with absolute surety, while it would matter little to the French how often it was blocked as long as it was clear the one day they wished to pass it. There is more point in the argument that a heavy squadron of battleships would have no very obvious objective east of the Red Sea; yet, even so, they could doubtless make things very unpleasant for

ARE WE READY FOR WAR?

us in India and elsewhere. Giving away the question of the eastern outlet, it may still be doubted if there is true strategical wisdom in concentrating our fleet to pen the enemy at Gibraltar. Why should we give up the offensive, and allow France and Russia—supposing them allied against us—to concentrate at their leisure? After all, if we keep to the Mediterranean, it is always possible that we might find the French fleet at sea and beat it, while the relatively low coal-endurance and speed of the Russian Black Sea Squadron would give us a very fair chance of dealing with it in like manner. Whereas if we sit down at the mouth of the Mediterranean, why should the war ever cease? Certainly it is difficult to see how we should be helping to defeat the enemy by abandoning to him the £54,000,000 of our annual trade to Mediterranean ports. Considering that the object of the enemy would be exactly to starve us out by destroying our trade, this policy would be more adapted to defeat ourselves.

On the other hand, if we want to command the Mediterranean, and carry the war up to the enemy's coast, we want a stronger squadron in that sea than we have at present. It is too much to expect that the Channel Fleet, with further to go, and probably less time to go in, could reinforce it before it fell in with a superior force. It might, with luck; but a wise policy will not leave the destinies of our Empire to luck. We must recognize the fact that the Mediterranean station, though not the nearest home, is the most important. There is to be found the strongest non-English fleet in the world—the combined French Mediterranean squadrons; and where the strongest enemy is, there should our strongest fleet be also. In

NAVAL POLICY

estimating the degree of force required, we must not regard the fact that the French Reserve Squadron has, at most seasons of the year, only part of its complement on board. The crews can be brought up to war strength at any moment from the depôt at Toulon, whereas our own crews cannot be so supplemented at Malta or Gibraltar. We ought, therefore, to keep in full commission a force equal in all respects to the French Active and Reserve Squadrons together. At the present moment we almost attain this standard, having twelve battleships to thirteen; but that includes the two battleships of the Particular Service Squadron, while the French numbers will shortly be increased as new ships are completed for the pennant. With regard to cruisers, the Mediterranean station, being the most important, should be supplied with newer, faster, and more powerful vessels than the *Blanche*—sent out this year—which even on trial made less than 17 knots, or the *Scout*, which has not even quick-firers. We have a dozen ships of the *Apollo* class lying in the basins at home which might be well employed in relieving these older craft. One destroyer, again, is not enough. There should be at least one for each French sea-going boat in commission. The Admiralty has, indeed, done well to send out more of this class lately; but since the experience of the *Ardent* appears to show Mediterranean waters very suitable for these delicate craft, at least half a dozen more might without disadvantage be added to these. We ought, also, to add vessels to neutralize the two battleships and three torpedo-craft of the Russian squadron in Mediterranean waters. These additions would probably bring up the squadron to its full

ARE WE READY FOR WAR?

requirements on a sudden outbreak of war. We could hardly expect the Admiralty to maintain, in the Mediterranean, a fleet equal to the full strength of France and Russia, whether in commission or not. The Channel Squadron should arrive in time to neutralize these; and, if more ships are wanted, there are the coastguard and portguard-ships, which have only to fill up with their complete crews. If we cannot mobilize fast enough to bring these ships, and those of the Fleet Reserves, into play in the first day or two of war, then we should do well to give our attention first to mobilization.

The word mobilization suggests another respect in which we may or may not be ready for war. All vessels placed in what is called the A Division of the Fleet Reserve are supposed to be available for sea within forty-eight hours. On the opening of war, this supposition would be put to the severest proof; otherwise we might be beaten by a ready enemy while still engaged in preparing great part of our fleet for sea. In future wars the power that is ready to strike the first blow will not unlikely gain thereby material, and still more moral, advantage which may easily turn out decisive. It was so with Germany and with Japan. France and China had doubtless tremendous reserves of strength, but instead of developing them, they found their initial unreadiness only the precursor of ever more irremediable confusion. It is not to be supposed that we are in so bad a state as China, or as France in 1870. Yet it would be a relief to be persuaded that we are as well prepared to put forth our whole strength without delay, without hitch, as were Japan and Germany.

What grounds have we for such a confidence? The

answer to this question, as to most others that bear on our readiness for war, is that we do not know. We are told that the ships are ready, but what little evidence is to be had points in the opposite direction. There is, indeed, an annual mobilization for the Naval Manœuvres, but the actual date of this is known for weeks beforehand, and the approximate date is always the same from year to year. Now France or Russia or Germany would not give us a month's notice of their intention to declare war, nor would they choose the exact moment when they knew we were mobilizing in any case for the Manœuvres. So that any results achieved at this season go for nothing as a real test of our preparation. When anything in the nature of a serious test is imposed, the dockyard authorities are usually found wanting. The *Swiftsure*, which is in the A Division of the Reserve, was recently called on for service, but she was found wanting; she could not be ready for some weeks. Or take again the commissioning of the Particular Service Squadron in January, 1896. Enthusiastic newspapers have spoken of this achievement as the fitting out of a squadron more powerful than any of Germany's within forty-eight hours. But if we descend to dates and figures, it was no more fitted out in forty-eight hours than it was a match for the German Navy. The announcement of the Admiralty's decision, and the lists of the principal officers, were published on January 8th. All the ships were officially supposed to be ready within forty-eight hours; it had even been announced by the *Army and Navy Gazette* three weeks before that all but the destroyers were to be commissioned in January. Yet in spite of the supposed readiness of the ships, they were

ARE WE READY FOR WAR?

not actually commissioned till January 14th. The first vessel left port rather over forty-eight hours after hoisting the pennant, and it was not until January 20th, twelve days after the order to mobilize, that the fleet was actually able to put to sea.

Now this, instead of being extolled as an extraordinary achievement, ought to have been the occasion of a searching inquiry into our whole arrangements for mobilization. If it is impossible that a number of ships can be got ready for sea within forty-eight hours, why does the Admiralty foster the delusion that they can? If it is possible, where was the fault, and whose was the blame, that these ships were kept six times as long fitting out as they should have been? It is true that there was a collision between a destroyer and a battleship, while another destroyer broke down. But that would be more, and not less, likely to happen in actual war. Moreover, if these ships were in the A Division of the Reserve, they should not have broken down; for presumably it is possible to keep the machinery overhauled and in order. There was also the fact that, Chatham being short of certain ratings, they had to be sent from Devonport by train. But what sort of organization is it that keeps ships at Chatham, and the men to take them to sea at Devonport? That, in itself, is a sign that our arrangements for mobilization are not what they should be. On this head there is no more emphatic testimony than that of the *Army and Navy Gazette*, which is, as a rule, no way disposed to be needlessly alarmist. "The system of skeleton crews and cadres for mobilization," says that service organ, "is of the most haphazard character. Much more remains to be done, if we are not to deceive ourselves, before we can feel that our system is as good as, for example, that of the German." Is it too much to ask of this country that it should be as ready for naval war as Germany?

It was suggested above that the first move of France —or, for that matter, perhaps of Germany also—in a war with this country would be to hurl a flotilla of torpedo-boats upon one or each of our naval ports. If the attack succeeded, it might heavily disable us at the very outset; if it failed, it would still cause considerable confusion, and call off attention from any other movement that might be contemplated. This danger would probably come upon us without warning, and almost certainly without declaration of war. There are always a number of ships moored to the jetties in Portsmouth Harbour inviting the torpedo. Are we prepared to meet this contingency? Again the answer is, we do not know. It is almost incredible that we should not be prepared, since the probability of this kind of attack has been the commonplace of alarmist prophets for years. There are flotillas of destroyers in commission attached to Portsmouth, Devonport, and Sheerness; but these would not necessarily be on the spot at the moment of attack. Then there are forts enough, as well as booms and similar defences; but it is doubtful whether the big guns of the former are adapted to hit moving torpedo-boats, while the latter would only be in position in war time. What precautions are to be taken in peace time against any such surprise must, of course, be left to the judgment of experts. But the inexpert public may, at least, ask for an assurance that precautions of some sort there are.

A further point arising out of this concerns the

ARE WE READY FOR WAR?

command of our naval ports. It is fairly obvious that if the command of a great organization like the defences of Portsmouth is to be effective, it must be centred in a single officer. It is also not altogether difficult to conclude that in the case of a naval port that officer ought to be a sailor. The defence of such places can only be efficiently carried out by the smooth and harmonious combination of troops ashore, forts ashore, mine-fields, torpedo-boats, and destroyers. Yet in our system the troops and forts are under the military authorities, the submarine mines—which are surely naval work—are given over to the Royal Engineers, with the assistance of militiamen recruited from the seafaring class, while the torpedo-defence is under the Admiral. How these different authorities are expected to work together efficiently at a moment's notice, only our wonderful Government offices can tell. Certainly it will not be through practice during peace, for such practice is conspicuously absent. Most incredible of all, the very ammunition of the fleet is supplied by the War Office, and not by the Admiralty, which is responsible for the fleets' movements. "The coast-defence of Great Britain," says the official report of an United States officer, "is notably the most inefficient of the European Powers. Owing to the divided control, lack of co-operation, absence of digested schemes for mutual support, and the mixing of naval and military duties, the defence is unwieldy in its administration, unprepared for sudden work, and labours under the disadvantage of placing military men in situations outside their legitimate sphere of action." A further disability of the British system of giving over shore-defence to military command is that a soldier will in many cases not possess the necessary knowledge of the weak points of attacking ships, nor be able so readily to detect their intention from any manœuvres they may go through. But it is useless to multiply disadvantages: briefly, our system of semi-military, semi-naval defence is as clumsy and chaotic as can be. Germany, France, Italy, have all placed their coast-defence in charge of an admiral for each district. The faults of our own organization, or disorganization, have been freely pointed out and fully recognized for at least ten years. To the official mind, it would appear, the recognition of an abuse compromises the necessity for its reform.

To come to an end of fault-finding, our whole Admiralty system appears expressly designed to be unready for war. Nobody is responsible for the sufficiency of our naval preparations, and nobody is responsible for the systematic employment of what preparation there is. In many lands, as is well known to all interested in foreign affairs, there exists such a thing as a General Staff, with a Chief of the Staff at its head. The Prussian General Staff—the creation of Von Moltke, from which all the others are derived—is simply described by Sir Charles Dilke as "nothing more than the application to military purposes of the principle on which civil businesses are conducted. In each case what is first needed is the best information upon the facts. Then plans are formed, anticipating those of others who are likely to become opponents."* A General Staff collects information as to the preparations, movements, and designs of other Powers, and arranges

* For a most detailed description of the functions of a General Staff, see Mr. Spenser Wilkinson in *The Brain of an Army*.

ARE WE READY FOR WAR?

how it is to meet them. It has a definite scheme for fighting any and every enemy. Thus, an English Chief of the Staff would know what force he wanted to fight France, what to fight Russia, what to fight France and Russia, and so on. He would also know how the force was to be disposed; where he intended to make his attack; how he proposed to meet probable attacks by the enemy. To the General Staff also is committed the training of officers for war. The Chief will have had a constant succession of officers through his hands; he will know their capabilities to a greater or less extent, and be able to advise as to the position in the general scheme which each is fitted to fill. In a word, the Chief of the Staff is a man whose business in life it is to organize war, and it is to be presumed that, such being his business, he will organize it well.

Now, if the Germany Army, with comparatively few and simple tasks before it, requires a professional organizer, with a staff of subordinate professional organizers behind him, to put it in readiness for its work, how much more does not the British Navy? The problems which it will have to face in war are of an infinite and world-wide conplexity; it is indispensable that they should have been thought out and provided against beforehand. At present it is difficult to believe and impossible to be sure that this has been done. It is quite true that there is attached to the Admiralty an Intelligence Department, presided over by a captain, which has functions analogous to those of one branch of the General Staff in continental countries. But this department, though strong in ability, is numerically weak. What is worse, it is weak in official stand-

NAVAL POLICY

ing and authority; the Director of Naval Intelligence can make representations, but he cannot command their adoption. He cannot even ensure a reasonable amount of attention for them, unless his superiors choose to bestow it. If the German Chief of the Staff represented that a certain force was necessary for a certain not improbable war, he would either have his way or he would decline to be responsible for the safety of the country in such a war. If the Director of Naval Intelligence did the same, his opinion would, like as not, be left to the mercy of the First Lord, to be over-ruled for the first party advantage, real or imaginary, that presented itself.

The truth is that in this country it is nobody's business to hold the Navy in readiness for war. Nobody is personally responsible, and therefore the thing is not done. The First Lord's professional advisers, the Naval Lords of the Admiralty, are doubtless responsible to him; so is the First Lord to the Cabinet, the Cabinet to the House of Commons, and the House to the country. But this 'House-that-Jack-built' of responsibility comes, in the end, to no responsibility at all. The naval advisers at one end are sincerely anxious that the Navy should be sufficient for all not impossible demands upon it, and know what these demands would entail. The general sense of the country at the other end is as anxious that the Navy should be sufficient for all emergencies, though not knowing how much sufficiency implies. Between the two is the solid buffer presented by the First Lord, the Cabinet, and the House of Commons. The First Lord is too often an eminent party hack, who has to be made room for in the Cabinet somehow, and is put

ARE WE READY FOR WAR?

into the Admiralty as being a position of dignity in which he can do his party neither much good, nor much harm. It must be remembered that the First Lord has no direct responsibility to the country. He is a member of the Cabinet, which stands or falls together. Mr. Goschen, in the debate on the 1896 Estimates, professed himself ready to take the full responsibility for measures affecting the Navy. It is a cheap kind of responsibility, for it is not the First Lord's responsibility at all, but the Cabinet's. The defeat of the Rosebery Government illustrates this point exactly. It was Sir Henry Campbell-Bannerman's administration of the War Office that was censured; but it was the whole Cabinet—not Sir Henry personally —that resigned. No doubt there might be a First Lord who, by some mental twist, preferred his country to his place and his party, and resigned if his colleagues refused to allow him the money necessary for the efficiency of the service. Lord Charles Beresford set the example as Junior Lord; but it is perhaps too much to expect of a First Lord and Cabinet Minister. He is content to pass the matter on to his colleagues of the Cabinet. They would be very happy to oblige him. But it is not so much their business to put the country in a proper state of defence, as to knock a penny off the income-tax, and put themselves, if possible, into another tenure of office. As the result, inadequate Estimates come year by year before the House of Commons. The few members who have studied naval questions explain that they are inadequate; the First Lord replies that the Admiralty has given, is giving, and will give the subject most careful consideration. The First Lord's party follows

NAVAL POLICY

him into the Lobby—it has to, or face a General Election—and the Estimates are passed.

It is not to be supposed that either the Sea Lords, or the First Lord, or the Cabinet, or the House, or the country, intends to leave the Navy insufficient to perform its duties. But it is nobody's duty particularly to see that it is sufficient. Each can shuffle off responsibility on to the next man, and each very naturally does so. Those who know, have not the power to bring the Navy up to its requirements; those who have the power—the private member of Parliament and his constituents—do not know. The result is inevitable and deplorable. Our fleet ought to be increased steadily, and on a reasoned plan, according to the requirements of probable war as computed by the best authority. In practice it declines for three or four years, and then there is a scare. Popular pressure is put upon the Government, and the First Lord, who complacently declared our force amply sufficient in one year, as complacently takes credit for increasing it in the next. If the scare is inspired by any definite danger, as was the case during the Crimean or Russo-Turkish Wars, or the Penjdeh incident on the Afghan frontier, it is usual to spend millions of money in the most wasteful way. Ships are bought up in a hurry, and naturally turn out extravagant failures. When the pressure of public opinion is exerted on the general ground of the inadequacy of the fleet, the money is spent more reasonably. Yet such a method of attending to the first interest of the country by fits and starts, is at its best highly undignified, and is especially discreditable to our successive Governments. It also has the bad result that when

ARE WE READY FOR WAR?

the moment's perturbation is passed, people and politicians alike become lethargic again; the Navy is again neglected until, in a few years, there is another scare. It is only by the greatest good luck that we have been able to see-saw thus through forty years without serious disaster.

Now if Parliament and the country were allowed to know the opinion of responsible experts about our naval strength, this most unbusinesslike conduct of our national affairs would become impossible at once. Let us imagine our Chief of the Staff—it does not matter what he is called—installed at the Admiralty. It is his duty, in case of war, to tell the First Lord how that war is to be fought and won. He knows, or thinks he knows, how many battleships, cruisers, and torpedo-craft, will be required for this war; what coaling-stations, and with what garrisons; what system of coast defence, and so on. He knows how much money this will cost. If the First Lord comes to him and offers to spend less money than the necessary minimum, he will object. If the First Lord thereon refuses to increase the money up to the sum necessary, the Chief of the Staff cannot force him to do so. But he can, and ought to, declare that he considers the provision granted him inadequate, and that he will not make himself responsible for the success of a campaign unless he gets more resources to do it with. The truth is that his view of the provision made by each year's Estimates ought to be accessible to members of Parliament and to the public. Is the Chief of the Staff ready to see us through a war on these Estimates? should be the first question of the debate. It may be a violation of the Constitution to bring him into the case; but, if so, then the Constitution ought to be altered. The country would then, in case of conflict between the expert adviser and the political First Lord, be left to decide between them. Supposing that the Chief of the Staff approved certain Estimates, which were afterwards found to be inadequate, then he ought to be broke. If the Cabinet insisted on giving less for the Navy than he wanted, and this were afterwards proved inadequate, then the Cabinet ought to be impeached. In either case, the full penalty ought to be exacted without mercy. We are prepared to confer upon those who thus serve us the highest honours we have to bestow; we should be prepared to punish them as remorselessly if they fail us in our supremest need.

If this system, or some analogous system, were adopted we might soon rest secure. To those responsible the adequacy or inadequacy of the Navy would mean their whole careers—just as at bottom it means the nation's whole career—and it would shortly be superfluous to ask whether or not we were ready for war.

There remains, however, one element of readiness which cannot be affected by any administrative change. That element is the force of popular opinion. In time of peace, popular opinion is most properly concerned with the strength of the Navy; it is, indeed, directly due to its expression that we are even as well prepared for war as we are. But those who have clamoured, and most rightly and necessarily clamoured, for an increase of the Navy in time of peace, must remember that their function ceases from the first moment of war. Public pressure on the Government

ARE WE READY FOR WAR?

to alter its plans in war time might easily be almost irresistible, and as easily quite fatal. It is conceivable, for example, that popular feeling might insist on keeping a powerful force in the Channel when strategy cried aloud that it should be sent elsewhere. To the lay mind it is a hard saying that we should be saved from invasion in the Channel by sending the Channel Squadron to the Mediterranean. It might happen that it was too hard a saying—that the Channel Squadron was kept useless at home, and that thereby we suffered a crushing defeat. Still more urgent might be the appeals of residents on the coast for protection from raiding and bombarding cruisers, but those appeals must perforce be disregarded and ought not to be made. We must all remember that we are not makers of war by profession, and if the hour of trial comes we must put our whole-hearted trust in those who are. All we can do is to insist with all our might in peace that we should be well prepared. War we must leave, and we may with all confidence leave, to the men who understand it. It is not an easy thing thus to sit still under anxiety and suffering: perhaps it is less easy than to go out and fight. But it is all that the plain citizen can do, and he ought to do it. Only in return he ought to be vouchsafed assurances that his countrymen who wage war on his behalf will be equipped so that they may do justice to themselves and to him. If he is but permitted to know what they require, it is most certain that he will be continually forward to give it.

APPENDIX

PARTICULARS OF
THE PRINCIPAL NAVIES OF THE WORLD

The subjoined tables give particulars of all the most important vessels in the principal navies. In addition to those described in Chapter IV., statements have been added of the force of Austria, Japan, and Spain. The first two, although not themselves of the first rank, might conceivably be engaged in a first-class war as the allies of other Powers. The Spanish figures have been given in view of possible complications with the United States.

Full information is not always given by foreign governments, and hence some spaces have been left blank. Trial speeds are given when obtainable and trustworthy, and rough estimates of coal endurance: both are subject to the considerations put forward respectively on pages 89 and 99. The coal endurance is generally reckoned at 10 knots, or at the vessel's most economical rate of steaming. Where a vessel is fitted to carry more coal than her normal stowage, the higher figure and coal endurance is given. This involves an increase in displacement, and a slight decrease in speed, until the extra quantity is burnt.

After the figures giving the thickness of armour, i means iron; c, compound plating; h, Harveyed steel; n, nickel steel; and s, steel hardened otherwise than by the Harvey process; solid steel armour is denoted by the figure alone, without any further description. M.L. after a gun means muzzle-loading; Q.F., quick-firing. Guns below 3 inches calibre are omitted, so as to avoid unending figures. Almost all vessels but the very oldest carry Hotchkisses and machine guns. Where ships are officially divided into classes, the classification has been adhered to for facility of reference; but it is sometimes misleading, as has been pointed out in previous pages.

BRITAIN.

BATTLESHIPS.

Name. FIRST CLASS.	Displacement.	Date of Completion.	Cost.	Armour. Side.	Armour. Bulkhead.	Armour. Gun Posit'n.	Armour. Deck.	Armament.	Speed.	Coal. Capacity.	Coal. Endurance.	Complem't.
	Tons.		£	In.	In.	In.	In.		Knots.	Tons.	Miles.	
Albion	12,900	(1899)	...	8 *h*	6 *h*	10 *h*	3	4 12-in. (wire), 12 6-in. Q.F., 16 12-pr. Q.F.	18¾	...	7600	700
Anson	10,600	1889	724,765	18 *c*	16 *c*	14 *c*	3	4 13½-in., 6 6-in.	17.2	1200	7100	515
Barfleur	10,500	1894	599,089	12 *c* & 4 *n*	12 *c*	9 *c*	2½	4 10-in., 10 4.7-in. Q.F.	17½	1240	10000	606
Benbow	10,600	1888	760,820	18 *c*	16 *c*	14 *c*	3	2 16¼-in., 10 6-in. Q.F.	16¾	1200	7100	525
Caesar	14,900	(1898)	865,533	9 *h*	14 *h*	14 *h*	4	4 12-in. (wire), 12 6-in. Q.F., 16 12-pr. Q.F.	17½	1850	7600	757
Camperdown	10,600	1889	769,456	18 *c*	16 *c*	14 *c*	3	4 13½-in., 6 6-in.	16.9	1200	7100	515
Canopus	12,900	(1898)		8 *h*	6 *h*	10 *h*	3	4 12-in. (wire), 12 6-in. Q.F., 16 12-pr. Q.F.	18¾	...	7600	700
Centurion	10,500	1893	608,098	12 *c* & 4 *n*	12 *c*	9 *c*	2½	4 10-in., 10 4.7-in. Q.F.	18½	1240	10000	622
Collingwood	9,300	1886	624,000	18 *c*	16 *c*	12 *c*	2½	4 12-in., 6 6-in. Q.F.	16½	1200	8500	480
Empress of India	14,150	1893	838,087	18 *c* & 4	16 *c*	17 *c*	3	4 13½-in., 10 6-in. Q.F.	17¾*	1450	7900	730
Glory	12,900	(1899)		8 *h*	6 *h*	10 *h*	3	4 12-in. (wire), 12 6-in. Q.F., 16 12-pr. Q.F.	18¾	...	7600	700
Goliath	12,900	(1898)	...	8 *h*	6 *h*	10 *h*	3	4 12-in. (wire), 12 6-in. Q.F., 16 12-pr. Q.F.	18¾	...	7600	700
Hannibal	14,900	(1897)	867,403	9 *h*	14 *h*	14 *h*	4	4 12-in. (wire), 12 6-in. Q.F., 16 12-pr. Q.F.	17½	1850	7600	757
Hood	14,150	1893	830,536	18 *c* & 5	17 *c*	18 *c*	3	4 13½-in., 10 6-in. Q.F.	17¾	1450	7900	730

* The ships of this class were not fully tested on trial, but the figure given is probably about their safe forced-draught speed.

Howe . .	10,300	1889	667,022	18 *c*	16 *c*	11½ *c*	3	4 13½-in., 6 6-in. . .	16¾	1200	7200	515
Illustrious . .	14,900	(1898)	885,945	9 *h*	14 *h*	14 *h*	4	4 12-in. (wire), 12 6-in. Q.F., 16 12-pr. Q.F. . .	17½	1850	7600	757
Jupiter . .	14,900	(1897)	893,816	9 *h*	14 *h*	14 *h*	4	4 12-in. (wire), 12 6-in. Q.F., 16 12-pr. Q.F. . .	17½	1850	7600	757
Magnificent . .	14,900	1895	912,291	9 *h*	14 *h*	14 *h*	4	4 12-in. (wire), 12 6-in. Q.F., 16 12-pr. Q.F. . .	17.6	1850	7600	757
Majestic . .	14,900	1895	910,632	9 *h*	14 *h*	14 *h*	4	4 12-in. (wire), 12 6-in. Q.F., 16 12-pr. Q.F. . .	17.9	1850	7600	757
Mars . .	14,900	(1897)	894,330	9 *h*	14 *h*	14 *h*	4	4 12-in. (wire), 12 6-in. Q.F., 16 12-pr. Q.F. . .	17½	1850	7600	757
Nile . .	11,940	1890	819,717	20 *c*	18 *c*	18 *c*	3	4 13½-in., 6 4.7-in. Q.F. .	16.7	1200	6500	558
Ocean .	12,900	(1899)	...	8 *h*	6 *h*	10 *h*	3	4 12-in. (wire), 12 6-in. Q.F., 16 12-pr. Q.F. . .	18¾	...	7600	700
Prince George .	14,900	1896	885,037	9 *h*	14 *h*	14 *h*	4	4 12-in. (wire), 12 6-in. Q.F., 16 12-pr. Q.F. . .	17½	1850	7600	757
Ramillies . .	14,150	1893	874,255	18 *c* & 4 *n*	16 *c*	17 *c*	3	4 13½-in., 10 6-in. Q.F. .	17¾	1450	7900	730
Renown . .	12,350	1896	696,425	8 *h*	10 *h*	10 *h*	3	4 10-in., 10 6-in. Q.F., 8 12-pr. Q.F. . .	18¾	1600	12000	674
Repulse . .	14,150	1894	841,274	18 *c* & 4 *n*	16 *c*	17 *c*	3	4 13½-in., 10 6-in. Q.F. .	17¾	1450	7900	730
Resolution . .	14,150	1893	852,755	18 *c* & 4	16 *c*	17 *c*	3	4 13½-in., 10 6-in. Q.F. .	17¾	1450	7900	730
Revenge . .	14,150	1895	852,755	18 *c* & 4 *n*	16 *c*	17 *c*	3	4 13½-in., 10 6-in. Q.F. .	17¾	1450	7900	730
Rodney . .	10,300	1888	669,278	18 *c*	16 *c*	11½ *c*	3	4 13½-in., 6 6-in. . .	16¾	1200	7200	515
Royal Oak . .	14,150	1894	877,378	18 *c* & 4 *n*	16 *c*	17 *c*	3	4 13½-in., 10 6-in. Q.F. .	17¾	1450	7900	730
Royal Sovereign .	14,150	1892	824,583	18 *c* & 4	16 *c*	17 *c*	3	4 13½-in., 10 6-in. Q.F. .	17¾	1450	7900	730
Sans Pareil .	10,470	1889	719,442	18 *c*	16 *c*	18 *c*	3	2 16¼-in., 1 10-in., 12 6-in. Q.F. . . .	17¾	1200	7000	583

BRITAIN—BATTLESHIPS (FIRST CLASS)—Continued.

Name.	Displacement. Tons.	Date of Completion.	Cost. £	Armour. Side. In.	Armour. Bulkhead. In.	Armour. Gun Posit'n. In.	Armour. Deck. In.	Armament.	Speed. Knots.	Coal. Capacity. Tons.	Coal. Endurance. Miles.	Complem't.
FIRST CLASS.—*Contd.*												
Trafalgar	11,940	1890	862,794	20 c	18 c	18 c	3	4 13½-in., 6 4·7-in. Q.F.	16.7	1200	6500	558
Victorious	14,900	1896	863,313	9 h	14 h	14 c	4	4 12-in. (wire), 12 6-in. Q.F., 16 12-pr. Q.F.	17½	1850	7600	757
SECOND CLASS.												
Agamemnon	8660	1883	504,065	18 i	16 i	16 i	3	4 12½-in. M.L, 2 6-in.	12.1	960	4100	410
Ajax	8660	1883	518,357	18 i	16 i	16 i	3	4 12½-in. M.L, 2 6-in.*	12.1	960	4100	410
Alexandra	9490	1877	514,324	12 i	8 i	12 i	2	8 10-in. M.L, 4 9·2-in., 6 4-in.	14.3	680	2700	680
Colossus	9420	1886	646,786	18 c	16 c	16 c	3	4 12-in., 5 6-in.	14.2	970	6200	396
Devastation	9330	1873	353,848	12 i	12 i	14 i	3	4 10-in.	14	1800	6000	420
Dreadnought	10,820	1875	592,573	14 i	13 i	14 i	3	4 12½-in. M.L.	13.7	1200	5250	440
Edinburgh	9420	1886	642,333	18 c	16 i	16 c	3	4 12-in., 5 6-in.	14.2	970	6200	396
Inflexible	11,880	1881	795,268	24 c	22 c	18 c	3	4 16-in. M.L, 8 4-in.	12¾	1300	5200	485
Neptune	9310	1878	600,000	12 i	8 i	13 i	3	4 12½-in. M.L, 2 9-in. M.L.	13.4	670	1480	465
Superb	9170	1880	443,000	12 i	10 i	10 i	1½	16 10-in. M.L, 6 4-in.	14½	970	1850	640
Téméraire	8540	1877	454,969	11 i	8 i	10 i	2	4 11-in. M.L, 4 10-in. M.L, 6 4-in.	13¾	620	2700	592
Thunderer	9330	1877	358,542	12 i	12 i	14 i	3	4 10-in.	14	1600	5300	420

* For these guns quick-firers of the same calibre are to be substituted.

PRINCIPAL NAVIES OF THE WORLD

THIRD CLASS AND COAST DEFENCE.

Audacious	6010	1869	246,482	8 i	5 i	6 i	...	10 9-in. M.L., 8 4-in.	11.6	500	1260	492
Belleisle	4870	1878	240,000	12 i	9 i	9 i	2	4 12-in. M.L.	11.9	520	1850	284
Bellerophon	7550	1866	322,701	6 i	5 i	6 i	...	10 8-in., 4 6-in.	12.2	650	1600	572
Conqueror	6200	1882	418,433	12 c	11½ c	12 c	2½	2 12-in., 4 6-in.	15.3	650	5200	335
Cyclops	3560	1871	154,026	8 i	9 i	10 i	1½	4 10-in. M.L.	9.9	270	1250	192
Glatton	4910	1872	219,529	12 i	12 i	14 i	3	2 12-in. M.L.	11	540	2000	192
Gorgon	3560	1872	138,567	8 i	9 i	10 i	1½	4 10-in. M.L.	9.9	270	1250	192
Hecate	3560	1872	140,593	8 i	9 i	10 i	1½	4 10-in. M.L.	9.9	270	1250	192
Hercules	8680	1868	361,134	9 i	6 i	9 i	...	8 10-in. M.L., 2 9-in. M.L., 4 7-in. M.L., 6 4.7-in. Q.F.	14.6	610	1700	630
Hero	6200	1888	397,271	12 c	11½ c	12 c	2½	2 12-in., 4 6-in.	15.2	650	5200	335
Hotspur	4010	1871	171,528	11 i	8 i	10 c	3	2 12-in. M.L., 2 6-in.	11¼	300	950	240
Hydra	3560	1872	141,372	8 i	9 i	10 i	1½	4 10-in. M.L.	9.9	270	1250	192
Invincible	6010	1870	239,441	8 i	5 i	6 i	...	10 9-in. M.L., 6 4-in.	11.6	500	1580	492
Iron Duke	6010	1871	196,479	8 i	5 i	6 i	...	10 9-in. M.L., 4 5-in.	12½	700	3900	492
Monarch	8320	1869	354,575	7 i	5 i	8 i	...	4 12-in. M.L., 2 9-in. M.L., 1 7-in. M.L., 4 12-pr. Q.F.	15	630	1500	570
Orion	4870	1882	292,229	12 i	9 i	9 i	2	4 12-in. M.L.	11.9	520	1850	284
Penelope	4470	1868	186,848	6 i	4½ i	5 i	...	8 8-in. M.L.	11	470	1360	360
Prince Albert	3880	1866	202,666	4½ i	5 i	4½ i	7¼	4 9-in. M.L.	9¾	230	950	175

295

NAVAL POLICY

BRITAIN—BATTLESHIPS (THIRD CLASS AND COAST DEFENCE)—*Continued.*

Name.	Displace-ment.	Date of Com-pletion.	Cost.	Armour.				Armament.	Speed.	Coal.		Com-plem't.
				Side.	Bulk-head.	Gun Posit'n.	Deck.			Capa-city.	Endur-ance.	
THIRD CLASS AND COAST DEFENCE. —*Contd.*	Tons.		£	In.	In.	In.	In.		Knots.	Tons.	Miles.	
Rupert	5440	1874	232,677	11 *i*	12 *i*	14 *i*	3	2 9.2-in., 2 6-in.	14	480	1350	232
Scorpion	2750	1865	110,573	4½ *i*	...	5 *i*	...	4 9-in. M.I.	8½	300	1150	151
Sultan	9290	1871	357,415	9 *i*	6 *i*	9 *i*	...	8 10-in. M.L., 4 9-in. M.I., 4 4.7-in. Q.F.	15	810	2150	661
Swiftsure	6910	1872	257,081	8 *i*	6 *i*	6 *i*	...	10 9-in. M.L., 8 4-in.	12.6	540	1650	476
Triumph	6640	1873	258,322	8 *i*	6 *i*	6 *i*	...	10 9-in. M.L., 4 5-in.	12.6	550	1700	476
Wivern	2750	1865	116,514	4½ *i*	...	5 *i*	...	4 9-in. M.I.	8½	300	1150	151

Also four old Ironclads—**Achilles, Agincourt, Minotaur, Northumberland**—classed as Armoured Cruisers; they have a miscellaneous armament, mostly muzzle-loading, 4½ to 5½ inches of iron armour, and 12 to 13 knots speed.

FIRST CLASS AND ARMOURED.

CRUISERS.

Name	Displace-ment.	Date of Com-pletion.	Cost.	Side.	Bulk-head.	Gun Posit'n.	Deck.	Armament.	Speed.	Capa-city.	Endur-ance.	Com-plem't.
Andromeda	11,000	(1898)	...	...	...	4½	6	16 6-in. Q.F., 14 12-pr. Q.F.	20½	2000	...	600
Aurora	5600	1889	284,550	10 *c*	16 *c*	...	3	2 9.2-in., 10 6-in. Q.F.	18¼	900	7000	484
Australia	5600	1888	259,390	10 *c*	16 *c*	...	3	2 9.2-in., 10 6-in. Q.F.	18.8	900	7000	484
Blake	9000	1892	449,471	...	...	6	6	2 9.2-in., 10 6-in. Q.F.	22	1800	15,000	590
Blenheim	9000	1891	425,591	...	...	6	6	2 9.2-in., 10 6-in. Q.F.	20	1800	15,000	590
Crescent	7700	1892	383,068	...	...	6	5	1 9.2-in., 12 6-in. Q.F.	19.7	1260	14,000	520

PRINCIPAL NAVIES OF THE WORLD

Name							Armament				
Diadem	11,000	(1898)	...	...	...	4¾	16 6-in. Q.F., 14 12-pr. Q.F.	20½	2000	...	600
Edgar	7350	1891	401,083	...	...	6	2 9.2-in., 10 6-in. Q.F.	20¼	1200	14,000	544
Endymion	7350	1892	350,459	...	...	6	2 9.2-in., 10 6-in. Q.F.	20	1200	14,000	544
Europa	11,000	(1898)	...	...	...	4¾	16 6-in. Q.F., 14 12-pr. Q.F.	20½	2000	...	600
Galatea	5600	1889	258,390	10 c	16 c	...	2 9.2-in., 10 6-in. Q.F.	19	900	7000	484
Gibraltar	7700	1893	347,634	...	...	6	2 9.2-in., 10 6-in. Q.F.	19.7	1260	14,000	520
Grafton	7350	1892	351,851	...	...	6	2 9.2-in., 10 6-in. Q.F.	20	1200	14,000	544
Hawke	7350	1891	365,491	...	...	6	2 9.2-in., 10 6-in. Q.F.	20	1200	14,000	544
Immortalité	5600	1889	278,500	10 c	16 c	...	2 9.2-in., 10 6-in. Q.F.	19¼	900	7000	484
Impérieuse	8400	1886	530,814	10 c	9 c	9 c	4 9.2-in., 10 6-in. Q.F.	16.7	1130	7000	527
Narcissus	5600	1889	257,390	10 c	16 c	...	2 9.2-in., 10 6-in. Q.F.	18½	900	7000	484
Niobe	11,000	(1898)	...	...	...	4½	16 6-in. Q.F., 14 12-pr. Q.F.	20½	2000	...	600
Orlando	5600	1888	266,812	10 c	16 c	...	2 9.2-in., 10 6-in.	17.1	900	7000	484
Powerful	14,200	1896	674,879	...	...	6	2 9.2-in., 12 6-in. Q.F., 16 12-pr. Q.F.	22	3000	25,000	894
Royal Arthur	7700	1891	402,414	...	...	6	1 9.2-in., 12 6-in. Q.F.	19.7	1260	14,000	520
St. George	7700	1893	377,204	...	...	6	2 9.2-in, 10 6-in. Q.F.	19.7	1260	14,000	520
Terrible	14,200	1896	681,419	...	...	6	2 9.2-in., 12.6-in. Q.F., 16 12-pr. Q.F.	22	3000	25,000	894
Theseus	7350	1892	347,577	...	...	6	2 9.2-in., 10 6-in. Q.F.	20	1200	14,000	544

BRITAIN—CRUISERS (FIRST CLASS AND ARMOURED)—*Continued*.

Name.	Displacement. Tons.	Date of completion.	Cost. £	Armour. Side. In.	Armour. Bulkhead. In.	Armour. Gun Posit'n. In.	Armour. Deck. In.	Armament.	Speed. Knots.	Coal. Capacity. Tons.	Coal. Endurance. Miles.	Complem't.
FIRST CLASS AND ARMOURED.—*Contd.*												
Undaunted	5600	1889	256,055	10*c*	16*c*	...	3	2 9.2-in., 10 6-in.	18.7	900	7000	484
Warspite	8400	1888	529,332	10*c*	9*c*	9*c*	3	4 9.2-in., 10 6-in.	16.7	1130	7000	527
SECOND CLASS.												
Æolus	3600	1892	208,450	...	...	...	2	2 6-in. Q.F., 6 4.7-in. Q.F.	19¾	535	8500	273
Amphion	4300	1883	160,500	...	...	...	1½	10 6-in. Q.F.	16.6	1000	10,000	309
Andromache	3400	1891	186,280	...	...	...	2	2 6-in. Q.F., 6 4.7-in. Q.F.	20	535	8500	273
Apollo	3400	1891	186,361	...	...	...	2	2 6-in. Q.F., 6 4.7-in. Q.F.	20	535	8500	273
Arethusa	4300	1882	145,198	...	...	...	1½	10 6-in.	16.6	1000	10,000	309
Arrogant	5800	(1897)	...	...	...	...	2*n*	4 6-in. Q.F., 6 4.7-in. Q.F., 8 12-pr. Q.F.	19½	500	...	450
Astræa	4360	1893	244,831	...	...	...	2	2 6-in. Q.F., 8 4.7-in. Q.F.	19¾	535	7000	318
Bonaventure	4360	1892	247,128	...	...	...	2	2 6-in. Q.F., 8 4.7-in. Q.F.	20	535	7000	318
Brilliant	3600	1892	204,228	...	...	...	2	2 6-in. Q.F., 6 4.7-in. Q.F.	19¾	535	8500	273
Cambrian	4360	1893	236,919	...	...	...	2	2 6-in. Q.F., 8 4.7-in. Q.F.	20.4	535	7000	318
Charybdis	4360	1894	237,344	...	...	...	2	2 6-in. Q.F., 8 4.7-in. Q.F.	20½	535	7000	318
Diana	5600	1896	249,332	...	...	...	3	5 6-in. Q.F., 6 4.7-in. Q.F., 8 12-pr. Q.F.	20	1000	...	450

PRINCIPAL NAVIES OF THE WORLD

Name			Displacement	Date	Cost			Torpedo Tubes	Guns	Speed	Coal		I.H.P.
Dido	.	5600	1896	252,278	...	...	3	5 6-in. Q.F., 6 4.7-in. Q.F., 8 12-pr. Q.F.	20	1000	...	450
Doris	.	5600	(1897)	254,029	...	...	3	5 6-in. Q.F., 6 4.7-in. Q.F., 8 12-pr. Q.F.	20	1000	...	450
Eclipse	.	5600	1896	279,345	...	...	3	5 6-in. Q.F., 6 4.7-in. Q.F., 8 12-pr. Q.F.	20	1000	...	450
Flora	.	4360	1894	241,819	...	...	2	2 6-in. Q.F., 8 4.7-in. Q.F.	19¼	535	7000	318
Forte	.	4360	1894	240,816	...	...	2	2 6-in. Q.F., 8 4.7-in. Q.F.	19.8	535	7000	318
Forth	.	4050	1886	201,952	...	...	3	2 8-in. 10 6-in.*	17.2	900	8750	326
Fox	.	4360	1894	244,078	...	...	2	2 6-in. Q.F., 8 4.7-in. Q.F.	19¾	535	7000	318
Furious	.	5800	(1897)	...	...	...	2″	4 6-in. Q.F., 6 4.7-in. Q.F., 8 12-pr. Q.F.	19½	500	...	450
Gladiator	.	5800	(1897)	...	...	...	2″	4 6-in. Q.F., 6 4.7-in. Q.F., 8 12-pr. Q.F.	19½	500	...	450
Hermione	.	4360	1894	223,267	...	...	2	2 6-in. Q.F., 8 4.7-in. Q.F.	19¼	535	7000	318
Indefatigable	.	3600	1892	181,024	...	...	2	2 6-in. Q.F., 6 4.7-in. Q.F.	19¾	535	8500	273
Intrepid	.	3600	1892	181,157	...	...	2	2 6-in. Q.F., 6 4.7-in. Q.F.	19¾	535	8500	273
Iphigenia	.	3600	1892	181,879	...	...	2	2 6-in. Q.F., 6 4.7-in. Q.F.	19¾	535	8500	273
Iris	.	3730	1878	213,186	...	...	...	13 5-in.	18	780	4500	280
Isis	.	5600	(1897)	252,067	...	...	3	5 6-in. Q.F., 6 4.7-in. Q.F., 8 12-pr. Q.F.	20	1000	...	450
Juno	.	5600	1896	254,097	...	...	3	5 6-in. Q.F., 6 4.7-in. Q.F., 8 12-pr. Q.F.	20	1000	...	450
Latona	.	3400	1891	171,068	...	...	2	2 6-in. Q.F., 6 4.7-in. Q.F.	20	535	8500	273
Leander	.	4300	1882	148,453	...	...	1½	10 6-in. Q.F.	16.6	1000	10,000	309

* For the 6-in. guns quick-firers of the same calibre are to be substituted.

299

NAVAL POLICY

BRITAIN—CRUISERS (SECOND CLASS)—*Continued*.

Name.	Displacement. Tons.	Date of Completion.	Cost. £	Armour. Side. In.	Armour. Bulkhead. In.	Armour. Gun Posit'n. In.	Armour. Deck. In.	Armament.	Speed. Knots.	Coal. Capacity. Tons.	Coal. Endurance. Miles.	Complem't.
SECOND CLASS. *Contd.*												
Melampus	3400	1890	171,635	...	...	...	2	2 6-in. Q.F., 6 4.7-in. Q.F.	20	535	8500	273
Mercury	3730	1879	213,252	...	...	...	...	13 5-in.	18	780	4500	280
Mersey	4050	1886	154,000	...	...	...	3	2 8-in., 10 6-in.*	17.3	900	8750	326
Minerva	5600	1896	244,046	...	...	...	...	5 6-in. Q.F., 6 4.7-in. Q.F., 8 12-pr. Q.F.	20	1000	...	450
Naiad	3400	1890	171,445	...	...	...	2	2 6-in. Q.F., 6 4.7-in. Q.F.	20	535	8500	273
Phaeton	4300	1884	145,198	...	...	...	1½	10 6-in. Q.F.	16.6	1000	10,000	309
Pique	3600	1891	184,108	...	...	...	2	2 6-in. Q.F., 6 4.7-in. Q.F.	19¾	535	8500	273
Rainbow	3600	1892	184,086	...	...	...	2	2 6-in. Q.F., 6 4.7-in. Q.F.	19¾	535	8500	273
Retribution	3600	1892	183,975	...	...	...	2	2 6-in. Q.F., 6 4.7-in. Q.F.	19¾	535	8500	273
Sappho	3400	1892	171,853				2	2 6-in. Q.F., 6 4.7-in. Q.F.	20	535	8500	273
Scylla	3400	1892	171,593	...	...	...	2	2 6-in. Q.F., 6 4.7-in. Q.F.	20	535	8500	273
Severn	4050	1886	212,621	...	...	...	3	2 8-in., 10 6-in.*	17.2	900	8750	326
Sirius	3600	1892	186,649	...	...	...	2	2 6-in. Q.F., 6 4.7-in. Q.F.	19¾	535	8500	273
Spartan	3600	1892	186,351	...	...	...	2	2 6-in. Q.F., 6 4.7-in. Q.F.	20	535	8500	273
Sybille	3400	1892	174,670	...	...	...	2	2 6-in. Q.F., 6 4.7-in. Q.F.	20	535	8500	273

* For the 6-in. guns quick-firers of the same calibre are to be substituted.

PRINCIPAL NAVIES OF THE WORLD

Talbot	.	5600	1896	273,856	...	3	5 6-in. Q.F., 6 4.7-in. Q.F., 8 12-pr. Q.F.	20	1000	...	450
Terpsichore	.	3600	1892	173,341	...	2	2 6-in. Q.F., 6 4.7-in. Q.F.	19¾	535	8500	273
Thames	.	4050	1886	205,452	...	3	2 8-in., 10 6-in.*	17.2	900	8750	326
Thetis	.	3600	1892	173,146	...	2	2 6-in. Q.F., 6 4.7-in. Q.F.	19¾	535	8500	273
Tribune	.	3600	1892	173,006	...	2	2 6-in. Q.F., 6 4.7-in. Q.F.	19¾	535	8500	273
Venus	.	5600	1896	249,938	...	3	5 6-in. Q.F., 6 4.7-in. Q.F., 8 12-pr. Q.F.	20	1000	...	450
Vindictive	.	5800	(1897)	...	...	2″	4 6-in. Q.F., 6 4.7-in. Q.F., 8 12-pr. Q.F.	19½	500	...	450

* For the 6-in. guns quick-firers of the same calibre are to be substituted.

Also ranked as First Class, three old Iron-Belted Cruisers—**Nelson, Northampton, Shannon**—with miscellaneous armament, and 10 to 12 knots speed.

As Second Class, five old Frigates—**Active, Boadicea, Inconstant, Raleigh, Volage**—with slow-firing armament, and 12 to 15 knots speed.

Of THIRD CLASS CRUISERS, the principal types are—**Pelorus** (and **Proserpine**), 2135 tons, 8 4-in. Q.F., 20 knots, 250 tons of coal, 200 men; **Pallas** (and **Pearl, Philomel, Phœbe**), 2575 tons, 8 4.7-in. Q.F., 19 knots, 440 tons of coal=6000 miles, and 190 men; **Barham** (and **Bellona**), 1830 tons, 6 4.7-in. Q.F., 18.6 and 17.8 knots respectively, 140 tons of coal=2600 miles, and 169 men; **Barracouta** (and **Barrosa, Blanche, Blonde**), 1580 tons, 6 4.7-in. Q.F., 16½ knots, 160 tons of coal = 3400 miles, and 159 men; **Magicienne** (and **Marathon, Melpomene**), 2950 tons, 6 6-in., 19 knots, 400 tons of coal=6000 miles, and 216 men; **Medea** (and **Medusa**), 2800 tons, 6 6-in., 19 knots, 400 tons of coal=8000 miles, and 216 men. Also twenty-nine vessels less modern—**Calliope, Calypso, Canada, Carysfort, Champion, Cleopatra, Comus, Conquest, Constance, Cordelia, Curaçoa, Caroline, Heroine, Pylades, Rapid, Royalist, Satellite, Archer, Brisk, Cossack, Mohawk, Porpoise, Racoon, Tartar, Fearless, Scout, Garnet, Ruby, Tourmaline**. Also numerous Sloops, Gunboats, Training-ships, Store-ships, and the like.

Also the following types of TORPEDO-GUNBOATS—**Dryad** (and **Halcyon, Harrier, Hazard, Hussar**), 1070 tons, 2 4.7-in. Q.F., 18¼ knots, 2500 miles coal endurance, and 115 men; **Alarm** (and **Antelope, Circe, Jaseur, Jason, Hebe, Leda, Niger, Onyx, Renard, Speedy**), 810 tons, 2 4.7-in. Q.F., 19¼ knots (Speedy, 20 knots), 2500 miles coal endurance, and 85 men; **Gossamer** (and **Gleaner,**

NAVAL POLICY

Salamander, Seagull, Sharpshooter, Sheldrake, Skipjack, Spanker, Speedwell, 735 tons, 2 4·7-in. Q.F., 19 knots, 3200 miles coal endurance, and 91 men; Grasshopper (and Rattlesnake, Sandfly, Spider), 525 tons (Rattlesnake, 550), 1 4-in. (Spider, 1 4-in. Q.F.), 19 knots (Rattlesnake, 18½), 2400 miles coal endurance (Rattlesnake, 3000) and 63 men.

Also seventy TORPEDO-BOAT DESTROYERS—Angler, Ardent, Ariel, Avon, Banshee, Bat, Bittern, Boxer, Brazen, Bruiser, Chamois, Charger, Conflict, Contest, Crane, Daring, Dasher, Decoy, Desperate, Dragon, Earnest, Electra, Fame, Ferret, Fervent, Flyfish, Foam, Griffon, Handy, Hardy, Hart, Hasty, Haughty, Havock, Hornet, Janus, Lightning, Locust, Lynx, Mallard, Opossum, Panther, Porcupine, Quail, Ranger, Recruit, Rocket, Salmon, Seal, Shark, Skate, Snapper, Sparrowhawk, Spitfire, Star, Starfish, Sturgeon, Sunfish, Surly, Swordfish, Teaser, Thrasher, Virago, Vulture, Whiting, Wizard, Wolf, Zebra, Zephyr. These are of 210 to 300 tons, of 26 to 31 knots speed, armed with four to six 12-and 6-pounders, of 2500 to 4000 miles coal endurance, and carry from 43 to 58 men.

There are forty-three sea-going TORPEDO-BOATS, twenty-six First Class, four Second Class, twenty Third Class, and seventy-three Vedettes. Also the Torpedo-depôt-ship and floating workshop, **Vulcan**, 6620 tons, 8 4-in. Q.F., 20 knots, 12,000 miles coal endurance, 387 men.

Besides the above, four First Class Cruisers (Diadem class), three Second Class (Eclipse class), and six Third Class (Pelorus class) are projected on the 1896 programme, besides twenty destroyers.

AUSTRIA.

BATTLESHIPS.

Name.	Displacement.	Date of Launch.	Cost.	Armour.			Armament.	Speed.	Coal.		Complem't.
				Belt.	Gun Posit'n.	Deck.			Capacity.	Endurance.	
	Tons.		£	In.	In.	In.		Knots.	Tons.	Miles.	
Budapest	5550	(1897)	339,062	10.6⅔ & 3½	9¾	2⅜	4 9.4-in., 6 5.9-in. Q.F.	17.2	500	...	...
Custoza	7060	1872	414,400	9	7	1½	8 10.2-in., 8 3½-in.	14	580	1620	567
Don Juan de Austria	3550	1875		8	6	1	8 8.2-in., 4 3½-in.	13	380	2000	440

302

PRINCIPAL NAVIES OF THE WORLD

Kaiser	5810	1871	337,200	6	5½	...	10 9-in. M.L., 6 3½-in.	13	450	1500	540
Kaiser Max	3566	1875	211,600	8	6	1	8 8.2-in., 4 3½-in.	13	380	2000	440
Kronprinz Rudolf	6870	1887	330,000	12	11	2¾	3 12-in., 6 4.7-in. Q.F.	16	650	...	492
Kronprinzessin Stephanie	5060	1887	300,000	9	8	1	2 12-in., 6 5.9-in.	16.3	510	...	510
Monarch	5550	1895	339,062	10.6 n	10.6 n	2½ n	4 9.4-in., 6 5.9-in. Q.F.	17.2	500	...	...
Prinz Eugen	3566	1877	...	8	6	1	8 8.2-in., 4 3½-in.	13	380	2000	440
Tegetthof	7390	1878	250,000	14	14	3	6 9.4-in. 5 5.9-in. Q.F.	16¼	670	3300	578
Wien	5510	(1897)	339,062	10.6 n	10.6 n	2½ n	4 9.4-in., 6 5.9-in. Q.F.	17.2	500	...	...

Also five River Monitors.

CRUISERS.

Kaiser Franz Josef	4064	1889	...	...	3½	2¼	2 9.4-in., 6 5.9-in.	19	660	4500	450
Kaiserin Elizabeth	4064	1890	...	...	3½	2¼	2 9.4-in., 6 5.9-in.	19	660	4500	450
Kaiserin Maria Teresa	5270	1893	304,187	4	4	2¼	2 9.4-in., 8 5.9-in. Q.F.	19	740	5200	450

FRANCE.

BATTLESHIPS.

Name.	Displacement.	Date of Launch.	Cost.	Armour. Belt.	Armour. Gun Posit'n.	Armour. Deck.	Armament.	Speed.	Coal. Capacity.	Coal. Endurance.	Complem't.
SEA-GOING.	Tons.		£	In.	In.	In.		Knots.	Tons.	Miles.	
Amiral Baudin	11,910	1883	600,000	$21\frac{1}{2}$	$16\frac{1}{2}$	4	3 $14\frac{1}{2}$-in., 4 6.3-in. Q.F., 8 $5\frac{1}{2}$-in. Q.F.	15	800	3000	630
Amiral Duperré	11,260	1879	570,000	$21\frac{1}{2}$	$15\frac{1}{2}$	$2\frac{1}{4}$	4 13.4-in., 1 6.3-in., 14 $5\frac{1}{2}$-in.	$14\frac{1}{4}$	850	...	664
Bouvet	12,205	1896	1,100,770	$15\frac{3}{4}$ s	$14\frac{1}{2}$ s	$3\frac{1}{2}$	2 12-in., 2 10.6-in., 8 $5\frac{1}{2}$-in. Q.F., 8 3.9-in. Q.F.	$17\frac{1}{2}$	800	4000	631
Bouvines	6610	1892	594,640	$17\frac{3}{4}$	$14\frac{1}{2}$	4	2 12-in., 8 3.9-in. Q.F.	16	300	...	323
Brennus	11,395	1891	991,767	$15\frac{3}{4}$ c & $4\frac{3}{4}$ c	$15\frac{3}{4}$ c	$4\frac{3}{4}$	3 13.4-in., 10 6.3-in. Q.F.	17.1	800	4300	696
Caiman	7640	1885	...	$19\frac{1}{2}$	$17\frac{3}{4}$	3	2 $16\frac{1}{2}$-in., 4 3.9-in. Q.F.	$14\frac{1}{2}$	800	...	504
Carnot	12,008	1895	1,070,088	$17\frac{3}{4}$	$14\frac{1}{2}$	$2\frac{3}{4}$	2 12-in., 2 10.6-in., 8 $5\frac{1}{2}$-in. Q.F.	$17\frac{1}{2}$	800	5000	625
Charlemagne	11,275	1895	1,096,432	$15\frac{3}{4}$ s	$15\frac{3}{4}$ s	$3\frac{1}{2}$	4 12-in., 10 $5\frac{1}{2}$-in. Q.F., 8 3.9-in. Q.F.	18	1100	7000	631
Charles Martel	11,882	1893	1,092,830	$17\frac{3}{4}$	$15\frac{3}{4}$	$3\frac{1}{2}$	2 12-in., 2 10.6-in., 8 $5\frac{1}{2}$-in. Q.F.	$17\frac{1}{2}$	800	5000	632
Courbet	10,810	1881	800,000	15	$9\frac{1}{2}$	$2\frac{1}{2}$	4 $12\frac{1}{2}$-in., 4 10.6-in., 6 $5\frac{1}{2}$-in.	15.4	900	3100	669
Dévastation	10,705	1879		15	$9\frac{1}{2}$	$2\frac{1}{2}$	4 $12\frac{1}{2}$-in., 4 10.6-in., 6 $5\frac{1}{2}$-in.	15.2	900	2800	685
Formidable	12,165	1885	467,520	$21\frac{1}{2}$	$17\frac{3}{4}$	3	3 $14\frac{1}{2}$-in., 4 6.3-in., 8 $5\frac{1}{2}$-in. Q.F.	16.2	1200	4000	640
Friedland	8990	1873	...	8	7	...	8 10.6-in., 8 $5\frac{1}{2}$-in.	$13\frac{1}{4}$	800	...	676

Gaulois . . .	11,275	1896	1,093,925	15¾ s	15¾ s	3½	4 12-in., 10 5½-in. Q.F., 8 3.9-in. Q.F. . .	18	1100	7000	631
Henri Quatre . . .	7000	(1898)	409,622	...	...	...	......	15	700	4500	...
Hoche . . .	10,997	1886	700,000	18	16	3	2 13.4-in., 2 10.6-in., 8 5½-in. Q.F. . . .	16	800	4000	631
Indomptable . . .	7635	1883		19½	17¾	3	2 16½-in., 4 3.9-in. Q.F. .	14.8	800	...	500
Jauréguiberry . . .	11,824	1893	1,069,536	17¾ & 4	14½	2¾	2 12-in., 2 10.6-in., 8 5½-in. Q.F. . . .	17½	800	...	624
Jemappes . . .	6590	1892	525,000	17¾	14½	4	2 13.4-in., 8 3.9-in., Q.F.	16.7	300	...	334
Magenta . . .	10,850	1890	760,960	18	16	3	4 13.4-in., 16 5½-in. Q.F.	16¼	800	4000	660
Marçeau . . .	10,850	1887	769,080	18	16	3	4 13.4-in., 16 5½-in. Q.F.	16.4	800	4000	660
Masséna . . .	11,924	1895	1,100,400	17¾ s	15¾ h	3½	2 12-in., 2 10.6-in., 8 5½-in. Q.F. . . .	17½	630	4000	610
Neptune . . .	10,980	1887	780,000	18	16	3	4 13.4-in., 16 5½-in. Q.F.	16	800	4000	660
Redoubtable . . .	9437	1876	...	14	9½	2½	8 10.6-in., 6 5½-in. . .	14.7	1000	2800	705
Requin . . .	7820	1885	...	19½	17¾	3	2 14½-in., 4 3.9-in. Q.F. .	14½	400	...	...
St. Louis . . .	11,275	(1897)	1,080,997	15¾ s	15¾ s	3½	4 12-in., 10 5½-in. Q.F. 8 3.9-in. Q.F. . .	18	1100	7000	631
Terrible . . .	7879	1881	...	19½	17¾	3	2 16½-in., 4 3.9-in. Q.F. .	14½	400	800	500
Tréhouart . . .	6610	1893	93,100	17¾	14½	4	2 12-in., 8 3.9-in. Q.F. .	17	300	...	323
Valmy . . .	6590	1892	578,957	17¾	14½	4	2 13.4-in., 8 3.9-in. Q.F.	16.7	300	...	334

Also eight old Wooden, Iron-plated Battleships—**Colbert, Marengo, Océan, Richelieu, Suffren, Trident, Triomphante, Victorieuse.**

Also eight Armoured Gunboats.

FRANCE—*Continued.*

CRUISERS.

Name.	Displacement.	Date of Launch.	Cost.	Armour. Belt.	Armour. Gun Posit'n.	Armour. Dock.	Armament.	Speed.	Coal. Capacity.	Coal. Endurance.	Complem't.
FIRST CLASS AND ARMOURED.	Tons.		£	In.	In.	In.		Knots.	Tons.	Miles.	
Bruix	4754	1894	409,622	$3\frac{3}{4}$	$3\frac{3}{4}$	2	2 7.4-in., 6 $5\frac{1}{2}$-in. Q.F.	19	413	4000	370
Cécille	5766	1888	299,666	...	...	4	8 6.3-in. Q.F., 10 $5\frac{1}{2}$-in. Q.F.	19	940	...	526
Chanzy	4754	1894	360,000	$3\frac{1}{2}$	$3\frac{3}{4}$	2	2 7.4-in., 6 $5\frac{1}{2}$-in. Q.F.	19	413	4000	370
Charner	4754	1893	353,200	$3\frac{1}{2}$	$3\frac{3}{4}$	2	2 7.4-in., 6 $5\frac{1}{2}$-in. Q.F.	19	413	4000	370
Châteaurenault	8018	(1898)	606,656	...	2	3	2 6.4-in. Q.F., 6 $5\frac{1}{2}$-in. Q.F.	23	1400	7500	625
D'Entrecasteaux	8114	1896	667,740	...	$2\frac{3}{4}$	4	2 9.4-in., 12 $5\frac{1}{2}$-in. Q.F.	19	1000	...	522
Dupuy de Lôme	6300	1890	416,000	4	4	2	2 7.4-in., 6 6.3-in. Q.F.	20	900	...	...
Guichen	8018	(1898)	611,945	...	2	3	2 6.4-in. Q.F., 6 $5\frac{1}{2}$-in. Q.F.	23	1400	7500	625
Jeanne d'Arc	11,300	(1898)	882,955	6	...	2	2 7.4-in., 8 $5\frac{1}{2}$-in.	23	...	15000	...
Latouche-Tréville	4754	1892	360,000	$3\frac{1}{2}$	$3\frac{3}{4}$	2	2 7.4-in., 6 $5\frac{1}{2}$-in. Q.F.	19	406	4000	370
Pothuau	5320	1895	384,000	$3\frac{1}{4}$	7	$3\frac{1}{2}$	2 7.4-in., 10 $5\frac{1}{2}$-in. Q.F.	19	538	...	461
Tage	7345	1886	...	...	...	...	8 6.3-in., 10 $5\frac{1}{2}$-in.	19	1000	...	530

SECOND CLASS.

Alger . . .	4122	1889	280,000	...	...	3½	4 6.3-in. Q.F., 6 5½-in. Q.F.	19½	860	...	407
Bugeaud . . .	3722	1893	308,650	...	...	3	6 6.3-in. Q.F., 4 3.9-in. Q.F.	19¼	580	587	358
Cassard . . .	3952	1894	318,712	...	...	3	6 6.3-in. Q.F., 4 3.9-in. Q.F.	19	610	...	385
Catinat . . .	4113	1894	324,992	...	...	2½	4 6.3-in. Q.F., 10 3.9-in. Q.F.	19	610	6000	394
Chasseloup-Laubat . .	3722	1893	256,320	...	...	3	6 6.3-in. Q.F., 4 3.9-in. Q.F.	19¼	587	...	358
D'Assas . . .	3952	1896	292,682	...	...	2½	6 6.3-in. Q.F., 4 3.9-in. Q.F.	19½	610	...	385
Davout . . .	3027	1890	221,827	...	...	3	6 6.3-in. Q.F., 4 3.9-in. Q.F.	20	600	...	336
Descartes . . .	3988	1894	334,725	...	...	1½	4 6.3-in. Q.F., 10 3.9-in. Q.F.	19	800	7000	378
Duchayla . . .	3952	...	315,835	...	...	2½	6 6.3-in. Q.F., 4 3.9-in. Q.F.	19¼	610	...	385
Friant . . .	3722	1893	308,750	...	...	3	6 6.3-in. Q.F., 4 3.9-in. Q.F.	19¼	587	...	358
Isly . . .	4160	1891	252,700	...	...	3	4 6.3-in. Q.F., 6 5½-in. Q.F.	18	880	...	374
Jean Bart . . .	4160	1889	283,240	...	...	3	4 6.3-in. Q.F., 6 5½-in. Q.F.	19	440	...	374
Pascal . . .	3988	1895	322,321	...	...	1½	4 6.3-in. Q.F., 10 3.9-in. Q.F.	19¼	800	7000	378
Protet . . .	4113	...	324,992	...	...	2	4 6.3-in. Q.F., 10 3.9-in. Q.F.	19	610	6000	394
Sfax . . .	4502	1884	200,000	...	...	1½	6 6.3-in., 10 5½-in. . .	16½	1000	7500	475
Suchet . . .	3430	1893	226,360	...	...	3	4 6.3-in. Q.F., 4 3.9-in. Q.F.	20	480	4800	335

Six older Second Class Cruisers.

Of modern **THIRD CLASS CRUISERS—Lavoisier, Galilée, Lisois,** 2275 to 2317 tons, 4 5½-in. and 2 3.9-in. Q.F., 20 knots, 225 to 248 men; **Cosmao, Lalande, Trond,** 1877 tons, 4 5½-in. Q.F., 20½ to 22 knots, 3000 miles, 220 men; **Coetlogon, Forbin, Surcouf,** 1848 tons, 4 5½-in. Q.F., 20 knots, 3000 miles, 210 men. Eighteen older.

Also six Torpedo-Cruisers, fifteen Torpedo-Gunboats, forty-six sea-going torpedo-boats, sixty-three first class, eighty-four second class, and fifty others.

GERMANY.
BATTLESHIPS.

Name.	Displacement. Metric Tons.	Date of Completion.	Cost. £	Armour. Belt. In.	Armour. Gun Posit'n. In.	Armour. Deck. In.	Armament.	Speed. Knots.	Coal. Capacity. Tons.	Coal. Endurance. Miles.	Complem't.
FIRST CLASS.											
Brandenburg	10,100	1891	606,500	15¾c	11¾c	2½	6 11-in., 6 4.1-in. Q.F., 8 3.4-in. Q.F.	16½	750	...	552
Kurfürst Friedrich Wilhelm	10,100	1891	653,000	15¾c	11¾c	2½	6 11-in., 6 4.1-in. Q.F., 8 3.4-in. Q.F.	15	750	...	552
Weissenburg	10,100	1891	659,475	15¾	11¾	2½	6 11-in., 6 4.1-in. Q.F., 8 3.4-in. Q.F.	17	750	...	552
Wörth	10,100	1892	595,250	15¾	11¾	2½	6 11-in., 6 4.1-in. Q.F., 8 3.4-in. Q.F.	17.2	750	...	552
Kaiser Friedrich III.	11,000	...	706,000	12h	10h	3	4 9.4-in., 18 5.9-in. Q.F., 12 3.4-in. Q.F.	18	750	...	590
SECOND CLASS.											
Baden	7441	1880	444,886	15¾	10	3	6 10.2-in., 6 3.4-in. Q.F.	14	700	...	376
Bayern	7441	1878	406,660	15¾	10	3	6 10.2-in., 6 3.4-in. Q.F.	14	700	...	376
Deutschland	7319	1874	412,022	10	8	2	8 10.2-in., 15.9-in., 64-in., 9 3.4-in. Q.F.	14½	710	3400	668
Kaiser	7531	1874	505,141	10	9	2	8 10.2-in., 15.9-in., 64-in., 9 3.4-in. Q.F.	14½	710	3400	668
Oldenburg	5200	1884	235,342	13c	8c	1	8 9.4-in., 2 3.4-in. Q.F.	13½	475	...	356
Sachsen	7441	1877	422,178	15¾	10	3	6 10.2-in., 6 3.4-in. Q.F.	14	700	...	376
Württemberg	7441	1878	402,512	15¾	10	3	6 10.2-in., 6 3.4-in. Q.F.	14	700	...	376

THIRD CLASS.

Ægir	3600	1895	233,500	9½ *h*	8 *h*	3	3 9.4-in., 10 3.4-in. Q.F.	16	225	...	255
Beowulf	3500	1890	175,000	9½	8	1	3 9.4-in., 8 3.4-in. Q.F.	16	225	...	266
Friedrich der Grosse	6770	1874	365,170	9¼	10	...	4 10.2-in., 2 6.6-in., 10 3.4-in. Q.F.	14	550	2500	537
Frithjof	3500	1891	175,000	9¼ *h*	7¾ *h*	3	3 9.4-in., 8 3.4-in. Q.F.	16	225	...	266
Hagen	3500	1893		9¼ *h*	7¾ *h*	3	3 9.4-in., 8 3.4-in. Q.F.	16	225	...	266
Heimdal	3500	1892	233,500	9¼ *h*	7¾ *h*	3	3 9.4-in., 8 3.4-in. Q.F.	16	225	...	266
Hildebrand	3500	1892	218,000	9¼ *h*	7¾ *h*	3	3 9.4-in., 8 3.4-in. Q.F.	16	225	...	266
König Wilhelm	9757	1868	505,141	12	6	...	20 5.9-in. Q.F., 18 3.4-in. Q.F.	14.7	700	1940	759
Odin	3600	1894	...	9½ *h*	7¾ *h*	3	3 9.4-in., 10 3.4-in. Q.F.	16	225	...	266
Preussen	6770	1873	531,904	9	10	...	4 10.2-in., 2 6.6-in., 10 3.4-in. Q.F.	14	550	2500	537
Siegfried	3500	1889	175,000	9½	7¾	3	3 9.4-in., 6 3.4-in. Q.F.	15	225	...	266

Also eleven **Armoured Gunboats—Basilisk, Biene, Camäleon, Crocodil, Hummel, Mücke, Natter, Salamander, Skorpion, Viper,** and **Wespe**—of 1109 tons displacement, 8-in. armour, 1 12-in. and 2 3.3-in. guns, and about 10 knots speed. A new ship is projected to replace the **Friedrich der Grosse,** at a cost of £700,000. The **Baden, Bayern, Sachsen,** and **Württemberg** are being re-engined, re-armed, and fitted with military masts.

CRUISERS.

FIRST CLASS.

Kaiserin Augusta	6331	1892		...	...	3½	12 5.9-in. Q.F., 8 3.4-in. Q.F.	21.8	...	...	427
Leipzig	10,300	...	...	8 *h*	8 *h*	3	4 9.4-in., 12 5.9-in. Q.F., 10 3.4-in. Q.F.	19	...	...	...

SECOND CLASS.

Gefion	4207	1893		...	...	3	8 5.9-in., 10 4.1-in. Q.F.	20	950	...	312

GERMANY—CRUISERS (SECOND CLASS)—*Continued.*

Name.	Displacement. Metric Tons.	Date of Completion.	Cost. £	Armour. Belt. In.	Armour. Gun Posit'n. In.	Armour. Deck. In.	Armament.	Speed. Knots.	Coal. Capacity. Tons.	Coal. Endurance. Miles.	Complem't.
SECOND CLASS.—*Contd.*											
Irene	4400	1887	222,000	...	...	3	4 5·9-in., 8 4·1-in. Q.F.	19.8	900	...	358
Prinzess Wilhelm	4400	1887	222,000	...	...	3	4 5·9-in., 8 4·1-in. Q.F.	18.7	900	...	358
(Three new vessels, to replace Freya, K., and F.)	6100	...		...	4½	4	2 8.2-in., 8 5·9-in. Q.F., 10 3·4-in. Q.F.	21	950	...	...
	6100	...		...	4½	4	2 8.2-in., 8 5·9-in. Q.F., 10 3·4-in. Q.F.	21	950	...	...
	6100	...		...	4½	4	2 8.2-in., 8 5·9-in. Q.F., 10 3·4-in. Q.F.	21	950	...	...

Two SECOND CLASS CRUISERS—M. and N.—are projected, to cost £375,000 apiece.

There are also six THIRD CLASS CRUISERS—**Bussard, Falke, Geier, Kondor, Kornoran,** and **See Adler**—of 1640 to 1857 tons, 8 4·1-in. Q.F. guns, and 15½ to 16¼ knots speed. Also fourteen smaller and older Third Class Cruisers, with Torpedo-boat Destroyers of speeds from 20 to 26 knots, sixty-four sea-going and eighty-one other torpedo-boats.

ITALY.

BATTLESHIPS.

FIRST CLASS.

PRINCIPAL NAVIES OF THE WORLD

Name	Tonnage	Date	I.H.P.	Speed	Armour	Tubes	Guns			
Duilio	11,138	1876	850,400	21½	18	2	4 100-ton M.L., 3 4.7-in. Q.F.	15	1000	3750	487
Emanuele Filiberto	9800	...	...	9¾ n	9¾ n	3	4 10-in., 8 6-in. Q.F., 8 4.7-in. Q.F.	18	1000	7500	509
Francesco Morosini	11,000	1885	770,680	18 c	18 c	3	4 17-in., 2 6-in., 4 4.7-in. Q.F.	17	850	4500	748
Italia	14,387	1880	1,167,680	16 partial	19 c	3¼	4 17-in., 8 6-in., 4 4.7-in. Q.F.	17.8	1650	6000	748
Lepanto	14,400	...	1,150,880	16 partial	19 c	3¼	4 17-in., 8 6-in., 4 4.7-in. Q.F.	18.4	1650	6000	785
Re Umberto	13,298	1888	1,058,500	4	18	3	4 13.5-in., 8 6-in. Q.F., 16 4.7-in. Q.F.	18.2	1200	...	409
Ruggiero di Lauria	11,000	1884	777,560	18 c	18 c	3	4 17-in., 2 6-in. Q.F., 4 4.7-in. Q.F.	17	850	4500	785
Sardegna	13,860	1890	1,057,440	4	14¼ c	3	4 13.5-in., 8 5.9-in. Q.F., 16 4.7-in. Q.F.	20.2	1200	...	785
Sicilia	13,375	1891	1,050,000	4	14¼ c	3	4 13.5-in., 8 5.9-in. Q.F., 16 4.7-in. Q.F.	19.2	1200	...	785

Also five Ironclads over thirty years old—**Affondatore, Ancona, Castelfidardo, Maria Pia,** and **San Martino**—of displacement between 4000 and 4500 tons, of 4½ to 5 inches iron armour, efficiently re-armed with quick-firers, and steaming 12 knots. The Duilio is to be re-boilered and re-armed like the Dandolo.

CRUISERS.

FIRST CLASS.

Name	Tonnage	Date	I.H.P.			Guns	Speed		
Carlo Alberto	6500	1895	...	6 n	6 n	1¼	12 5.9-in. Q.F., 6 4.7-in. Q.F.	20	1000	460
Marco Polo	4583	1890	344,400	4	4	1	6 5.9-in. Q.F., 10 4.7-in. Q.F.	19	630	315
Garibaldi	6840	...	520,000	6 n	6 n	1½	2 9.8-in., 10 5.9-in. Q.F., 6 4.7-in. Q.F.	20	1000	460
Varese	6840	...	520,000	6 n	6 n	1½	2 9.8-in., 10 5.9-in. Q.F., 6 4.7-in. Q.F.	20	1000	460
Vettor Pisani	6500	1895	...	6 n	6 n	1¼	12 5.9-in. Q.F., 6 4.7-in. Q.F.	20	1000	460

NAVAL POLICY

ITALY—CRUISERS—*Continued.*

Name.	Displacement. Metric Tons.	Date of Completion.	Cost. £	Armour. Belt. In.	Armour. Gun Posit'n. In.	Armour. Deck. In.	Armament.	Speed. Knots.	Coal. Capacity. Tons.	Coal. Endurance. Miles.	Complem't.
SECOND CLASS.											
Etna	3530	1885	226,720	...	5	1½	2 9.8-in., 6 5.9-in. Q.F.	17.8	630	...	...
Fieramosca	3600	1888	240,120	...	5	1½	2 9.8-in., 6 5.9-in. Q.F.	17.5	590	...	...
Stromboli	3475	1886	220,080	...	5	1½	2 9.8-in., 6 5.9-in. Q.F.	17	630	...	...
Vesuvio	3427	1886	218,320	...	5	1½	2 9.8-in., 6 5.9-in. Q.F.	17	600	...	...

Also thirteen **THIRD CLASS CRUISERS**—**Piemonte**, 2500 tons, 3-in. armour on gun positions and deck, 6 6.6-in. and 6 4.7-in. Q.F., 21 knots; **Puglia**, 2550 tons, 4½-in. on guns and 1-in. deck, 4 5.9-in. and 6 4.7-in. Q.F., 20 knots; **Giovanni Bausan**, 3063 tons, 5-in. on guns and 1-in. deck, 2 9.8-in., 6 5.9-in. Q.F., 17.5 knots; **Calabria**, **Elba**, **Etruria**, **Liguria**, **Lombardia**, **Umbria**, 2280 to 2730 tons, 4½-in. on guns and 2-in. deck, 4 5.9-in. and 6 4.7-in. Q.F., 17 to 19.8 knots; **Amerigo Vespucci**, **Cristoforo Colombo**, **Dogali**, and **Flavio Gioja**, less powerful.

Also sixteen **TORPEDO-GUNBOATS**, of speeds from 18 to 23 knots.

JAPAN.
BATTLESHIPS.

	Displacement. Metric Tons.	Date of Completion.	Cost. £	Armour. Belt. In.	Armour. Gun Posit'n. In.	Armour. Deck. In.	Armament.	Speed. Knots.	Coal. Capacity. Tons.	Coal. Endurance. Miles.	Complem't.
Chin-Yuen-Yo	7400	1882	Captured.	14	12	3	4 12-in., 2 5.9-in.	14	1000	...	250
Fuji	12,450	1896	...	18 h	14 h	2½	4 12-in., 10 6-in. Q.F.	18	1100	9000	...
Yashima	12,450	1896	...	18 h	14 h	2½	4 12-in., 10 6-in. Q.F.	18	1100	9000	...

The **Fu-Sō**, **Hi-yei**, **Kon-go**, and **Rio-jo**, small and old Battleships, are hardly fitted for modern war; the Hi-yei and Kon-go are used as Training-ships. Projected are two Battleships of 15,140 tons, to carry 4 11.8-in. and 12 5.9-in. Q.F. guns.

PRINCIPAL NAVIES OF THE WORLD

CRUISERS.

Akitsushima	3150	1892	...	4½	3	4 6-in. Q.F., 6 4.7-in. Q.F.	19	...	330
Chiyoda	2450	1889	...	4½	...	10 4.7-in. Q.F.	17.5	420	300
Hashidate	4277	1891	...	12	2	1 12.5-in., 11 4.7-in. Q.F.	17	400	350
Itsukushima	4277	1891	...	12	2	1 12.5-in., 11 4.7-in. Q.F.	17	400	350
Izumi (late Esmeralda)	2716	1878	...	22	5	2 10-in., 6 4.7-in. Q.F.	17.9	400	300
Matsushima	4277	1890	...	12	2	1 12.5-in., 11 4.7-in. Q.F.	17.5	400	350
Naniwa	3650	1885	...	1½	3	2 10-in., 6 5.9-in.	18.7	800	350
Ta Kachito	3700	1885	...	1½	3	2 10-in., 6 5.9-in.	18.7	800	350
Yoshino	4150	1892	...	4½	4½	4 6-in. Q.F., 8 4.7-in. Q.F.	23	1000	300

Also **Akashi** and **Suma** (building), 2700 tons, 2-in. deck, 2 6-in. and 6 4.7-in. Q.F., 20 knots. Also three smaller Cruisers, and two Torpedo-Gunboats. Projected, four Cruisers of 7500 tons, three of 4500, two of 3000, and smaller vessels.

RUSSIA.

BATTLESHIPS.

FIRST CLASS.									
Catherine II.	10,180	1886	900,000	16c	14c	3	6 12-in., 7 6-in.	15½	886	325
Georgi Pobiedonosek	10,280	1892	431,000	16	12	...	6 12-in., 7 6-in. Q.F.	16¼	700	500
Navarin	9476	1891	772,995	16	12	...	4 12-in., 8 6-in.	16	1200	...
Oslabya	12,674	(1899)	...	9	...	...	4 10-in., 8 6-in. Q.F.	17½	1750	...

NAVAL POLICY

RUSSIA—BATTLESHIPS (FIRST CLASS)—*Continued.*

Name.	Displacement. Metric Tons.	Date of Completion.	Cost. £	Armour. Belt. In.	Armour. Gun Posit'n In.	Armour. Deck. In.	Armament.	Speed. Knots.	Coal. Capacity. Tons.	Coal. Endurance. Miles.	Complem't.
FIRST CLASS—*Contd.*											
Peresviet	12,674	(1899)	...	9	...	...	4 10-in., 8 6-in. Q.F.	17½	1750	...	...
Petropavlovsk	10,960	1894	1,098,000	15¾	10h	3½	4 12-in., 8 8-in. (or 12 6-in. Q.F.)	17½	900	...	...
Poltava	10,960	1894	1,098,000	15¾	10h	3½	4 12-in., 8 8-in. (or 12 6-in. Q.F.)	17½	900	...	...
Sevastopol	10,960	1895	1,098,000	15¾	10h	3½	4 12-in., 8 8-in. (or 12 6-in. Q.F.)	17½	900	...	...
Sinope	10,180	1887	900,000	16c	14c	3	6 12-in., 7 6-in.	16	886	...	325
Tchesme	10,180	1886	900,000	16c	14c	3	6 12-in., 7 6-in.	15	886	...	325
Tri Sviatitelia	12,480	1893	...	18	16	3	4 12-in., 12 6-in. Q.F., 4 4-in. Q.F.	...	1000	...	582
SECOND CLASS.											
Alexander II.	8440	1887	...	14c	10c	2½	2 12-in., 4 9-in., 8 6-in.	...	1200	...	604
Dvenadzat Apostoloff	8076	1890	...	14c	12c	2½	4 12-in., 4 6-in.	16.6	800	...	500
Gangoot	6592	1890	...	16c	7.8	2½	1 12-in., 4 9-in., 4 6-in.	14.7	500	...	528
Nicolai I.	8440	1888	453,000	14c	10c	2½	2 12-in., 4 9-in., 8 6-in.	14.8	...	...	604
Peter Veliky	8749	1872	...	14	8	3	4 12-in.	14½	1200	...	436
Rostislav	8880	(1898)	...	15¾c	15¾c	3	4 10-in., 8 5.9-in. Q.F.	16	800	...	...
Sissoi Veliky	8880	1894	796,333	15¾c	15¾c	3	4 12-in., 6 5.9-in. Q.F.	16	550	...	...

PRINCIPAL NAVIES OF THE WORLD

THIRD CLASS OR COAST DEFENCE.

Admiral Chicagoff	3493	1868	...	6	6	...	2 11-in.	10½	300	...	264
Admiral Greig	3462	1868	...	4½	6	...	3 11-in.	10	300	...	280
Admiral Lazareff	3462	1867	...	4½	6	...	3 11-in.	10	300	...	280
Admiral Oushakoff	4126	(1897)	410,000	10	8	3	2 9-in., 4 6-in. Q.F.	16	400	2500	318
Admiral Seniavin	4126	(1897)	410,000	10	8	3	2 9-in., 4 6-in. Q.F.	16	400	2500	318
Admiral Spiridoff	3493	1868	...	6	6	...	2 11-in.	10½	300	...	264
Charodeika	1881	1867	...	4½	6	1	4 9-in.	8	250	...	171
General Admiral Apraxine	4126	(1898)	...	10	8	3	2 9-in., 4 6-in. Q.F.	16	400	2500	318
Kniaz Pojarski	5007	1867	...	4½	4½	...	2 8-in., 2 6-in.	11	600	...	452
Kreml	3480	1864	...	4½	4½	...	8 8-in., 6 6-in.	9	...	...	...
Netron Menya	3494	1864	...	4½	4½	...	14 8-in.	9	500	...	...

A First Class Battleship of the Oslabya type is projected. There are also four Armoured Gunboats—**Gremiastchy, Grosiastchy, Khrabry, Otvazny**—of 1500 tons, 5-in. belt and 1¾-in. deck, 1 9-in. and 1 6-in. gun, and 15 knots; two circular Coast Defence Ironclads—**Novgorod** and **Vice-Admiral Popoff**—and eleven Armoured Monitors, all ineffective.

CRUISERS.

FIRST CLASS—ARMOURED.

Admiral Nachimoff	7782	1885	572,000	10c	8c	3	8 8-in., 10 6-in.	16.7	1200	8000	567
Dmitri Donskoi	5893	1883	...	6	...	2½	2 8-in., 4 6-in. Q.F., 10 4.7-in., Q.F.	16¼	400	4800	551
General Admiral	4126	1873	...	6	...	...	6 8-in., 2 6-in.	14.2	1000	...	312

NAVAL POLICY

RUSSIA—CRUISERS (FIRST CLASS—ARMOURED)—*Continued*.

Name.	Displacement. Metric Tons.	Date of Completion.	Cost. £	Armour. Belt. In.	Armour. Gun Posit'n. In.	Armour. Deck. In.	Armament.	Speed. Knots.	Coal. Capacity. Tons.	Coal. Endurance. Miles.	Complem't.
FIRST CLASS—ARMOURED—*Contd.*											
Gerzog Edinburski	4604	1875	...	6	6	...	4 8-in., 5 6-in.	15.2	1000	...	500
Minin	5740	1878	...	7	8	...	4 8-in., 12 6-in.	14	1200	...	450
Pamyat Azova	6000	1888	350,000	9c	8c	2¼	2 8-in., 13 6-in.	18.8	1000	10,000	525
Rossia	12,130	(1898)	...	10	...	2¼	4 8-in., 16 6-in. Q.F., 6 4.7-in. Q.F.	20	2500	20,000	725
Rurik	10,923	1894	...	10c	...	2½	4 8-in., 16 6-in. Q.F., 6 4.7-in. Q.F.	18.7	2000	20,000	768
Vladimir Monomach	5796	1882	...	6c	...	2	4 8-in., 12 6-in.	15.2	400	...	550
SECOND CLASS.											
Admiral Korniloff	5000	1887	296,000	...	...	2½	2 8-in., 14 6-in.	17.5	1100	...	425
Pamyat Merkuriya	3050	1880	...	...	...	...	6 6-in.	16	1100	...	200
Svietlana	3828	(1898)	...	...	...	1¾	8 5.9-in. Q.F.	20	1000	...	...
THIRD CLASS.											
Rynda	2950	1885	...	...	...	1½	10 6-in.	14.8	710	...	322

Two Second Class Cruisers are projected. There are also two obsolete Third Class Cruisers, besides older Corvettes and Sloops. Also eight Torpedo-Gunboats—**Captain Sacken, Gaidamak, Griden, Kazarsky, Lieutenant Ilyen, Posadnik, Voevoda, Vzadnidk**—armed with light quick-firers, and steaming 18.5 to 22 knots per hour. Nine Auxiliary Steamers of the Black Sea Company, and fifteen of the Volunteer Fleet.

PRINCIPAL NAVIES OF THE WORLD

SPAIN.

BATTLESHIPS.

Numancia . . .	7395	1863	315,600	$5\frac{1}{2}i$	$5i$	...	8 10-in. M.L., 7 8-in. M.L.	8	1100	...	600
Pelayo . . .	9900	1887	...	$17\frac{3}{4}$	$19\frac{1}{4}$	4	2 12½-in., 2 11-in., 1 6.2-in., 12 4.7-in.	16	800	5000	600
Vitoria . . .	7250	1865	...	$5\frac{1}{2}i$	$5i$	...	8 9-in. M.L., 3 8-in. M.L.	11	875	...	561

CRUISERS.

FIRST CLASS AND ARMOURED.

Alfonso XIII. .	5000	1891	...	...	...	4½	4 7.8-in., 6 4.7-in.	20	1200	...	276
Almirante Oquendo .	7000	1891	600,000	12	10½	3	2 11-in., 10 5½-in. Q.F.	20	1200	10,000	500
Cardinal Cisneros .	7000	1896	600,000	12	10½	2	2 11-in., 10 5½-in. Q.F.	20	1200	10,000	500
Cataluña . .	7000	...	600,000	12	10½	2	2 11-in., 10 5½-in. Q.F.	20	1200	10,000	484
Emperador Carlos V.	9090	1895	734,000	6½	10	2	2 11-in., 8 5½-in. Q.F.	20	1700	12,000	535
Infanta Maria Theresa	7000	1890	600,000	12	10½	3	2 11-in., 10 5½-in. Q.F.	20¼	1200	10,000	500
Princesa de Asturias	7000	...	600,000	12	10½	2	2 11-in., 10 5½-in. Q.F.	20	1200	10,000	500
Vizcaya . .	7000	1891	600,000	12	10½	3	2 11-in., 10 5½-in. Q.F.	20	1200	10,000	500

UNITED STATES.
BATTLESHIPS.

Name.	Displacement. Metric Tons.	Date of Completion.	Cost. £	Armour. Belt. In.	Armour. Gun Posit'n. In.	Armour. Deck. In.	Armament.	Speed. Knots.	Coal. Capacity. Tons.	Coal. Endurance. Miles.	Complem't.
FIRST CLASS.											
Indiana	10,288	1893	604,000	18½	17 & 6	3	4 13-in., 8 8-in., 6 4-in. Q.F.	16	400	16,000	...
Iowa	11,300	(1897)	900,000	14	15	3	4 12-in., 8 8-in.	16.5	2000	6000	...
Kearsage	11,500	(1898)	800,000	15″	17 & 6″	5″	4 12-in., 4 8-in., 14 5-in. Q.F.	16	410	6000	520
Kentucky	11,500	(1898)	800,000	15″	17 & 6″	5″	4 12-in., 4 8-in., 14 5-in. Q.F.	16	410	6000	520
Massachusetts	10,288	1893	604,000	18½	17 & 6	3	4 13-in., 8 8-in., 4 6-in. Q.F.	16	400	16,000	...
Oregon	10,288	1893	636,000	18½	17 & 6	3	4 13-in., 8 8-in., 4 6-in. Q.F.	16	400	16,000	...
SECOND CLASS.											
Texas	6300	1892	495,000	12	12	3	2 12-in., 6 6-in.	17	850	8500	400
THIRD CLASS.											
Amphitrite	3990	1883	...	9	11½	2	4 10-in., 2 4-in. Q.F.	12	300	...	155
Katahdin	2050	1893	186,000	6	18	6	......	17	...	...	...
Miantonomoh	3990	1876	272,000	7	11½	2	4 10-in., 2 4-in. Q.F.	10¼	330	...	155
Monadnock	3990	1883	272,000	9	11½	2	4 10-in.	12	330	...	155
Monterey	4138	1891	...	13	14	3	2 12-in., 2 10-in.	13.6	200	...	211

PRINCIPAL NAVIES OF THE WORLD

CRUISERS.

ARMOURED.											
Brooklyn	9250	1895	700,000	3	8	6	8 8-in., 12 5-in. Q.F.	21	1650	15,000	500
Maine	6682	1890	517,600	12	12	4	4 10-in., 6 6-in.	19	822	7000	400
New York	8500	1891	597,000	4	10	6	6 8-in., 12 4-in. Q.F.	21	750	13,500	484
UNARMOURED.											
Atlanta	3189	1884	123,600	...	...	...	2 8-in., 6 6-in.	16¼	490	...	...
Baltimore	4600	1888	210,000	...	...	...	4 8-in., 6 6-in.	20½	400	12,000	...
Boston	3189	1884	123,200	...	...	...	2 8-in., 6 6-in.	15	490	...	...
Charleston	4040	1888	...	...	...	...	2 8-in., 6 6-in.	18½	328	...	...
Chicago	4500	1885	177,800	...	...	...	4 8-in., 8 6-in.	16¼	940	5000	...
Cincinnati	3183	1892	220,000	...	...	...	1 6-in., 10 5-in. Q.F.	19	556	4500	...
Columbia	7475	1892	545,000	...	...	...	1 8-in., 2 6-in. Q.F.	22¾	2000	13,000	...
Minneapolis	7475	1893	421,000	...	...	...	1 8-in., 2 6-in. Q.F.	22¾	2000	13,000	...
Newark	4083	1890	250,000	...	...	...	12 6-in.	19	850	10,000	...
Olympia	5800	1892	477,600	...	...	...	4 8-in., 10 5-in. Q.F.	21½	1300	13,000	...
Philadelphia	4413	1889	265,000	...	...	...	12 6-in.	19½	1175	7000	...
Raleigh	3183	1892	228,600	...	...	...	1 6-in., 10 5-in. Q.F.	19	556	4,500	...

INDEX

Achilles, 17.
——— "Admiral" class, 71, 117.
Almirante Condell, 26.
Almirante Lynch, 26.
Andrea Doria, 145.
"Apollo" class, 94.
Aquidaban, 27.
Armaments, Comparative tables of, 162-3, 165, 167, 172-3.
Armour, 35-6, 61, 117, 129, 138, 152.
Armstrong, Lord, 19, 24.
Arrogant, 97.
"Astræa" class, 95.
"Aurora" class, 41, 93.
Australia and France, 239.
Australian Defence, 249.

Balfour, Rt. Hon. A. J., 6.
Barfleur, 64.
Barham, 42.
Battleships, Classification of, 55, 64, 71, 76, 87, 90, 109, 129, 137.
Belleville's boilers, 47.
Bellona, 42.
Beresford, Lord Charles, 218, 227, 285.
Blake, 88.
Blanco Encalada, 26.
Blenheim, 88.
Blockades, 194-9.
Bouvet, 110.
Brassey, Mr. T. A., 134, 228, 230.
Breech-loaders *v.* Muzzle-loaders, 79, 161.

Brennus, 112, 114.
Brooklyn, 154.
Buenos-Aires, 97.
Canada, Defence of, 256.
Canet guns, 129.
Centurion, 64.
Channel Squadron—
  French, 215, 270, 272.
  British, 269, 270-1.
Charlemagne, 109.
China-Japanese War, Lessons of, 29, 33, 44, 62.
China Squadron, 241-2.
Coaling stations, 260-1.
Coast-defenders, French, 119-120.
Collingwood, 24, 71.
Colomb, Sir John, 9, 52.
Colomb, Admiral P., vi., 49.
Colossus, 77.
Comet, 16.
Commerce, Destruction and maintenance of, 191-193.
Commerce-destroyers—
  American, 156.
  French, 123.
Comparative tables of—
  Armaments, 162-3, 165, 167, 172-3.
  Navies, 160, 172, 178.
  Speed and endurance, 168-9, 175, 177.
Congress, 16.
Cruisers, 82, 85, 91, 93, 121, 133, 140, 148, 154, 156, 172.

Cumberland, 16.

Devastation, 78.
"Diadem" class, 87.
Dilke, Sir Charles, 6, 229, 282.
Dupuy-de-Lôme, 121.

"Eclipse" class, 96, 206.
"Edgar" class, 90.
Edinburgh, 77.
Elements of force in warships, 13.
Elliot, Admiral Sir George, 234.
Esmeralda, 84.

Forced draught, 41.
Foreign seamanship, 215.
Forster, Mr. Arnold, 9, 265.
Fournier, Admiral, 122.
France, Disposition of forces, 268.
— Relations of, 186.
French Navy, 107, 116.
Foreign Squadrons—
　British, China, 241-2.
　Mediterranean, 215, 268.
　Pacific, 243.

General Staff required, 282.
German Navy, 136.
— hostility, 183, 189, 210.
Georgi Pobiedonosek, 130.
Gibraltar, Defence of, 264.
Goschen, Rt. Hon. J. G., 4, 179, 203, 234.
Guns, Improvement in, 19.
— Pneumatic dynamite, 31.
— Quick-firing, 24, 27, 129, 162.

Harcourt, Sir William, 8, 182.
Harveyed plates, 37, 166.
Havock, 101.
Holtzer shot, 37.
Hood, 62.
Hornet, 101.
Hotchkiss gun, 25, 113.
Huascar, 33.

"Impossible Programme, An," 272.
Increase of strength imperative, 190.
India, Defence of, 255.
Induced draught, 44.
Inflexible, 23, 36.
Iowa, 153.
Isolation of England, 189.
Italian Navy, 143.

Jauréguiberry, 111.

Kaiser Friedrich III., 138.
Kaiserin Augusta, 141.
Kearsage, 49, 151.
Kentucky, 151.
Krupp guns, 68.

Magnificent, 44, 57, 59.
Mahan, Captain, 156.
Maine, 155.
Majestic, 17.
Malta, Defence of, 264.
Marines, 233.
Massachusetts, 38.
"Medea" class, 98.
Mediterranean, Abandonment of, Objections to, 272.
Mediterranean Squadron, 215, 268.
Mercantile Marine, British, 229.
Mercury, 84.
Merrimac, 16, 22, 36.
Monitor, 36.
Muzzle-loaders in British Navy, 78-9.

Naval Estimates, 1896, Debate on, 4.
— Reserve, Deficiencies of, 221, 231.
— — Failure of, 278.
— Reserves, Superiority of Foreign 224.
— Volunteers, 233.
Navies, Comparative tables of, 160, 172, 178.
— Foreign, 107, 126, 136, 143, 149.
Nictheroy, 32.
Nile, 66.

INDEX

Nordenfeldt, 25.

Officers and men, 212.
— Deficient supply of, 219, 226; Suggested remedies, 226, 228.

Pacific Squadron, 243.
Pallas, 40.
Particular Service Squadron, 268, 278.
"Pearl" class, 97.
Pelorus, 99.
Piemonte, 99.
Pneumatic dynamite gun, 31.
Powerful, 46.
Precautions against surprise imperative, 280.
Public opinion, Pressure of, 286.

Rattler, 16, 39.
Rattlesnake, 40.
Rawson, Admiral, 256.
Re Umberto, 145.
Readiness for war nobody's business, 284.
Rédoubtable, 116.
Reed, Sir Edward, 23, 61.
Relative strength of navies, 158, 205.
Renown, 32, 45.
Reserve Squadron, 215.
Rifling, Superiority of, 18.
Rossia, 133.
Royal Sovereign, 22, 42, 62, 64.
Rurik, 133.
Russia, Relations of, 186.
Russian Navy, 126.

Sans Pareil, 67.
See Adler, 137, 142.
Sempaio, 27.
Shipbuilding policy, 179.
Speed and endurance, Comparative tables of, 168-9, 175, 177.
Steam-power, Advance in, 39.

Terrible, 48, 85.
Thunderer, 78.
Thursfield, Mr., vi.
Torpedo craft, 25, 100, 125, 135, 142, 148, 157, 178, 195.
— destroyers, 34, 100, 104, 135, 197.
Torpedoes in warfare, 33.
Trafalgar, 66.
Turret ships, 78, 81.

United States Navy, Growth of, 149.

Vesuvius, 32.
Vulcan, 99.

War, Britain's unreadiness for, 267.
Warrior, 17.
Water-tube boilers, 46.
West Indies, Defence of, 259.
White, Sir William, 24, 61.
Wilkinson, Mr. Spenser, vi, 52, 191.
Williams, Mr. Harry, 45.
Wilson, Mr. H. W., 33.
Wire guns, 21.

Zalinski, Lieutenant, 31.

PLYMOUTH
WILLIAM BRENDON AND SON
PRINTERS

A CATALOGUE OF BOOKS AND ANNOUNCEMENTS OF METHUEN AND COMPANY PUBLISHERS : LONDON 36 ESSEX STREET W.C.

CONTENTS

	PAGE
FORTHCOMING BOOKS, .	2
POETRY,	9
ENGLISH CLASSICS,	10
ILLUSTRATED BOOKS, .	11
HISTORY, .	12
BIOGRAPHY,	14
GENERAL LITERATURE,	15
SCIENCE,	18
PHILOSOPHY, .	19
THEOLOGY,	20
LEADERS OF RELIGION,	21
FICTION,	22
BOOKS FOR BOYS AND GIRLS, .	31
THE PEACOCK LIBRARY,	32
UNIVERSITY EXTENSION SERIES,	32
SOCIAL QUESTIONS OF TO-DAY,	34
CLASSICAL TRANSLATIONS, .	35
EDUCATIONAL BOOKS,	36

OCTOBER 1896

October 1896.

Messrs. Methuen's
ANNOUNCEMENTS

Poetry

RUDYARD KIPLING

BALLADS. By RUDYARD KIPLING. *Crown 8vo.* 6s.
    150 copies on hand-made paper. *Demy 8vo.* 21s.
    30 copies on Japanese paper. *Demy 8vo.* 42s.

The enormous success of 'Barrack Room Ballads' justifies the expectation that this volume, so long postponed, will have an equal, if not a greater, success.

GEORGE WYNDHAM

SHAKESPEARE'S POEMS. Edited, with an Introduction and Notes, by GEORGE WYNDHAM, M.P. *Crown 8vo.* 3s. 6d.
[*English Classics.*

W. E. HENLEY

ENGLISH LYRICS. Selected and Edited by W. E. HENLEY. *Crown 8vo. Buckram.* 6s.
    Also 15 copies on Japanese paper. *Demy 8vo.* £2, 2s.

Few announcements will be more welcome to lovers of English verse than the one that Mr. Henley is bringing together into one book the finest lyrics in our language. The volume will be produced with the same care that made 'Lyra Heroica' delightful to the hand and eye.

'Q'

POEMS AND BALLADS. By 'Q,' Author of 'Green Bays, etc. *Crown 8vo. Buckram.* 3s. 6d.
    25 copies on Japanese paper. *Demy 8vo.* 21s.

History, Biography, and Travel

CAPTAIN HINDE

THE FALL OF THE CONGO ARABS. By SIDNEY L. HINDE. With Portraits and Plans. *Demy 8vo.* 12s. 6d.

This volume deals with the recent Belgian Expedition to the Upper Congo, which developed into a war between the State forces and the Arab slave-raiders in Central Africa. Two white men only returned alive from the three years' war—Commandant Dhanis and the writer of this book, Captain Hinde. During the greater part of the time spent by Captain Hinde in the Congo he was amongst cannibal races in little-known regions, and, owing to the peculiar circumstances of his position, was enabled to see a side of native history shown to few Europeans. The war terminated in the complete defeat of the Arabs, seventy thousand of whom perished during the struggle.

S. BARING GOULD

THE LIFE OF NAPOLEON BONAPARTE. By S. BARING GOULD. With over 450 Illustrations in the Text and 13 Photogravure Plates. *Large quarto.* 36s.

This study of the most extraordinary life in history is written rather for the general reader than for the military student, and while following the main lines of Napoleon's career, is concerned chiefly with the development of his character and his personal qualities. Special stress is laid on his early life—the period in which his mind and character took their definite shape and direction.

The great feature of the book is its wealth of illustration. There are over 450 illustrations, large and small, in the text, and there are also more than a dozen full page photogravures. Every important incident of Napoleon's career has its illustration, while there are a large number of portraits of his contemporaries, reproductions of famous pictures, of contemporary caricatures, of his handwriting, etc. etc.

It is not too much to say that no such magnificent book on Napoleon has ever been published.

VICTOR HUGO

THE LETTERS OF VICTOR HUGO. Translated from the French by F. CLARKE, M.A. *In Two Volumes. Demy 8vo.* 10s. 6d. each. *Vol. I.*

This is the first volume of one of the most interesting and important collection of letters ever published in France. The correspondence dates from Victor Hugo's boyhood to his death, and none of the letters have been published before. The arrangement is chiefly chronological, but where there is an interesting set of letters to one person these are arranged together. The first volume contains, among others, (1) Letters to his father; (2) to his young wife; (3) to his confessor, Lamennais; (4) a very important set of about fifty letters to Sainte-Beuve; (5) letters about his early books and plays.

J. M. RIGG

ST. ANSELM OF CANTERBURY: A CHAPTER IN THE HISTORY OF RELIGION. By J. M. RIGG, of Lincoln's Inn, Barrister-at-Law. *Demy 8vo.* 7s. 6d.

This work gives for the first time in moderate compass a complete portrait of St. Anselm, exhibiting him in his intimate and interior as well as in his public life. Thus, while the great ecclesiastico-political struggle in which he played so prominent a part is fully dealt with, unusual prominence is given to the profound and subtle speculations by which he permanently influenced theological and metaphysical thought; while it will be a surprise to most readers to find him also appearing as the author of some of the most exquisite religious poetry in the Latin language.

EDWARD GIBBON

THE DECLINE AND FALL OF THE ROMAN EMPIRE. By EDWARD GIBBON. A New Edition, edited with Notes, Appendices, and Maps by J. B. BURY, M.A., Fellow of Trinity College, Dublin. *In Seven Volumes. Demy 8vo, gilt top.* 8s. 6d. each. *Crown 8vo.* 6s. each. *Vol. II.*

Messrs. Methuen's Announcements

W. M. FLINDERS PETRIE

A HISTORY OF EGYPT, FROM THE EARLIEST TIMES TO THE PRESENT DAY. Edited by W. M. FLINDERS PETRIE, D.C.L., LL.D., Professor of Egyptology at University College. *Fully Illustrated. In Six Volumes. Crown 8vo. 6s. each.*

Vol. II. XVII.-XVIII. DYNASTIES. W. M. F. PETRIE.

'A history written in the spirit of scientific precision so worthily represented by Dr. Petrie and his school cannot but promote sound and accurate study, and supply a vacant place in the English literature of Egyptology.'—*Times.*

J. WELLS

A SHORT HISTORY OF ROME. By J. WELLS, M.A., Fellow and Tutor of Wadham Coll., Oxford. With 4 Maps. *Crown 8vo. 3s. 6d. 350 pp.*

This book is intended for the Middle and Upper Forms of Public Schools and for Pass Students at the Universities. It contains copious Tables, etc.

H. DE B. GIBBINS

THE HISTORY OF ENGLISH INDUSTRY. By H. DE B. GIBBINS, M.A. With 5 Maps. *Demy 8vo. 10s. 6d. Pp.* 450.

This book is written with the view of affording a clear view of the main facts of English Social and Industrial History placed in due perspective. Beginning with prehistoric times, it passes in review the growth and advance of industry up to the nineteenth century, showing its gradual development and progress. The author has endeavoured to place before his readers the history of industry as a connected whole in which all these developments have their proper place. The book is illustrated by Maps, Diagrams, and Tables, and aided by copious Footnotes.

MRS. OLIPHANT

THOMAS CHALMERS. By Mrs. OLIPHANT. *Second Edition. Crown 8vo. 3s. 6d.* [*Leaders of Religion.*

Naval and Military

DAVID HANNAY

A SHORT HISTORY OF THE ROYAL NAVY, FROM EARLY TIMES TO THE PRESENT DAY. By DAVID HANNAY. *Illustrated. Demy 8vo.* 15s.

This book aims at giving an account not only of the fighting we have done at sea, but of the growth of the service, of the part the Navy has played in the development of the Empire, and of its inner life. The author has endeavoured to avoid the mistake of sacrificing the earlier periods of naval history—the very interesting wars with Holland in the seventeenth century, for instance, or the American War of 1779-1783—to the later struggle with Revolutionary and Imperial France.

COL. COOPER KING
A SHORT HISTORY OF THE BRITISH ARMY. By Lieut.-Colonel COOPER KING, of the Staff College, Camberley. *Illustrated.* *Demy 8vo.* 7s. 6d.

This volume aims at describing the nature of the different armies that have been formed in Great Britain, and how from the early and feudal levies the present standing army came to be. The changes in tactics, uniform, and armament are briefly touched upon, and the campaigns in which the army has shared have been so far followed as to explain the part played by British regiments in them.

G. W. STEEVENS
NAVAL POLICY: WITH A DESCRIPTION OF ENGLISH AND FOREIGN NAVIES. By G. W. STEEVENS. *Demy 8vo.* 6s.

This book is a description of the British and other more important navies of the world, with a sketch of the lines on which our naval policy might possibly be developed. It describes our recent naval policy, and shows what our naval force really is. A detailed but non-technical account is given of the instruments of modern warfare—guns, armour, engines, and the like—with a view to determine how far we are abreast of modern invention and modern requirements. An ideal policy is then sketched for the building and manning of our fleet; and the last chapter is devoted to docks, coaling-stations, and especially colonial defence.

Theology

F. B. JEVONS
AN INTRODUCTION TO THE HISTORY OF RELIGION. By F. B. JEVONS, M.A., Litt.D., Fellow of the University of Durham. *Demy 8vo.* 12s. 6d.

This is the third number of the series of 'Theological Handbooks' edited by Dr. Robertson of Durham, in which have already appeared Dr. Gibson's 'XXXIX. Articles' and Mr. Ottley's 'Incarnation.'

Mr. F. B. Jevons' 'Introduction to the History of Religion' treats of early religion, from the point of view of Anthropology and Folk-lore; and is the first attempt that has been made in any language to weave together the results of recent investigations into such topics as Sympathetic Magic, Taboo, Totemism, Fetishism, etc., so as to present a systematic account of the growth of primitive religion and the development of early religious institutions.

W. YORKE FAUSSETT
THE *DE CATECHIZANDIS RUDIBUS* OF ST. AUGUSTINE. Edited, with Introduction, Notes, etc., by W. YORKE FAUSSETT, M.A., late Scholar of Balliol Coll. *Crown 8vo.* 3s. 6d.

An edition of a Treatise on the Essentials of Christian Doctrine, and the best methods of impressing them on candidates for baptism. The editor bestows upon this patristic work the same care which a treatise of Cicero might claim. There is a general Introduction, a careful Analysis, a full Commentary, and other useful matter. No better introduction to the study of the Latin Fathers, their style and diction, could be found than this treatise, which also has no lack of modern interest.

General Literature

C. F. ANDREWS

CHRISTIANITY AND THE LABOUR QUESTION. By C. F. ANDREWS, B.A. *Crown 8vo.* 2s. 6d.

R. E. STEEL

MAGNETISM AND ELECTRICITY. By R. ELLIOTT STEEL, M.A., F.C.S. With Illustrations. *Crown 8vo.* 4s. 6d.

G. LOWES DICKINSON

THE GREEK VIEW OF LIFE. By G. L. DICKINSON, Fellow of King's College, Cambridge. *Crown 8vo.* 2s. 6d.
[*University Extension Series.*

J. A. HOBSON

THE PROBLEM OF THE UNEMPLOYED. By J. A. HOBSON, B.A., Author of 'The Problems of Poverty.' *Crown 8vo.* 2s. 6d.
[*Social Questions Series.*

S. E. BALLY

GERMAN COMMERCIAL CORRESPONDENCE. By S. E. BALLY, Assistant Master at the Manchester Grammar School. *Crown 8vo.* 2s.
[*Commercial Series.*

L. F. PRICE

ECONOMIC ESSAYS. By L. F. PRICE, M.A., Fellow of Oriel College, Oxford. *Crown 8vo.* 6s.

This book consists of a number of Studies in Economics and Industrial and Social Problems.

Fiction

MARIE CORELLI'S ROMANCES

FIRST COMPLETE AND UNIFORM EDITION

Large crown 8vo. 6s.

MESSRS. METHUEN beg to announce that they have commenced the publication of a New and Uniform Edition of MARIE CORELLI'S Romances. This Edition is revised by the Author, and contains new Prefaces. The volumes are being issued at short intervals in the following order :—

1. A ROMANCE OF TWO WORLDS.   2. VENDETTA.
3. THELMA.   4. ARDATH.
5. THE SOUL OF LILITH.   6. WORMWOOD.
7. BARABBAS.   8. THE SORROWS OF SATAN.

BARING GOULD
DARTMOOR IDYLLS. By S. BARING GOULD. *Cr. 8vo.* 6s.

GUAVAS THE TINNER. By S. BARING GOULD, Author of 'Mehalah,' 'The Broom Squire,' etc. Illustrated. *Crown 8vo.* 6s.

THE PENNYCOMEQUICKS. By S. BARING GOULD. New Edition. *Crown 8vo.* 6s.

A new edition, uniform with the Author's other novels.

LUCAS MALET
THE CARISSIMA. By LUCAS MALET, Author of 'The Wages of Sin,' etc. *Crown 8vo.* 6s.

This is the first novel which Lucas Malet has written since her very powerful 'The Wages of Sin.'

ARTHUR MORRISON
A CHILD OF THE JAGO. By ARTHUR MORRISON. Author of 'Tales of Mean Streets.' *Crown 8vo.* 6s.

This, the first long story which Mr. Morrison has written, is like his remarkable 'Tales of Mean Streets,' a realistic study of East End life.

W. E. NORRIS
CLARISSA FURIOSA. By W. E. NORRIS, 'Author of 'The Rogue,' etc. *Crown 8vo.* 6s.

L. COPE CORNFORD
CAPTAIN JACOBUS: A ROMANCE OF HIGHWAYMEN. By L. COPE CORNFORD. Illustrated. *Crown 8vo.* 6s.

J. BLOUNDELLE BURTON
DENOUNCED. By J. BLOUNDELLE BURTON, Author of 'In the Day of Adversity,' etc. *Crown 8vo.* 6s.

J. MACLAREN COBBAN
WILT THOU HAVE THIS WOMAN? By J. M. COBBAN, Author of 'The King of Andaman.' *Crown 8vo.* 6s.

J. F. BREWER
THE SPECULATORS. By J. F. BREWER. *Crown 8vo.* 6s.

A. BALFOUR
BY STROKE OF SWORD. By ANDREW BALFOUR. *Crown 8vo.* 6s.

MESSRS. METHUEN'S ANNOUNCEMENTS

M. A. OWEN

THE DAUGHTER OF ALOUETTE. By MARY A. OWEN. *Crown 8vo.* 6s.

A story of life among the American Indians.

RONALD ROSS

THE SPIRIT OF STORM. By RONALD ROSS, Author of 'The Child of Ocean.' *Crown 8vo.* 6s.

A romance of the Sea.

J. A. BARRY

IN THE GREAT DEEP: TALES OF THE SEA. By J. A. BARRY. Author of 'Steve Brown's Bunyip.' *Crown 8vo.* 6s.

JAMES GORDON

THE VILLAGE AND THE DOCTOR. By JAMES GORDON. *Crown 8vo.* 6s.

BERTRAM MITFORD

THE SIGN OF THE SPIDER. By BERTRAM MITFORD. *Crown 8vo.* 3s. 6d.

A story of South Africa.

A. SHIELD

THE SQUIRE OF WANDALES. By A. SHIELD. *Crown 8vo.* 3s. 6d.

G. W. STEEVENS

MONOLOGUES OF THE DEAD. By G. W. STEEVENS. *Foolscap 8vo.* 3s. 6d.

A series of Soliloquies in which famous men of antiquity—Julius Cæsar, Nero, Alcibiades, etc., attempt to express themselves in the modes of thought and language of to-day.

S. GORDON

A HANDFUL OF EXOTICS. By S. GORDON. *Crown 8vo.* 3s. 6d.

A volume of stories of Jewish life in Russia.

P. NEUMANN

THE SUPPLANTER. By P. NEUMANN. *Crown 8vo.* 3s. 6d.

EVELYN DICKINSON

THE SIN OF ANGELS. By EVELYN DICKINSON. *Crown 8vo.* 3s. 6d.

H. A. KENNEDY

A MAN WITH BLACK EYELASHES. By H. A. KENNEDY. *Crown 8vo.* 3s. 6d.

A LIST OF

MESSRS. METHUEN'S PUBLICATIONS

Poetry

Rudyard Kipling. BARRACK-ROOM BALLADS; And Other Verses. By RUDYARD KIPLING. *Ninth Edition. Crown 8vo. 6s.*

'Mr. Kipling's verse is strong, vivid, full of character. . . . Unmistakable genius rings in every line.'—*Times.*

'"Barrack-Room Ballads" contains some of the best work that Mr. Kipling has ever done, which is saying a good deal. "Fuzzy-Wuzzy," "Gunga Din," and "Tommy," are, in our opinion, altogether superior to anything of the kind that English literature has hitherto produced.'—*Athenæum.*

'The ballads teem with imagination, they palpitate with emotion. We read them with laughter and tears; the metres throb in our pulses, the cunningly ordered words tingle with life; and if this be not poetry, what is?'—*Pall Mall Gazette.*

"Q." THE GOLDEN POMP: A Procession of English Lyrics from Surrey to Shirley, arranged by A. T. QUILLER COUCH. *Crown 8vo. Buckram. 6s.*

A delightful volume: a really golden "Pomp."'—*Spectator.*

"Q." GREEN BAYS: Verses and Parodies. By "Q.," Author of 'Dead Man's Rock,' etc. *Second Edition. Crown 8vo. 3s. 6d.*

'The verses display a rare and versatile gift of parody, great command of metre, and a very pretty turn of humour.'—*Times.*

H. C. Beeching. LYRA SACRA: An Anthology of Sacred Verse. Edited by H. C. BEECHING, M.A. *Crown 8vo. Buckram. 6s.*

'An anthology of high excellence.'—*Athenæum.*
'A charming selection, which maintains a lofty standard of excellence.'—*Times.*

W. B. Yeats. AN ANTHOLOGY OF IRISH VERSE. Edited by W. B. YEATS. *Crown 8vo. 3s. 6d.*

'An attractive and catholic selection.'—*Times.*
'It is edited by the most original and most accomplished of modern Irish poets, and against his editing but a single objection can be brought, namely, that it excludes from the collection his own delicate lyrics.'—*Saturday Review.*

E. Mackay. A SONG OF THE SEA: MY LADY OF DREAMS, AND OTHER POEMS. By ERIC MACKAY, Author of 'The Love Letters of a Violinist.' *Second Edition. Fcap. 8vo, gilt top. 5s.*

'Everywhere Mr. Mackay displays himself the master of a style marked by all the characteristics of the best rhetoric. He has a keen sense of rhythm and of general balance; his verse is excellently sonorous.'—*Globe.*
'Throughout the book the poetic workmanship is fine.'—*Scotsman.*

Ibsen. BRAND. A Drama by HENRIK IBSEN. Translated by WILLIAM WILSON. *Second Edition. Crown 8vo.* 3s. 6d.

'The greatest world-poem of the nineteenth century next to "Faust." It is in the same set with "Agamemnon," with "Lear," with the literature that we now instinctively regard as high and holy.'—*Daily Chronicle.*

"**A. G.**" VERSES TO ORDER. By "A. G." *Cr. 8vo.* 2s. 6d. net.

A small volume of verse by a writer whose initials are well known to Oxford men.

'A capital specimen of light academic poetry. These verses are very bright and engaging, easy and sufficiently witty.'—*St. James's Gazette.*

F. Langbridge. BALLADS OF THE BRAVE: Poems of Chivalry, Enterprise, Courage, and Constancy, from the Earliest Times to the Present Day. Edited, with Notes, by Rev. F. LANGBRIDGE. *Crown 8vo. Buckram.* 3s. 6d. *School Edition.* 2s. 6d.

'A very happy conception happily carried out. These "Ballads of the Brave" are intended to suit the real tastes of boys, and will suit the taste of the great majority.'—*Spectator.* 'The book is full of splendid things.'—*World.*

Lang and Craigie. THE POEMS OF ROBERT BURNS. Edited by ANDREW LANG and W. A. CRAIGIE. With Portrait. *Demy 8vo, gilt top.* 6s.

This edition contains a carefully collated Text, numerous Notes, critical and textual, a critical and biographical Introduction, and a Glossary.

'Among the editions in one volume, Mr. Andrew Lang's will take the place of authority.'—*Times.*

'To the general public the beauty of its type, and the fair proportions of its pages, as well as the excellent chronological arrangement of the poems, should make it acceptable enough. Mr. Lang and his publishers have certainly succeeded in producing an attractive popular edition of the poet, in which the brightly written biographical introduction is not the least notable feature.'—*Glasgow Herald.*

English Classics

Edited by W. E. HENLEY.

'Very dainty volumes are these; the paper, type, and light-green binding are all very agreeable to the eye. *Simplex munditiis* is the phrase that might be applied to them.'—*Globe.*

'The volumes are strongly bound in green buckram, are of a convenient size, and pleasant to look upon, so that whether on the shelf, or on the table, or in the hand the possessor is thoroughly content with them.'—*Guardian.*

'The paper, type, and binding of this edition are in excellent taste, and leave nothing to be desired by lovers of literature.'—*Standard.*

THE LIFE AND OPINIONS OF TRISTRAM SHANDY. By LAWRENCE STERNE. With an Introduction by CHARLES WHIBLEY, and a Portrait. 2 vols. 7s.

THE COMEDIES OF WILLIAM CONGREVE. With an Introduction by G. S. STREET, and a Portrait. 2 vols. 7s.

MESSRS. METHUEN'S LIST

THE ADVENTURES OF HAJJI BABA OF ISPAHAN.
By JAMES MORIER. With an Introduction by E. G. BROWNE, M.A.,
and a Portrait. 2 vols. 7s.

THE LIVES OF DONNE, WOTTON, HOOKER, HER-
BERT, AND SANDERSON. By IZAAK WALTON. With an
Introduction by VERNON BLACKBURN, and a Portrait. 3s. 6d.

THE LIVES OF THE ENGLISH POETS. By SAMUEL
JOHNSON, LL.D. With an Introduction by J. H. MILLAR, and a
Portrait. 3 vols. 10s. 6d.

Illustrated Books

Jane Barlow. THE BATTLE OF THE FROGS AND MICE,
translated by JANE BARLOW, Author of 'Irish Idylls,' and pictured
by F. D. BEDFORD. *Small 4to.* 6s. *net.*

S. Baring Gould. A BOOK OF FAIRY TALES retold by S.
BARING GOULD. With numerous illustrations and initial letters by
ARTHUR J. GASKIN. *Second Edition. Crown 8vo. Buckram.* 6s.

'Mr. Baring Gould has done a good deed, and is deserving of gratitude, in re-writing
in honest, simple style the old stories that delighted the childhood of "our fathers
and grandfathers." We do not think he has omitted any of our favourite stories,
the stories that are commonly regarded as merely "old fashioned." As to the form
of the book, and the printing, which is by Messrs. Constable, it were difficult to
commend overmuch.'—*Saturday Review.*

S. Baring Gould. OLD ENGLISH FAIRY TALES. Collected and edited by S. BARING GOULD. With Numerous Illustrations by F. D. BEDFORD. *Second Edition. Crown 8vo. Buckram.* 6s.

'A charming volume, which children will be sure to appreciate. The stories have
been selected with great ingenuity from various old ballads and folk-tales, and,
having been somewhat altered and readjusted, now stand forth, clothed in Mr.
Baring Gould's delightful English, to enchant youthful readers. All the tales
are good.'—*Guardian.*

S. Baring Gould. A BOOK OF NURSERY SONGS AND
RHYMES. Edited by S. BARING GOULD, and Illustrated by the
Birmingham Art School. *Buckram, gilt top. Crown 8vo.* 6s.

'The volume is very complete in its way, as it contains nursery songs to the number
of 77, game-rhymes, and jingles. To the student we commend the sensible introduction, and the explanatory notes. The volume is superbly printed on soft,
thick paper, which it is a pleasure to touch; and the borders and pictures are, as
we have said, among the very best specimens we have seen of the Gaskin school.'
—*Birmingham Gazette.*

H. C. Beeching. A BOOK OF CHRISTMAS VERSE. Edited by H. C. BEECHING, M.A., and Illustrated by WALTER CRANE. *Crown 8vo, gilt top.* 5s.

A collection of the best verse inspired by the birth of Christ from the Middle Ages to the present day. A distinction of the book is the large number of poems it contains by modern authors, a few of which are here printed for the first time.

'An anthology which, from its unity of aim and high poetic excellence, has a better right to exist than most of its fellows.'—*Guardian.*

History

Gibbon. THE DECLINE AND FALL OF THE ROMAN EMPIRE. By EDWARD GIBBON. A New Edition, Edited with Notes, Appendices, and Maps, by J. B. BURY, M.A., Fellow of Trinity College, Dublin. *In Seven Volumes. Demy 8vo. Gilt top.* 8s. 6d. each. *Also crown 8vo.* 6s. *each.* Vol. I.

'The time has certainly arrived for a new edition of Gibbon's great work.... Professor Bury is the right man to undertake this task. His learning is amazing, both in extent and accuracy. The book is issued in a handy form, and at a moderate price, and it is admirably printed.'—*Times.*

'The edition is edited as a classic should be edited, removing nothing, yet indicating the value of the text, and bringing it up to date. It promises to be of the utmost value, and will be a welcome addition to many libraries.'—*Scotsman.*

'This edition, so far as one may judge from the first instalment, is a marvel of erudition and critical skill, and it is the very minimum of praise to predict that the seven volumes of it will supersede Dean Milman's as the standard edition of our great historical classic.'—*Glasgow Herald.*

'The beau-ideal Gibbon has arrived at last.'—*Sketch.*

'At last there is an adequate modern edition of Gibbon.... The best edition the nineteenth century could produce.'—*Manchester Guardian.*

Flinders Petrie. A HISTORY OF EGYPT, FROM THE EARLIEST TIMES TO THE PRESENT DAY. Edited by W. M. FLINDERS PETRIE, D.C.L., LL.D., Professor of Egyptology at University College. *Fully Illustrated. In Six Volumes. Crown 8vo.* 6s. *each.*

Vol. I. PREHISTORIC TIMES TO XVI. DYNASTY. W. M. F. Petrie. *Second Edition.*

'A history written in the spirit of scientific precision so worthily represented by Dr. Petrie and his school cannot but promote sound and accurate study, and supply a vacant place in the English literature of Egyptology.'—*Times.*

Flinders Petrie. EGYPTIAN TALES. Edited by W. M. FLINDERS PETRIE. Illustrated by TRISTRAM ELLIS. *In Two Volumes. Crown 8vo.* 3s. 6d. *each.*

'A valuable addition to the literature of comparative folk-lore. The drawings are really illustrations in the literal sense of the word.'—*Globe.*
'It has a scientific value to the student of history and archæology.'—*Scotsman.*
'Invaluable as a picture of life in Palestine and Egypt.'—*Daily News.*

Flinders Petrie. EGYPTIAN DECORATIVE ART. By W. M. FLINDERS PETRIE, D.C.L. With 120 Illustrations. *Crown 8vo. 3s. 6d.*

'Professor Flinders Petrie is not only a profound Egyptologist, but an accomplished student of comparative archæology. In these lectures, delivered at the Royal Institution, he displays both qualifications with rare skill in elucidating the development of decorative art in Egypt, and in tracing its influence on the art of other countries. Few experts can speak with higher authority and wider knowledge than the Professor himself, and in any case his treatment of his subject is full of learning and insight.'—*Times*.

S. Baring Gould. THE TRAGEDY OF THE CÆSARS. The Emperors of the Julian and Claudian Lines. With numerous Illustrations from Busts, Gems, Cameos, etc. By S. BARING GOULD, Author of 'Mehalah,' etc. *Third Edition. Royal 8vo. 15s.*

'A most splendid and fascinating book on a subject of undying interest. The great feature of the book is the use the author has made of the existing portraits of the Caesars, and the admirable critical subtlety he has exhibited in dealing with this line of research. It is brilliantly written, and the illustrations are supplied on a scale of profuse magnificence.'—*Daily Chronicle*.

'The volumes will in no sense disappoint the general reader. Indeed, in their way, there is nothing in any sense so good in English. . . . Mr. Baring Gould has presented his narrative in such a way as not to make one dull page.'—*Athenæum*.

A. Clark. THE COLLEGES OF OXFORD: Their History, their Traditions. By Members of the University. Edited by A. CLARK, M.A., Fellow and Tutor of Lincoln College. *8vo. 12s. 6d.*

'A work which will certainly be appealed to for many years as the standard book on the Colleges of Oxford.'—*Athenæum*.

Perrens. THE HISTORY OF FLORENCE FROM 1434 TO 1492. By F. T. PERRENS. Translated by HANNAH LYNCH. *8vo. 12s. 6d.*

A history of Florence under the domination of Cosimo, Piero, and Lorenzo de Medicis.

'This is a standard book by an honest and intelligent historian, who has deserved well of all who are interested in Italian history.'—*Manchester Guardian*.

E. L. S. Horsburgh. THE CAMPAIGN OF WATERLOO. By E. L. S. HORSBURGH, B.A. *With Plans. Crown 8vo. 5s.*

'A brilliant essay—simple, sound, and thorough.'—*Daily Chronicle*.
'A study, the most concise, the most lucid, the most critical that has been produced.'
—*Birmingham Mercury*.
'A careful and precise study, a fair and impartial criticism, and an eminently readable book.'—*Admiralty and Horse Guards Gazette*.

H. B. George. BATTLES OF ENGLISH HISTORY. By H. B. GEORGE, M.A., Fellow of New College, Oxford. *With numerous Plans. Third Edition. Crown 8vo. 6s.*

'Mr. George has undertaken a very useful task—that of making military affairs intelligible and instructive to non-military readers—and has executed it with laudable intelligence and industry, and with a large measure of success.'—*Times*.
'This book is almost a revelation; and we heartily congratulate the author on his work and on the prospect of the reward he has well deserved for so much conscientious and sustained labour.'—*Daily Chronicle*.

O. Browning. A SHORT HISTORY OF MEDIÆVAL ITALY, A.D. 1250-1530. By OSCAR BROWNING, Fellow and Tutor of King's College, Cambridge. *Second Edition. In Two Volumes.* Crown 8vo. 5s. each.

    VOL. I. 1250-1409.—Guelphs and Ghibellines.
    VOL. II. 1409-1530.—The Age of the Condottieri.

'A vivid picture of mediæval Italy.'—*Standard.*
'Mr. Browning is to be congratulated on the production of a work of immense labour and learning.'—*Westminster Gazette.*

O'Grady. THE STORY OF IRELAND. By STANDISH O'GRADY, Author of 'Finn and his Companions.' *Cr. 8vo.* 2s. 6d.

'Most delightful, most stimulating. Its racy humour, its original imaginings, make it one of the freshest, breeziest volumes.'—*Methodist Times.*
'A survey at once graphic, acute, and quaintly written.'—*Times.*

Biography

R. L. Stevenson. VAILIMA LETTERS. By ROBERT LOUIS STEVENSON. With an Etched Portrait by WILLIAM STRANG, and other Illustrations. *Second Edition. Crown 8vo. Buckram.* 7s. 6d.

'The Vailima Letters are rich in all the varieties of that charm which have secured for Stevenson the affection of many others besides "journalists, fellow-novelists, and boys."'—*The Times.*
'Few publications have in our time been more eagerly awaited than these "Vailima Letters," giving the first fruits of the correspondence of Robert Louis Stevenson. But, high as the tide of expectation has run, no reader can possibly be disappointed in the result.'—*St. James's Gazette.*
'For the student of English literature these letters indeed are a treasure. They are more like "Scott's Journal" in kind than any other literary autobiography.'—*National Observer.*

F. W. Joyce. THE LIFE OF SIR FREDERICK GORE OUSELEY. By F. W. JOYCE, M.A. With Portraits and Illustrations. *Crown 8vo.* 7s. 6d.

'All the materials have been well digested, and the book gives us a complete picture of the life of one who will ever be held in loving remembrance by his personal friends, and who in the history of music in this country will always occupy a prominent position on account of the many services he rendered to the art.'—*Musical News.*
'This book has been undertaken in quite the right spirit, and written with sympathy, insight, and considerable literary skill.'—*Times.*

W. G. Collingwood. THE LIFE OF JOHN RUSKIN. By W. G. COLLINGWOOD, M.A., Editor of Mr. Ruskin's Poems. With numerous Portraits, and 13 Drawings by Mr. Ruskin. *Second Edition.* 2 vols. 8vo. 32s.

'No more magnificent volumes have been published for a long time.'—*Times.*
'It is long since we had a biography with such delights of substance and of form. Such a book is a pleasure for the day, and a joy for ever.'—*Daily Chronicle.*
'A noble monument of a noble subject. One of the most beautiful books about one of the noblest lives of our century.'—*Glasgow Herald.*

C. Waldstein. JOHN RUSKIN: a Study. By CHARLES WALDSTEIN, M.A., Fellow of King's College, Cambridge. With a Photogravure Portrait after Professor HERKOMER. *Post 8vo.* 5s.

'A thoughtful, impartial, well-written criticism of Ruskin's teaching, intended to separate what the author regards as valuable and permanent from what is transient and erroneous in the great master's writing.'—*Daily Chronicle.*

W. H. Hutton. THE LIFE OF SIR THOMAS MORE. By W. H. HUTTON, M.A., Author of 'William Laud.' *With Portraits. Crown 8vo.* 5s.

'The book lays good claim to high rank among our biographies. It is excellently, even lovingly, written.'—*Scotsman.*
'An excellent monograph.'—*Times.*
'A most complete presentation.'—*Daily Chronicle.*

M. Kaufmann. CHARLES KINGSLEY. By M. KAUFMANN, M.A. *Crown 8vo. Buckram.* 5s.

A biography of Kingsley, especially dealing with his achievements in social reform.
'The author has certainly gone about his work with conscientiousness and industry.—*Sheffield Daily Telegraph.*

A. F. Robbins. THE EARLY LIFE OF WILLIAM EWART GLADSTONE. By A. F. ROBBINS. *With Portraits. Crown 8vo.* 6s.

'Considerable labour and much skill of presentation have not been unworthily expended on this interesting work.'—*Times.*

Clark Russell. THE LIFE OF ADMIRAL LORD COLLINGWOOD. By W. CLARK RUSSELL, Author of 'The Wreck of the Grosvenor.' With Illustrations by F. BRANGWYN. *Third Edition. Crown 8vo.* 6s.

'A most excellent and wholesome book, which we should like to see in the hands of every boy in the country.'—*St. James's Gazette.*
'A really good book.'—*Saturday Review.*

Southey. ENGLISH SEAMEN (Howard, Clifford, Hawkins. Drake, Cavendish). By ROBERT SOUTHEY. Edited, with an Introduction, by DAVID HANNAY. *Second Edition. Crown 8vo.* 6s.

'Admirable and well-told stories of our naval history.'—*Army and Navy Gazette.*
'A brave, inspiring book.'—*Black and White.*
'The work of a master of style, and delightful all through.'—*Daily Chronicle.*

General Literature

S. Baring Gould. OLD COUNTRY LIFE. By S. BARING GOULD, Author of 'Mehalah,' etc. With Sixty-seven Illustrations by W. PARKINSON, F. D. BEDFORD, and F. MASEY. *Large Crown 8vo.* 10s. 6d. *Fifth and Cheaper Edition.* 6s.

'"Old Country Life," as healthy wholesome reading, full of breezy life and movement, full of quaint stories vigorously told, will not be excelled by any book to be published throughout the year. Sound, hearty, and English to the core.'—*World.*

S. Baring Gould. HISTORIC ODDITIES AND STRANGE EVENTS. By S. BARING GOULD. *Third Edition. Crown 8vo. 6s.*

'A collection of exciting and entertaining chapters. The whole volume is delightful reading.'—*Times.*

S. Baring Gould. FREAKS OF FANATICISM. By S. BARING GOULD. *Third Edition. Crown 8vo. 6s.*

'Mr. Baring Gould has a keen eye for colour and effect, and the subjects he has chosen give ample scope to his descriptive and analytic faculties. A perfectly fascinating book.'—*Scottish Leader.*

S. Baring Gould. A GARLAND OF COUNTRY SONG: English Folk Songs with their Traditional Melodies. Collected and arranged by S. BARING GOULD and H. FLEETWOOD SHEPPARD. *Demy 4to. 6s.*

S. Baring Gould. SONGS OF THE WEST: Traditional Ballads and Songs of the West of England, with their Traditional Melodies. Collected by S. BARING GOULD, M.A., and H. FLEETWOOD SHEPPARD, M.A. Arranged for Voice and Piano. In 4 Parts (containing 25 Songs each), *Parts I., II., III., 3s. each. Part IV., 5s. In one Vol., French morocco, 15s.*

'A rich collection of humour, pathos, grace, and poetic fancy.'—*Saturday Review.*

S. Baring Gould. YORKSHIRE ODDITIES AND STRANGE EVENTS. *Fourth Edition. Crown 8vo. 6s.*

S. Baring Gould. STRANGE SURVIVALS AND SUPERSTITIONS. With Illustrations. By S. BARING GOULD. *Crown 8vo. Second Edition. 6s.*

'We have read Mr. Baring Gould's book from beginning to end. It is full of quaint and various information, and there is not a dull page in it.'—*Notes and Queries.*

S. Baring Gould. THE DESERTS OF SOUTHERN FRANCE. By S. BARING-GOULD. With numerous Illustrations by F. D. BEDFORD, S. HUTTON, etc. *2 vols. Demy 8vo. 32s.*

This book is the first serious attempt to describe the great barren tableland that extends to the south of Limousin in the Department of Aveyron, Lot, etc., a country of dolomite cliffs, and cañons, and subterranean rivers. The region is full of prehistoric and historic interest, relics of cave-dwellers, of mediæval robbers, and of the English domination and the Hundred Years' War.

'His two richly-illustrated volumes are full of matter of interest to the geologist, the archæologist, and the student of history and manners.'—*Scotsman.*

'It deals with its subject in a manner which rarely fails to arrest attention.'—*Times.*

R. S. Baden-Powell. THE DOWNFALL OF PREMPEH. A Diary of Life with the Native Levy in Ashanti, 1895. By Lieut.-Col. BADEN-POWELL. With 21 Illustrations, a Map, and a Special Chapter on the Political and Commercial Position of Ashanti by Sir GEORGE BADEN-POWELL, K.C.M.G., M.P. *Demy 8vo. 10s. 6d.*

'A compact, faithful, most readable record of the campaign.'—*Daily News.*
'A bluff and vigorous narrative.'—*Glasgow Herald.*
'A really interesting book.'—*Yorkshire Post.*

W. E. Gladstone. THE SPEECHES AND PUBLIC ADDRESSES OF THE RT. HON. W. E. GLADSTONE, M.P. Edited by A. W. HUTTON, M.A., and H. J. COHEN, M.A. With Portraits. *8vo. Vols. IX. and X.* 12s. 6d. each.

Henley and Whibley. A BOOK OF ENGLISH PROSE. Collected by W. E. HENLEY and CHARLES WHIBLEY. *Cr. 8vo.* 6s.

'A unique volume of extracts—an art gallery of early prose.'—*Birmingham Post.*
'An admirable companion to Mr. Henley's "Lyra Heroica."'—*Saturday Review.*
'Quite delightful. The choice made has been excellent, and the volume has been most admirably printed by Messrs. Constable. A greater treat for those not well acquainted with pre-Restoration prose could not be imagined.'—*Athenæum.*

J. Wells. OXFORD AND OXFORD LIFE. By Members of the University. Edited by J. WELLS, M.A., Fellow and Tutor of Wadham College. *Crown 8vo.* 3s. 6d.

This work contains an account of life at Oxford—intellectual, social, and religious—a careful estimate of necessary expenses, a review of recent changes, a statement of the present position of the University, and chapters on Women's Education, aids to study, and University Extension.
'We congratulate Mr. Wells on the production of a readable and intelligent account of Oxford as it is at the present time, written by persons who are possessed of a close acquaintance with the system and life of the University.'—*Athenæum.*

W. M. Dixon. A PRIMER OF TENNYSON. By W. M. DIXON, M.A., Professor of English Literature at Mason College. *Crown 8vo.* 2s. 6d.

'Much sound and well-expressed criticism and acute literary judgments. The bibliography is a boon.'—*Speaker.*
'No better estimate of the late Laureate's work has yet been published. His sketch of Tennyson's life contains everything essential; his bibliography is full and concise: his literary criticism is most interesting.'—*Glasgow Herald.*

W. A. Craigie. A PRIMER OF BURNS. By W. A. CRAIGIE. *Crown 8vo.* 2s. 6d.

This book is planned on a method similar to the 'Primer of Tennyson.' It has also a glossary.
'A valuable addition to the literature of the poet.'—*Times.*
'An excellent short account.'—*Pall Mall Gazette.*
'An admirable introduction.'—*Globe.*

L. Whibley. GREEK OLIGARCHIES: THEIR ORGANISATION AND CHARACTER. By L. WHIBLEY, M.A., Fellow of Pembroke College, Cambridge. *Crown 8vo.* 6s.

'An exceedingly useful handbook: a careful and well-arranged study of an obscure subject.'—*Times.*
'Mr. Whibley is never tedious or pedantic.'—*Pall Mall Gazette.*

W. B. Worsfold. SOUTH AFRICA: Its History and its Future. By W. BASIL WORSFOLD, M.A. *With a Map. Crown 8vo.* 6s.

'An intensely interesting book.'—*Daily Chronicle.*
'A monumental work compressed into a very moderate compass.'—*World.*

C. H. Pearson. ESSAYS AND CRITICAL REVIEWS. By C. H. PEARSON, M.A., Author of 'National Life and Character.' Edited, with a Biographical Sketch, by H. A. STRONG, M.A., LL.D. With a Portrait. *Demy 8vo.* 10s. 6d.

'These fine essays illustrate the great breadth of his historical and literary sympathies and the remarkable variety of his intellectual interests.'—*Glasgow Herald.*
'Remarkable for careful handling, breadth of view, and thorough knowledge.'—*Scotsman.*
'Charming essays.'—*Spectator.*

Ouida. VIEWS AND OPINIONS. By OUIDA. *Crown 8vo. Second Edition.* 6s.

'Ouida is outspoken, and the reader of this book will not have a dull moment. The book is full of variety, and sparkles with entertaining matter.'—*Speaker.*

J. S. Shedlock. THE PIANOFORTE SONATA: Its Origin and Development. By J. S. SHEDLOCK. *Crown 8vo.* 5s.

'This work should be in the possession of every musician and amateur, for it not only embodies a concise and lucid history of the origin of one of the most important forms of musical composition, but, by reason of the painstaking research and accuracy of the author's statements, it is a very valuable work for reference.'—*Athenæum.*

E. M. Bowden. THE EXAMPLE OF BUDDHA: Being Quotations from Buddhist Literature for each Day in the Year. Compiled by E. M. BOWDEN. With Preface by Sir EDWIN ARNOLD. *Third Edition.* 16mo. 2s. 6d.

J. Beever. PRACTICAL FLY-FISHING, Founded on Nature, by JOHN BEEVER, late of the Thwaite House, Coniston. A New Edition, with a Memoir of the Author by W. G. COLLINGWOOD, M.A. *Crown 8vo.* 3s. 6d.

A little book on Fly-Fishing by an old friend of Mr. Ruskin.

Science

Freudenreich. DAIRY BACTERIOLOGY. A Short Manual for the Use of Students. By Dr. ED. VON FREUDENREICH. Translated from the German by J. R. AINSWORTH DAVIS, B.A., F.C.P. *Crown 8vo.* 2s. 6d.

Chalmers Mitchell. OUTLINES OF BIOLOGY. By P. CHALMERS MITCHELL, M.A., F.Z.S. *Fully Illustrated. Crown 8vo.* 6s.

A text-book designed to cover the new Schedule issued by the Royal College of Physicians and Surgeons.

G. Massee. A MONOGRAPH OF THE MYXOGASTRES. By GEORGE MASSEE. With 12 Coloured Plates. *Royal 8vo.* 18s. net.

'A work much in advance of any book in the language treating of this group of organisms. It is indispensable to every student of the Myxogastres. The coloured plates deserve high praise for their accuracy and execution.'—*Nature.*

Philosophy

L. T. Hobhouse. THE THEORY OF KNOWLEDGE. By L. T. HOBHOUSE, Fellow and Tutor of Corpus College, Oxford. *Demy 8vo.* 21s.

'The most important contribution to English philosophy since the publication of Mr. Bradley's "Appearance and Reality." Full of brilliant criticism and of positive theories which are models of lucid statement.'—*Glasgow Herald.*

An elaborate and often brilliantly written volume. The treatment is one of great freshness, and the illustrations are particularly numerous and apt.'—*Times.*

W. H. Fairbrother. THE PHILOSOPHY OF T. H. GREEN. By W. H. FAIRBROTHER, M.A., Lecturer at Lincoln College, Oxford. *Crown 8vo.* 3s. 6d.

This volume is expository, not critical, and is intended for senior students at the Universities and others, as a statement of Green's teaching, and an introduction to the study of Idealist Philosophy.

'In every way an admirable book. As an introduction to the writings of perhaps the most remarkable speculative thinker whom England has produced in the present century, nothing could be better than Mr. Fairbrother's exposition and criticism.'—*Glasgow Herald.*

F. W. Bussell. THE SCHOOL OF PLATO: its Origin and its Revival under the Roman Empire. By F. W. BUSSELL, M.A., Fellow and Tutor of Brasenose College, Oxford. *Demy 8vo.* Two volumes. 7s. 6d. each. Vol. I.

'A highly valuable contribution to the history of ancient thought.'—*Glasgow Herald.*

'A clever and stimulating book, provocative of thought and deserving careful reading.'—*Manchester Guardian.*

F. S. Granger. THE WORSHIP OF THE ROMANS. By F. S. GRANGER, M.A., Litt.D., Professor of Philosophy at University College, Nottingham. *Crown 8vo.* 6s.

The author has attempted to delineate that group of beliefs which stood in close connection with the Roman religion, and among the subjects treated are Dreams, Nature Worship, Roman Magic, Divination, Holy Places, Victims, etc. Thus the book is, apart from its immediate subject, a contribution to folk-lore and comparative psychology.

'A scholarly analysis of the religious ceremonies, beliefs, and superstitions of ancient Rome, conducted in the new instructive light of comparative anthropology.'—*Times.*

Theology

E. C. S. Gibson. THE XXXIX. ARTICLES OF THE CHURCH OF ENGLAND. Edited with an Introduction by E. C. S. GIBSON, D.D., Vicar of Leeds, late Principal of Wells Theological College. *In Two Volumes. Demy 8vo. 7s. 6d. each.* Vol. I. *Articles I.-VIII.*

'The tone maintained throughout is not that of the partial advocate, but the faithful exponent.'—*Scotsman.*
'There are ample proofs of clearness of expression, sobriety of judgment, and breadth of view. . . . The book will be welcome to all students of the subject, and its sound, definite, and loyal theology ought to be of great service.'—*National Observer.*
'So far from repelling the general reader, its orderly arrangement, lucid treatment, and felicity of diction invite and encourage his attention.'—*Yorkshire Post.*

R. L. Ottley. THE DOCTRINE OF THE INCARNATION. By R. L. OTTLEY, M.A., late fellow of Magdalen College, Oxon., Principal of Pusey House. *In Two Volumes. Demy 8vo. 15s.*

'Learned and reverent: lucid and well arranged.'—*Record.*
'Accurate, well ordered, and judicious.'—*National Observer.*
'A clear and remarkably full account of the main currents of speculation. Scholarly precision . . . genuine tolerance . . . intense interest in his subject—are Mr. Ottley's merits.'—*Guardian.*

S. R. Driver. SERMONS ON SUBJECTS CONNECTED WITH THE OLD TESTAMENT. By S. R. DRIVER, D.D., Canon of Christ Church, Regius Professor of Hebrew in the University of Oxford. *Crown 8vo. 6s.*

'A welcome companion to the author's famous "Introduction." No man can read these discourses without feeling that Dr. Driver is fully alive to the deeper teaching of the Old Testament.'—*Guardian.*

T. K. Cheyne. FOUNDERS OF OLD TESTAMENT CRITICISM: Biographical, Descriptive, and Critical Studies. By T. K. CHEYNE, D.D., Oriel Professor of the Interpretation of Holy Scripture at Oxford. *Large crown 8vo. 7s. 6d.*

This important book is a historical sketch of O. T. Criticism in the form of biographical studies from the days of Eichhorn to those of Driver and Robertson Smith. It is the only book of its kind in English.
'A very learned and instructive work.'—*Times.*

C. H. Prior. CAMBRIDGE SERMONS. Edited by C. H. PRIOR, M.A., Fellow and Tutor of Pembroke College. *Crown 8vo. 6s.*

A volume of sermons preached before the University of Cambridge by various preachers, including the Archbishop of Canterbury and Bishop Westcott.
'A representative collection. Bishop Westcott's is a noble sermon.'—*Guardian.*

H. C. Beeching. SERMONS TO SCHOOLBOYS. By H. C. BEECHING, M.A., Rector of Yattendon, Berks. With a Preface by Canon SCOTT HOLLAND. *Crown 8vo. 2s. 6d.*

Seven sermons preached before the boys of Bradfield College.

MESSRS. METHUEN'S LIST 21

E. B. Layard. RELIGION IN BOYHOOD. Notes on the Religious Training of Boys. With a Preface by J. R. ILLINGWORTH. By E. B. LAYARD, M.A. 18*mo*. 1*s*.

Devotional Books.

With Full-page Illustrations. Fcap. 8vo. Buckram. 3s. 6d. Padded morocco, 5s.

THE IMITATION OF CHRIST. By THOMAS À KEMPIS. With an Introduction by DEAN FARRAR. Illustrated by C. M. GERE, and printed in black and red. *Second Edition*.

'Amongst all the innumerable English editions of the "Imitation," there can have been few which were prettier than this one, printed in strong and handsome type by Messrs. Constable, with all the glory of red initials, and the comfort of buckram binding.'—*Glasgow Herald.*

THE CHRISTIAN YEAR. By JOHN KEBLE. With an Introduction and Notes by W. LOCK, M.A., Sub-Warden of Keble College, Ireland Professor at Oxford, Author of the 'Life of John Keble.' Illustrated by R. ANNING BELL.

'The present edition is annotated with all the care and insight to be expected from Mr. Lock. The progress and circumstances of its composition are detailed in the Introduction. There is an interesting Appendix on the MSS. of the "Christian Year," and another giving the order in which the poems were written. A "Short Analysis of the Thought" is prefixed to each, and any difficulty in the text is explained in a note.—*Guardian.*

'The most acceptable edition of this ever-popular work.'—*Globe.*

Leaders of Religion

Edited by H. C. BEECHING, M.A. *With Portraits, crown 8vo.*

A series of short biographies of the most prominent leaders of religious life and thought of all ages and countries.

3/6

The following are ready—

CARDINAL NEWMAN. By R. H. HUTTON.

JOHN WESLEY. By J. H. OVERTON, M.A.

BISHOP WILBERFORCE. By G. W. DANIEL, M.A.

CARDINAL MANNING. By A. W. HUTTON, M.A.

CHARLES SIMEON. By H. C. G. MOULE, M.A.

JOHN KEBLE. By WALTER LOCK, M.A.

THOMAS CHALMERS. By Mrs. OLIPHANT.

LANCELOT ANDREWES. By R. L. OTTLEY, M.A.

AUGUSTINE OF CANTERBURY. By E. L. Cutts, D.D.
WILLIAM LAUD. By W. H. Hutton, M.A.
JOHN KNOX. By F. M'Cunn.
JOHN HOWE. By R. F. Horton, D.D.
BISHOP KEN. By F. A. Clarke, M.A.
GEORGE FOX, THE QUAKER. By T. Hodgkin, D.C.L.

Other volumes will be announced in due course.

Fiction

SIX SHILLING NOVELS

Marie Corelli's Novels

Crown 8vo. 6s. each.

A ROMANCE OF TWO WORLDS. *Fourteenth Edition.*

VENDETTA. *Eleventh Edition.*

THELMA. *Fourteenth Edition.*

ARDATH. *Tenth Edition.*

THE SOUL OF LILITH. *Ninth Edition.*

WORMWOOD. *Eighth Edition.*

BARABBAS: A DREAM OF THE WORLD'S TRAGEDY. *Twenty-fifth Edition.*

'The tender reverence of the treatment and the imaginative beauty of the writing have reconciled us to the daring of the conception, and the conviction is forced on us that even so exalted a subject cannot be made too familiar to us, provided it be presented in the true spirit of Christian faith. The amplifications of the Scripture narrative are often conceived with high poetic insight, and this "Dream of the World's Tragedy" is, despite some trifling incongruities, a lofty and not inadequate paraphrase of the supreme climax of the inspired narrative.'—*Dublin Review.*

THE SORROWS OF SATAN. *Twenty-ninth Edition.*

'A very powerful piece of work. . . . The conception is magnificent, and is likely to win an abiding place within the memory of man. . . . The author has immense command of language, and a limitless audacity. . . . This interesting and remarkable romance will live long after much of the ephemeral literature of the day is forgotten. . . . A literary phenomenon . . . novel, and even sublime.'—W. T. Stead in the *Review of Reviews.*

Anthony Hope's Novels

Crown 8vo. 6s. each.

THE GOD IN THE CAR. *Seventh Edition.*

'A very remarkable book, deserving of critical analysis impossible within our limit; brilliant, but not superficial; well considered, but not elaborated; constructed with the proverbial art that conceals, but yet allows itself to be enjoyed by readers to whom fine literary method is a keen pleasure; true without cynicism, subtle without affectation, humorous without strain, witty without offence, inevitably sad, with an unmorose simplicity.'—*The World.*

A CHANGE OF AIR. *Fourth Edition.*

'A graceful, vivacious comedy, true to human nature. The characters are traced with a masterly hand.'—*Times.*

A MAN OF MARK. *Third Edition.*

'Of all Mr. Hope's books, "A Man of Mark" is the one which best compares with "The Prisoner of Zenda." The two romances are unmistakably the work of the same writer, and he possesses a style of narrative peculiarly seductive, piquant, comprehensive, and—his own.'—*National Observer.*

THE CHRONICLES OF COUNT ANTONIO. *Third Edition.*

'It is a perfectly enchanting story of love and chivalry, and pure romance. The outlawed Count is the most constant, desperate, and withal modest and tender of lovers, a peerless gentleman, an intrepid fighter, a very faithful friend, and a most magnanimous foe. In short, he is an altogether admirable, lovable, and delightful hero. There is not a word in the volume that can give offence to the most fastidious taste of man or woman, and there is not, either, a dull paragraph in it. The book is everywhere instinct with the most exhilarating spirit of adventure, and delicately perfumed with the sentiment of all heroic and honourable deeds of history and romance.'—*Guardian.*

S. Baring Gould's Novels

Crown 8vo. 6s. each.

'To say that a book is by the author of "Mehalah" is to imply that it contains a story cast on strong lines, containing dramatic possibilities, vivid and sympathetic descriptions of Nature, and a wealth of ingenious imagery.'—*Speaker.*

'That whatever Mr. Baring Gould writes is well worth reading, is a conclusion that may be very generally accepted. His views of life are fresh and vigorous, his language pointed and characteristic, the incidents of which he makes use are striking and original, his characters are life-like, and though somewhat exceptional people, are drawn and coloured with artistic force. Add to this that his descriptions of scenes and scenery are painted with the loving eyes and skilled hands of a master of his art, that he is always fresh and never dull, and under such conditions it is no wonder that readers have gained confidence both in his power of amusing and satisfying them, and that year by year his popularity widens.'—*Court Circular.*

ARMINELL: A Social Romance. *Fourth Edition.*

URITH: A Story of Dartmoor. *Fourth Edition.*

'The author is at his best.'—*Times.*
'He has nearly reached the high water-mark of "Mehalah."'—*National Observer.*

MESSRS. METHUEN'S LIST

IN THE ROAR OF THE SEA. *Fifth Edition.*

'One of the best imagined and most enthralling stories the author has produced.'
—*Saturday Review.*

MRS. CURGENVEN OF CURGENVEN. *Fourth Edition.*

' A novel of vigorous humour and sustained power.'—*Graphic.*
' The swing of the narrative is splendid.'—*Sussex Daily News*

CHEAP JACK ZITA. *Third Edition.*

' A powerful drama of human passion.'—*Westminster Gazette.*
' A story worthy the author.'—*National Observer.*

THE QUEEN OF LOVE. *Fourth Edition.*

' The scenery is admirable, and the dramatic incidents are most striking.'—*Glasgow Herald.*
' Strong, interesting, and clever.'—*Westminster Gazette.*
' You cannot put it down until you have finished it.'—*Punch.*
' Can be heartily recommended to all who care for cleanly, energetic, and interesting fiction.'—*Sussex Daily News.*

KITTY ALONE. *Fourth Edition.*

' A strong and original story, teeming with graphic description, stirring incident, and, above all, with vivid and enthralling human interest.'—*Daily Telegraph.*
' Brisk, clever, keen, healthy, humorous, and interesting.'—*National Observer.*
' Full of quaint and delightful studies of character.'—*Bristol Mercury.*

NOÉMI : A Romance of the Cave-Dwellers. Illustrated by R. CATON WOODVILLE. *Third Edition.*

' "Noémi" is as excellent a tale of fighting and adventure as one may wish to meet. All the characters that interfere in this exciting tale are marked with properties of their own. The narrative also runs clear and sharp as the Loire itself.'—*Pall Mall Gazette.*
' Mr. Baring Gould's powerful story is full of the strong lights and shadows and vivid colouring to which he has accustomed us.'—*Standard.*

THE BROOM-SQUIRE. Illustrated by FRANK DADD. *Third Edition.*

' A strain of tenderness is woven through the web of his tragic tale, and its atmosphere is sweetened by the nobility and sweetness of the heroine's character.'—*Daily News.*
' A story of exceptional interest that seems to us to be better than anything he has written of late.'—*Speaker.* ' A powerful and striking story.'—*Guardian.*
' A powerful piece of work.'—*Black and White.*

Gilbert Parker's Novels

Crown 8vo. 6s. each.

PIERRE AND HIS PEOPLE. *Third Edition.*

' Stories happily conceived and finely executed. There is strength and genius in Mr. Parker's style.'—*Daily Telegraph.*

MRS. FALCHION. *Third Edition.*

'A splendid study of character.'—*Athenæum.*
'But little behind anything that has been done by any writer of our time.'—*Pall Mall Gazette.*
'A very striking and admirable novel.'—*St. James's Gazette.*

THE TRANSLATION OF A SAVAGE.

'The plot is original and one difficult to work out; but Mr. Parker has done it with great skill and delicacy. The reader who is not interested in this original, fresh, and well-told tale must be a dull person indeed.'—*Daily Chronicle.*
'A strong and successful piece of workmanship. The portrait of Lali, strong, dignified, and pure, is exceptionally well drawn.'—*Manchester Guardian.*

THE TRAIL OF THE SWORD. *Fourth Edition.*

'Everybody with a soul for romance will thoroughly enjoy "The Trail of the Sword."'—*St. James's Gazette.*
'A rousing and dramatic tale. A book like this, in which swords flash, great surprises are undertaken, and daring deeds done, in which men and women live and love in the old straightforward passionate way, is a joy inexpressible to the reviewer, brain-weary of the domestic tragedies and psychological puzzles of everyday fiction; and we cannot but believe that to the reader it will bring refreshment as welcome and as keen.'—*Daily Chronicle.*

WHEN VALMOND CAME TO PONTIAC: The Story of a Lost Napoleon. *Third Edition.*

'Here we find romance—real, breathing, living romance, but it runs flush with our own times, level with our own feelings. Not here can we complain of lack of inevitableness or homogeneity. The character of Valmond is drawn unerringly; his career, brief as it is, is placed before us as convincingly as history itself. The book must be read, we may say re-read, for any one thoroughly to appreciate Mr. Parker's delicate touch and innate sympathy with humanity.'—*Pall Mall Gazette.*
'The one work of genius which 1895 has as yet produced.'—*New Age.*

AN ADVENTURER OF THE NORTH: The Last Adventures of 'Pretty Pierre.'

'The present book is full of fine and moving stories of the great North, and it will add to Mr. Parker's already high reputation.'—*Glasgow Herald.*
'The new book is very romantic and very entertaining—full of that peculiarly elegant spirit of adventure which is so characteristic of Mr. Parker, and of that poetic thrill which has given him warmer, if less numerous, admirers than even his romantic story-telling gift has done.'—*Sketch.*

THE SEATS OF THE MIGHTY. *Illustrated. Fourth Edition.*

'The best thing he has done; one of the best things that any one has done lately.'—*St. James's Gazette.*
'Mr. Parker seems to become stronger and easier with every serious novel that he attempts.... In "The Seats of the Mighty" he shows the matured power which his former novels have led us to expect, and has produced a really fine historical novel.... The great creation of the book is Doltaire.... His character is drawn with quite masterly strokes, for he is a villain who is not altogether a villain, and who attracts the reader, as he did the other characters, by the extraordinary brilliance of his gifts, and by the almost unconscious acts of nobility which he performs.... Most sincerely is Mr. Parker to be congratulated on the finest novel he has yet written.'—*Athenæum.*

MESSRS. METHUEN'S LIST

'Mr. Parker's latest book places him in the front rank of living novelists. "The Seats of the Mighty" is a great book.'—*Black and White.*

'One of the strongest stories of historical interest and adventure that we have read for many a day. . . . Through all Mr. Parker moves with an assured step, whilst in his treatment of his subject there is that happy blending of the poetical with the prosaic which has characterised all his writings. A notable and successful book.' —*Speaker.*

'The story is very finely and dramatically told. . . . In none of his books has his imaginative faculty appeared to such splendid purpose as here. Captain Moray, Alixe, Gabord, Vauban—above all, Doltaire—and, indeed, every person who takes part in the action of the story are clearly conceived and finely drawn and individualised.—*Scotsman.*

'An admirable romance. The glory of a romance is its plot, and this plot is crowded with fine sensations, which have no rest until the fall of the famous old city and the final restitution of love.'—*Pall Mall Gazette.*

Conan Doyle. ROUND THE RED LAMP. By A. CONAN DOYLE, Author of 'The White Company,' 'The Adventures of Sherlock Holmes,' etc. *Fourth Edition. Crown 8vo. 6s.*

'The book is, indeed, composed of leaves from life, and is far and away the best view that has been vouchsafed us behind the scenes of the consulting-room. It is very superior to "The Diary of a late Physician."'—*Illustrated London News.*

Stanley Weyman. UNDER THE RED ROBE. By STANLEY WEYMAN, Author of 'A Gentleman of France.' With Twelve Illustrations by R. Caton Woodville. *Eighth Edition. Crown 8vo. 6s.*

'A book of which we have read every word for the sheer pleasure of reading, and which we put down with a pang that we cannot forget it all and start again.'— *Westminster Gazette.*

'Every one who reads books at all must read this thrilling romance, from the first page of which to the last the breathless reader is haled along. An inspiration of "manliness and courage."—*Daily Chronicle.*

'A delightful tale of chivalry and adventure, vivid and dramatic, with a wholesome modesty and reverence for the highest.'—*Globe.*

Mrs. Clifford. A FLASH OF SUMMER. By MRS. W. K. CLIFFORD, Author of 'Aunt Anne,' etc. *Second Edition. Crown 8vo. 6s.*

'The story is a very sad and a very beautiful one, exquisitely told, and enriched with many subtle touches of wise and tender insight. It will, undoubtedly, add to its author's reputation—already high—in the ranks of novelists.'—*Speaker.*

'We must congratulate Mrs. Clifford upon a very successful and interesting story, told throughout with finish and a delicate sense of proportion, qualities which, indeed, have always distinguished the best work of this very able writer.'— *Manchester Guardian.*

Emily Lawless. HURRISH. By the Honble. EMILY LAWLESS, Author of 'Maelcho,' etc. *Fifth Edition. Crown 8vo. 6s.*

A reissue of Miss Lawless' most popular novel, uniform with 'Maelcho.'

Emily Lawless. MAELCHO: a Sixteenth Century Romance. By the Honble. EMILY LAWLESS, Author of 'Grania,' 'Hurrish,' etc. *Second Edition. Crown 8vo. 6s.*

'A really great book.'—*Spectator.*

'There is no keener pleasure in life than the recognition of genius. Good work is commoner than it used to be, but the best is as rare as ever. All the more gladly, therefore, do we welcome in "Maelcho" a piece of work of the first order, which we do not hesitate to describe as one of the most remarkable literary achievements of this generation. Miss Lawless is possessed of the very essence of historical genius.'—*Manchester Guardian.*

J. H. Findlater. THE GREEN GRAVES OF BALGOWRIE. By JANE H. FINDLATER. *Third Edition. Crown 8vo. 6s.*

'A powerful and vivid story.'—*Standard.*
'A beautiful story, sad and strange as truth itself.'—*Vanity Fair.*
'A work of remarkable interest and originality.'—*National Observer.*
'A really original novel.'—*Journal of Education.*
'A very charming and pathetic tale.'—*Pall Mall Gazette.*
'A singularly original, clever, and beautiful story.'—*Guardian.*
'"The Green Graves of Balgowrie" reveals to us a new Scotch writer of undoubted faculty and reserve force.'—*Spectator.*
'An exquisite idyll, delicate, affecting, and beautiful.'—*Black and White.*
'Permeated with high and noble purpose. It is one of the most wholesome stories we have met with, and cannot fail to leave a deep and lasting impression.'—*Newsagent.*

E. F. Benson. DODO: A DETAIL OF THE DAY. By E. F. BENSON. *Sixteenth Edition. Crown 8vo. 6s.*

'A delightfully witty sketch of society.'—*Spectator.*
'A perpetual feast of epigram and paradox.'—*Speaker.*
'By a writer of quite exceptional ability.'—*Athenæum.*
'Brilliantly written.'—*World.*

E. F. Benson. THE RUBICON. By E. F. BENSON, Author of 'Dodo.' *Fifth Edition. Crown 8vo. 6s.*

'Well written, stimulating, unconventional, and, in a word, characteristic.'—*Birmingham Post.*
'An exceptional achievement; a notable advance on his previous work.'—*National Observer.*

M. M. Dowie. GALLIA. By MÉNIE MURIEL DOWIE, Author of 'A Girl in the Carpathians.' *Third Edition. Crown 8vo. 6s.*

'The style is generally admirable, the dialogue not seldom brilliant, the situations surprising in their freshness and originality, while the subsidiary as well as the principal characters live and move, and the story itself is readable from title-page to colophon.'—*Saturday Review.*
'A very notable book; a very sympathetically, at times delightfully written book.'—*Daily Graphic.*

Mrs. Oliphant. SIR ROBERT'S FORTUNE. By MRS. OLIPHANT. *Crown 8vo. 6s.*

'Full of her own peculiar charm of style and simple, subtle character-painting come her new gift, the delightful story before us. The scene mostly lies in the moors, and at the touch of the authoress a Scotch moor becomes a living thing, strong tender, beautiful, and changeful.'—*Pall Mall Gazette.*

Mrs. Oliphant. THE TWO MARYS. By MRS. OLIPHANT. *Second Edition. Crown 8vo. 6s.*

W. E. Norris. MATTHEW AUSTIN. By W. E. NORRIS, Author of 'Mademoiselle de Mersac,' etc. *Fourth Edition. Crown 8vo. 6s.*

'"Matthew Austin" may safely be pronounced one of the most intellectually satisfactory and morally bracing novels of the current year.'—*Daily Telegraph.*

W. E. Norris. HIS GRACE. By W. E. NORRIS. *Third Edition. Crown 8vo. 6s.*

'Mr. Norris has drawn a really fine character in the Duke of Hursthourne, at once unconventional and very true to the conventionalities of life, weak and strong in a breath, capable of inane follies and heroic decisions, yet not so definitely portrayed as to relieve a reader of the necessity of study.'—*Athenæum.*

W. E. Norris. THE DESPOTIC LADY AND OTHERS. By W. E. NORRIS. *Crown 8vo.* 6s.

'A budget of good fiction of which no one will tire.'—*Scotsman.*
'An extremely entertaining volume—the sprightliest of holiday companions.'—*Daily Telegraph*

H. G. Wells. THE STOLEN BACILLUS, and other Stories. By H. G. WELLS, Author of 'The Time Machine.' *Crown 8vo.* 6s.

'The ordinary reader of fiction may be glad to know that these stories are eminently readable from one cover to the other, but they are more than that; they are the impressions of a very striking imagination, which, it would seem, has a great deal within its reach.'—*Saturday Review.*

Arthur Morrison. TALES OF MEAN STREETS. By ARTHUR MORRISON. *Fourth Edition. Crown 8vo.* 6s.

'Told with consummate art and extraordinary detail. He tells a plain, unvarnished tale, and the very truth of it makes for beauty. In the true humanity of the book lies its justification, the permanence of its interest, and its indubitable triumph.'—*Athenæum.*
'A great book. The author's method is amazingly effective, and produces a thrilling sense of reality. The writer lays upon us a master hand. The book is simply appalling and irresistible in its interest. It is humorous also; without humour it would not make the mark it is certain to make.'—*World.*

J. Maclaren Cobban. THE KING OF ANDAMAN: A Saviour of Society. By J. MACLAREN COBBAN, Author of 'The Red Sultan,' etc. *Crown 8vo.* 6s.

'An unquestionably interesting book. It would not surprise us if it turns out to be the most interesting novel of the season, for it contains one character, at least, who has in him the root of immortality, and the book itself is ever exhaling the sweet savour of the unexpected. . . . Plot is forgotten and incident fades, and only the really human endures, and throughout this book there stands out in bold and beautiful relief its high-souled and chivalric protagonist, James the Master of Hutcheon, the King of Andaman himself.'—*Pall Mall Gazette.*
'A most original and refreshing story. James Hutcheon is a personage whom it is good to know and impossible to forget. He is beautiful within and without, whichever way we take him.'—*Spectator.*
'"The King of Andaman," is a book which does credit not less to the heart than the head of its author.'—*Athenæum.*
'The fact that Her Majesty the Queen has been pleased to gracefully express to the author of "The King of Andaman" her interest in his work will doubtless find for it many readers.'—*Vanity Fair.*

H. Morrah. A SERIOUS COMEDY. By HERBERT MORRAH. *Crown 8vo.* 6s.

'There are many delightful places in this volume, which is well worthy of its title. The theme has seldom been presented with more freshness or more force.'—*Scotsman.*

L. B. Walford. SUCCESSORS TO THE TITLE. By MRS. WALFORD, Author of 'Mr. Smith,' etc. *Second Edition. Crown 8vo.* 6s.

'The story is fresh and healthy from beginning to finish; and our liking for the two simple people who are the successors to the title mounts steadily, and ends almost in respect.'—*Scotsman.*
'The book is quite worthy to be ranked with many clever predecessors. It is excellent reading.'—*Glasgow Herald.*

T. L. Paton. A HOME IN INVERESK. By T. L. PATON. *Crown 8vo.* 6s.

'A distinctly fresh and fascinating novel.'—*Montrose Standard.*
'A book which bears marks of considerable promise.'—*Scotsman.*
'A pleasant and well-written story.'—*Daily Chronicle.*

John Davidson. MISS ARMSTRONG'S AND OTHER CIRCUMSTANCES. By JOHN DAVIDSON. *Crown 8vo.* 6s.

'Throughout the volume there is a strong vein of originality, a strength in the handling, and a knowledge of human nature that are worthy of the highest praise.' —*Scotsman.*

J. B. Burton. IN THE DAY OF ADVERSITY. By J. BLOUNDELLE BURTON, Author of 'The Hispaniola Plate,' etc. *Crown 8vo.* 6s.

'Unusually interesting and full of highly dramatic situations.'—*Guardian.*
'A well-written story, drawn from that inexhaustible mine, the time of Louis XIV. —*Pall Mall Gazette.*

H. Johnston. DR. CONGALTON'S LEGACY. By HENRY JOHNSTON. *Crown 8vo.* 6s.

'The story is redolent of humour, pathos, and tenderness, while it is not without a touch of tragedy.'—*Scotsman.*
A worthy and permanent contribution to Scottish creative literature.'—*Glasgow Herald.*

Julian Corbett. A BUSINESS IN GREAT WATERS. By JULIAN CORBETT, Author of 'For God and Gold,' 'Kophetua XIIIth.,' etc. *Crown 8vo.* 6s.

'In this stirring story Mr. Julian Corbett has done excellent work, welcome alike for its distinctly literary flavour, and for the wholesome tone which pervades it. Mr. Corbett writes with immense spirit, and the book is a thoroughly enjoyable one in all respects. The salt of the ocean is in it, and the right heroic ring resounds through its gallant adventures.'—*Speaker.*

C. Phillips Woolley. THE QUEENSBERRY CUP. A Tale of Adventure. By CLIVE PHILLIPS WOOLLEY, Author of 'Snap,' Editor of 'Big Game Shooting.' *Illustrated.* *Crown 8vo.* 6s.

'A book which will delight boys: a book which upholds the healthy schoolboy code of morality.'—*Scotsman.*
'A brilliant book. Dick St. Clair, of Caithness, is an almost ideal character—a combination of the mediæval knight and the modern pugilist.'—*Admiralty and Horseguards Gazette.*

Robert Barr. IN THE MIDST OF ALARMS. By ROBERT BARR, Author of 'From Whose Bourne,' etc. *Third Edition. Crown 8vo.* 6s.

'A book which has abundantly satisfied us by its capital humour.'—*Daily Chronicle.*
'Mr. Barr has achieved a triumph whereof he has every reason to be proud.'—*Pall Mall Gazette.*

L. Daintrey. THE KING OF ALBERIA. A Romance of the Balkans. By LAURA DAINTREY. *Crown 8vo.* 6s.

Miss Daintrey seems to have an intimate acquaintance with the people and politics of the Balkan countries in which the scene of her lively and picturesque romance is laid. On almost every page we find clever touches of local colour which differentiate her book unmistakably from the ordinary novel of commerce. The story is briskly told, and well conceived.'—*Glasgow Herald.*

Mrs. Pinsent. CHILDREN OF THIS WORLD. By ELLEN F. PINSENT, Author of 'Jenny's Case.' *Crown 8vo.* 6s.

'Mrs. Pinsent's new novel has plenty of vigour, variety, and good writing. There are certainty of purpose, strength of touch, and clearness of vision.'—*Athenæum.*

Clark Russell. MY DANISH SWEETHEART. By W. CLARK RUSSELL, Author of 'The Wreck of the Grosvenor,' etc. *Illustrated. Fourth Edition. Crown 8vo.* 6s.

G. Manville Fenn. AN ELECTRIC SPARK. By G. MANVILLE FENN, Author of 'The Vicar's Wife,' 'A Double Knot,' etc. *Second Edition. Crown 8vo.* 6s.

'A simple and wholesome story.'—*Manchester Guardian.*

R. Pryce. TIME AND THE WOMAN. By RICHARD PRYCE, Author of 'Miss Maxwell's Affections,' 'The Quiet Mrs. Fleming,' etc. *Second Edition. Crown 8vo.* 6s.

'Mr. Pryce's work recalls the style of Octave Feuillet, by its clearness, conciseness, its literary reserve.'—*Athenæum.*

Mrs. Watson. THIS MAN'S DOMINION. By the Author of 'A High Little World.' *Second Edition. Crown 8vo.* 6s.

Marriott Watson. DIOGENES OF LONDON and other Sketches. By H. B. MARRIOTT WATSON, Author of 'The Web of the Spider.' *Crown 8vo. Buckram.* 6s.

'By all those who delight in the uses of words, who rate the exercise of prose above the exercise of verse, who rejoice in all proofs of its delicacy and its strength, who believe that English prose is chief among the moulds of thought, by these Mr. Marriott Watson's book will be welcomed.'—*National Observer.*

M. Gilchrist. THE STONE DRAGON. By MURRAY GILCHRIST. *Crown 8vo. Buckram.* 6s.

'The author's faults are atoned for by certain positive and admirable merits. The romances have not their counterpart in modern literature, and to read them is a unique experience.'—*National Observer.*

E. Dickinson. A VICAR'S WIFE. By EVELYN DICKINSON. *Crown 8vo.* 6s.

E. M. Gray. ELSA. By E. M'QUEEN GRAY. *Crown 8vo.* 6s.

THREE-AND-SIXPENNY NOVELS

Crown 8vo. **3/6**

DERRICK VAUGHAN, NOVELIST. By EDNA LYALL.
MARGERY OF QUETHER. By S. BARING GOULD.
JACQUETTA. By S. BARING GOULD.
SUBJECT TO VANITY. By MARGARET BENSON.
THE MOVING FINGER. By MARY GAUNT.
JACO TRELOAR. By J. H. PEARCE.

AUT DIABOLUS AUT NIHIL. By X. L.
THE COMING OF CUCULAIN. A Romance of the Heroic Age of Ireland. By STANDISH O'GRADY. *Illustrated*.
THE GODS GIVE MY DONKEY WINGS. By ANGUS EVAN ABBOTT.
THE STAR GAZERS. By G. MANVILLE FENN.
THE POISON OF ASPS. By R. ORTON PROWSE.
THE QUIET MRS. FLEMING. By R. PRYCE.
THE PLAN OF CAMPAIGN. By F. MABEL ROBINSON.
DISENCHANTMENT. By F. MABEL ROBINSON.
MR. BUTLER'S WARD. By F. MABEL ROBINSON.
A LOST ILLUSION. By LESLIE KEITH.
A REVEREND GENTLEMAN. By J. M. COBBAN.
A DEPLORABLE AFFAIR. By W. E. NORRIS.
A CAVALIER'S LADYE. By Mrs. DICKER.

HALF-CROWN NOVELS 2/6
A Series of Novels by popular Authors.

1. HOVENDEN, V.C. By F. MABEL ROBINSON.
2. ELI'S CHILDREN. By G. MANVILLE FENN.
3. A DOUBLE KNOT. By G. MANVILLE FENN.
4. DISARMED. By M. BETHAM EDWARDS.
5. A MARRIAGE AT SEA. By W. CLARK RUSSELL.
6. IN TENT AND BUNGALOW. By the Author of 'Indian Idylls.'
7. MY STEWARDSHIP. By E. M'QUEEN GRAY.
8. JACK'S FATHER. By W. E. NORRIS.
9. JIM B.

Lynn Linton. THE TRUE HISTORY OF JOSHUA DAVIDSON, Christian and Communist. By E. LYNN LINTON. *Eleventh Edition. Post 8vo.* 1s.

Books for Boys and Girls 3/6
A Series of Books by well-known Authors, well illustrated.

1. THE ICELANDER'S SWORD. By S. BARING GOULD.
2. TWO LITTLE CHILDREN AND CHING. By EDITH E. CUTHELL.

MESSRS. METHUEN'S LIST

3. TODDLEBEN'S HERO. By M. M. BLAKE.
4. ONLY A GUARD ROOM DOG. By EDITH E. CUTHELL.
5. THE DOCTOR OF THE JULIET. By HARRY COLLINGWOOD.
6. MASTER ROCKAFELLAR'S VOYAGE. By W. CLARK RUSSELL.
7. SYD BELTON: Or, The Boy who would not go to Sea. By G. MANVILLE FENN.

The Peacock Library

A Series of Books for Girls by well-known Authors, handsomely bound in blue and silver, and well illustrated. **3/6**

1. A PINCH OF EXPERIENCE. By L. B. WALFORD.
2. THE RED GRANGE. By Mrs. MOLESWORTH.
3. THE SECRET OF MADAME DE MONLUC. By the Author of 'Mdle Mori.'
4. DUMPS. By Mrs. PARR, Author of 'Adam and Eve.'
5. OUT OF THE FASHION. By L. T. MEADE.
6. A GIRL OF THE PEOPLE. By L. T. MEADE.
7. HEPSY GIPSY. By L. T. MEADE. 2s. 6d.
8. THE HONOURABLE MISS. By L. T. MEADE.
9. MY LAND OF BEULAH. By Mrs. LEITH ADAMS.

University Extension Series

A series of books on historical, literary, and scientific subjects, suitable for extension students and home-reading circles. Each volume is complete in itself, and the subjects are treated by competent writers in a broad and philosophic spirit.

Edited by J. E. SYMES, M.A.,
Principal of University College, Nottingham.
Crown 8vo. Price (with some exceptions) 2s. 6d.
The following volumes are ready:—

THE INDUSTRIAL HISTORY OF ENGLAND. By H. DE B. GIBBINS, M.A., late Scholar of Wadham College, Oxon., Cobden Prizeman. *Fourth Edition. With Maps and Plans.* 3s.

'A compact and clear story of our industrial development. A study of this concise but luminous book cannot fail to give the reader a clear insight into the principal phenomena of our industrial history. The editor and publishers are to be congratulated on this first volume of their venture, and we shall look with expectant interest for the succeeding volumes of the series.'—*University Extension Journal.*

A HISTORY OF ENGLISH POLITICAL ECONOMY. By
L. L. PRICE, M.A., Fellow of Oriel College, Oxon. *Second Edition.*

PROBLEMS OF POVERTY: An Inquiry into the Industrial
Conditions of the Poor. By J. A. HOBSON, M.A. *Third Edition.*

VICTORIAN POETS. By A. SHARP.

THE FRENCH REVOLUTION. By J. E. SYMES, M.A.

PSYCHOLOGY. By F. S. GRANGER, M.A., Lecturer in Philosophy at University College, Nottingham.

THE EVOLUTION OF PLANT LIFE: Lower Forms. By
G. MASSEE, Kew Gardens. *With Illustrations.*

AIR AND WATER. Professor V. B. LEWES, M.A. *Illustrated.*

THE CHEMISTRY OF LIFE AND HEALTH. By C. W.
KIMMINS, M.A. Camb. *Illustrated.*

THE MECHANICS OF DAILY LIFE. By V. P. SELLS, M.A.
Illustrated.

ENGLISH SOCIAL REFORMERS. H. DE B. GIBBINS, M.A.

ENGLISH TRADE AND FINANCE IN THE SEVENTEENTH CENTURY. By W. A. S. HEWINS, B.A.

THE CHEMISTRY OF FIRE. The Elementary Principles of
Chemistry. By M. M. PATTISON MUIR, M.A. *Illustrated.*

A TEXT-BOOK OF AGRICULTURAL BOTANY. By M. C.
POTTER, M.A., F.L.S. *Illustrated.* 3s. 6d.

THE VAULT OF HEAVEN. A Popular Introduction to
Astronomy. By R. A. GREGORY. *With numerous Illustrations.*

METEOROLOGY. The Elements of Weather and Climate.
By H. N. DICKSON, F.R.S.E., F.R. Met. Soc. *Illustrated.*

A MANUAL OF ELECTRICAL SCIENCE. By GEORGE
J. BURCH, M.A. *With numerous Illustrations.* 3s.

THE EARTH. An Introduction to Physiography. By EVAN
SMALL, M.A. *Illustrated.*

INSECT LIFE. By F. W. THEOBALD, M.A. *Illustrated.*

ENGLISH POETRY FROM BLAKE TO BROWNING. By
W. M. DIXON, M.A.

ENGLISH LOCAL GOVERNMENT. By E. JENKS, M.A.,
Professor of Law at University College, Liverpool.

Social Questions of To-day

Edited by H. DE B. GIBBINS, M.A.

Crown 8vo.   2s. 6d.   **2/6**

A series of volumes upon those topics of social, economic, and industrial interest that are at the present moment foremost in the public mind. Each volume of the series is written by an author who is an acknowledged authority upon the subject with which he deals.

The following Volumes of the Series are ready:—

TRADE UNIONISM—NEW AND OLD. By G. HOWELL, Author of 'The Conflicts of Capital and Labour.' *Second Edition.*

THE CO-OPERATIVE MOVEMENT TO-DAY. By G. J. HOLYOAKE, Author of 'The History of Co-operation.' *Second Edition.*

MUTUAL THRIFT. By Rev. J. FROME WILKINSON, M.A., Author of 'The Friendly Society Movement.'

PROBLEMS OF POVERTY: An Inquiry into the Industrial Conditions of the Poor. By J. A. HOBSON, M.A. *Third Edition.*

THE COMMERCE OF NATIONS. By C. F. BASTABLE, M.A., Professor of Economics at Trinity College, Dublin.

THE ALIEN INVASION. By W. H. WILKINS, B.A., Secretary to the Society for Preventing the Immigration of Destitute Aliens.

THE RURAL EXODUS. By P. ANDERSON GRAHAM.

LAND NATIONALIZATION. By HAROLD COX, B.A.

A SHORTER WORKING DAY. By H. DE B. GIBBINS and R. A. HADFIELD, of the Hecla Works, Sheffield.

BACK TO THE LAND: An Inquiry into the Cure for Rural Depopulation. By H. E. MOORE.

TRUSTS, POOLS AND CORNERS: As affecting Commerce and Industry. By J. STEPHEN JEANS, M.R.I., F.S.S.

THE FACTORY SYSTEM. By R. COOKE TAYLOR.

THE STATE AND ITS CHILDREN. By GERTRUDE TUCKWELL.

WOMEN'S WORK. By LADY DILKE, MISS BULLEY, and MISS WHITLEY.

MUNICIPALITIES AT WORK. The Municipal Policy of Six Great Towns, and its Influence on their Social Welfare. By FREDERICK DOLMAN.

SOCIALISM AND MODERN THOUGHT. By M. KAUFMANN.

THE HOUSING OF THE WORKING CLASSES. By R. F. BOWMAKER.

MODERN CIVILISATION IN SOME OF ITS ECONOMIC ASPECTS. By W. CUNNINGHAM, D.D., Fellow of Trinity College, Cambridge.

Classical Translations

Edited by H. F. FOX, M.A., Fellow and Tutor of Brasenose College, Oxford.

Messrs. Methuen are issuing a New Series of Translations from the Greek and Latin Classics. They have enlisted the services of some of the best Oxford and Cambridge Scholars, and it is their intention that the Series shall be distinguished by literary excellence as well as by scholarly accuracy.

ÆSCHYLUS—Agamemnon, Chöephoroe, Eumenides. Translated by LEWIS CAMPBELL, LL.D., late Professor of Greek at St. Andrews. 5s.

CICERO—De Oratore I. Translated by E. N. P. MOOR, M.A., Assistant Master at Clifton. 3s. 6d.

CICERO—Select Orations (Pro Milone, Pro Murena, Philippic II., In Catilinam). Translated by H. E. D. BLAKISTON, M.A., Fellow and Tutor of Trinity College, Oxford. 5s.

CICERO—De Natura Deorum. Translated by F. BROOKS, M.A., late Scholar of Balliol College, Oxford. 3s. 6d.

LUCIAN—Six Dialogues (Nigrinus, Icaro-Menippus, The Cock, The Ship, The Parasite, The Lover of Falsehood). Translated by S. T. IRWIN, M.A., Assistant Master at Clifton; late Scholar of Exeter College, Oxford. 3s. 6d.

SOPHOCLES—Electra and Ajax. Translated by E. D. A. MORSHEAD, M.A., late Scholar of New College, Oxford; Assistant Master at Winchester. 2s. 6d.

TACITUS—Agricola and Germania. Translated by R. B. TOWNSHEND, late Scholar of Trinity College, Cambridge. 2s. 6d.

Educational Books

CLASSICAL

TACITI AGRICOLA. With Introduction, Notes, Map, etc. By R. F. DAVIS, M.A., Assistant Master at Weymouth College. *Crown 8vo.* 2s.

TACITI GERMANIA. By the same Editor. *Crown 8vo.* 2s.

HERODOTUS: EASY SELECTIONS. With Vocabulary. By A. C. LIDDELL, M.A., Assistant Master at Nottingham High School. *Fcap. 8vo.* 1s. 6d.

SELECTIONS FROM THE ODYSSEY. By E. D. STONE, M.A., late Assistant Master at Eton. *Fcap. 8vo.* 1s. 6d.

PLAUTUS: THE CAPTIVI. Adapted for Lower Forms by J. H. FREESE, M.A., late Fellow of St. John's, Cambridge. 1s. 6d.

DEMOSTHENES AGAINST CONON AND CALLICLES. Edited with Notes, and Vocabulary, by F. DARWIN SWIFT, M.A., formerly Scholar of Queen's College, Oxford; Assistant Master at Denstone College. *Fcap. 8vo.* 2s.

GERMAN

A COMPANION GERMAN GRAMMAR. By H. DE B. GIBBINS, M.A., Assistant Master at Nottingham High School. *Crown 8vo.* 1s. 6d.

GERMAN PASSAGES FOR UNSEEN TRANSLATION. By E. M'QUEEN GRAY. *Crown 8vo.* 2s. 6d.

SCIENCE

THE WORLD OF SCIENCE. Including Chemistry, Heat, Light, Sound, Magnetism, Electricity, Botany, Zoology, Physiology, Astronomy, and Geology. By R. ELLIOT STEEL, M.A., F.C.S. 147 Illustrations. *Second Edition. Crown 8vo.* 2s. 6d.

'Mr. Steel's Manual is admirable in many ways. The book is well calculated to attract and retain the attention of the young.'—*Saturday Review.*

'If Mr. Steel is to be placed second to any for this quality of lucidity, it is only to Huxley himself; and to be named in the same breath with this master of the craft of teaching is to be accredited with the clearness of style and simplicity of arrangement that belong to thorough mastery of a subject.'—*Parents' Review.*

ELEMENTARY LIGHT. By R. E. STEEL. With numerous Illustrations. *Crown 8vo.* 4s. 6d.

ENGLISH

ENGLISH RECORDS. A Companion to the History of England. By H. E. MALDEN, M.A. *Crown 8vo.* 3s. 6d.

A book which aims at concentrating information upon dates, genealogy, officials, constitutional documents, etc., which is usually found scattered in different volumes.

THE ENGLISH CITIZEN: HIS RIGHTS AND DUTIES. By H. E. MALDEN, M.A. 1s. 6d.

'The book goes over the same ground as is traversed in the school books on this subject written to satisfy the requirements of the Education code. It would serve admirably the purposes of a text-book, as it is well based in historical facts, and keeps quite clear of party matters.'—*Scotsman.*

METHUEN'S COMMERCIAL SERIES.

Edited by H. DE B. GIBBINS, M.A.

BRITISH COMMERCE AND COLONIES FROM ELIZABETH TO VICTORIA. By H. DE B. GIBBINS, M.A., Author of 'The Industrial History of England,' etc. etc. 2s.

COMMERCIAL EXAMINATION PAPERS. By H. DE B. GIBBINS, M.A. 1s. 6d.

THE ECONOMICS OF COMMERCE. By H. DE B. GIBBINS, M.A. 1s. 6d.

A MANUAL OF FRENCH COMMERCIAL CORRESPONDENCE. By S. E. BALLY, Modern Language Master at the Manchester Grammar School. 2s.

A FRENCH COMMERCIAL READER. By S. E. BALLY. 2s.

COMMERCIAL GEOGRAPHY, with special reference to Trade Routes, New Markets, and Manufacturing Districts. By L. W. LYDE, M.A., of the Academy, Glasgow. 2s.

A PRIMER OF BUSINESS. By S. JACKSON, M.A. 1s. 6d.

COMMERCIAL ARITHMETIC. By F. G. TAYLOR, M.A. 1s. 6d.

WORKS BY A. M. M. STEDMAN, M.A.

INITIA LATINA: Easy Lessons on Elementary Accidence. *Second Edition. Fcap. 8vo.* 1s.

FIRST LATIN LESSONS. *Fourth Edition. Crown 8vo.* 2s.

FIRST LATIN READER. With Notes adapted to the Shorter Latin Primer and Vocabulary. *Second Edition. Crown 8vo.* 1s. 6d.

EASY SELECTIONS FROM CAESAR. Part I. The Helvetian War. 18mo. 1s.

EASY SELECTIONS FROM LIVY. Part I. The Kings of Rome. 18mo. 1s. 6d.

EASY LATIN PASSAGES FOR UNSEEN TRANSLATION. *Third Edition. Fcap. 8vo.* 1s. 6d.

EXEMPLA LATINA. First Lessons in Latin Accidence. With Vocabulary. *Crown 8vo.* 1s.

EASY LATIN EXERCISES ON THE SYNTAX OF THE SHORTER AND REVISED LATIN PRIMER. With Vocabulary. *Fourth Edition. Crown 8vo.* 2s. 6d. Issued with the consent of Dr. Kennedy.

THE LATIN COMPOUND SENTENCE: Rules and Exercises. *Crown 8vo.* 1s. 6d. With Vocabulary. 2s.

NOTANDA QUAEDAM: Miscellaneous Latin Exercises on Common Rules and Idioms. *Second Edition. Fcap. 8vo.* 1s. 6d. With Vocabulary, 2s.

LATIN VOCABULARIES FOR REPETITION: Arranged according to Subjects. *Fourth Edition. Fcap. 8vo.* 1s. 6d.

A VOCABULARY OF LATIN IDIOMS AND PHRASES. 18mo. 1s.

STEPS TO GREEK. 18mo. 1s.

EASY GREEK PASSAGES FOR UNSEEN TRANSLATION. *Fcap. 8vo.* 1s. 6d.

GREEK VOCABULARIES FOR REPETITION. Arranged according to Subjects. *Second Edition. Fcap. 8vo.* 1s. 6d.

GREEK TESTAMENT SELECTIONS. For the use of Schools. *Third Edition.* With Introduction, Notes, and Vocabulary. *Fcap. 8vo.* 2s. 6d.

MESSRS. METHUEN'S LIST

STEPS TO FRENCH. 18*mo*. 8*d*.

FIRST FRENCH LESSONS. *Crown* 8*vo*. 1*s*.

EASY FRENCH PASSAGES FOR UNSEEN TRANSLATION. *Second Edition*. *Fcap*. 8*vo*. 1*s*. 6*d*.

EASY FRENCH EXERCISES ON ELEMENTARY SYNTAX. With Vocabulary. *Crown* 8*vo*. 2*s*. 6*d*.

FRENCH VOCABULARIES FOR REPETITION : Arranged according to Subjects. *Third Edition*. *Fcap*. 8*vo*. 1*s*.

SCHOOL EXAMINATION SERIES.

EDITED BY A. M. M. STEDMAN, M.A.

Crown 8*vo*. 2*s*. 6*d*.

FRENCH EXAMINATION PAPERS IN MISCELLANEOUS GRAMMAR AND IDIOMS. By A. M. M. STEDMAN, M.A. *Sixth Edition*.

A KEY, issued to Tutors and Private Students only, to be had on application to the Publishers. *Second Edition*. *Crown* 8*vo*. 6*s*. *net*.

LATIN EXAMINATION PAPERS IN MISCELLANEOUS GRAMMAR AND IDIOMS. By A. M. M. STEDMAN, M.A. *Fourth Edition*. KEY issued as above. 6*s*. *net*.

GREEK EXAMINATION PAPERS IN MISCELLANEOUS GRAMMAR AND IDIOMS. By A. M. M. STEDMAN, M.A. *Third Edition*. KEY issued as above. 6*s*. *net*.

GERMAN EXAMINATION PAPERS IN MISCELLANEOUS GRAMMAR AND IDIOMS. By R. J. MORICH, Manchester. *Third Edition*. KEY issued as above. 6*s*. *net*.

HISTORY AND GEOGRAPHY EXAMINATION PAPERS. By C. H. SPENCE, M.A., Clifton Coll.

SCIENCE EXAMINATION PAPERS. By R. E. STEEL, M.A., F.C.S., Chief Natural Science Master, Bradford Grammar School. *In two vols*. Part I. Chemistry; Part II. Physics.

GENERAL KNOWLEDGE EXAMINATION PAPERS. By A. M. M. STEDMAN, M.A. *Second Edition*. KEY issued as above. 7*s*. *net*.

www.ingramcontent.com/pod-product-compliance
Lightning Source LLC
Chambersburg PA
CBHW032044220426
43664CB00008B/853